I0142134

SEVEN SUTRAS

TO

SELF LIBERATION

Sharon Moriarty, M.S.E.E.

Gateway To Eternity Publications

Reno, San Francisco, Cork

http://www.GatewayToEternity.com

Copyright © 2016 Sharon Moriarty

Published on Amazon and CreateSpace

ISBN : 978-0-9971179-2-9

Library Of Congress Control Number (LCCN) : 2016906962

GATEWAY TO ETERNITY PUBLICATIONS

http://www.GatewayToEternity.com

SEVEN SUTRAS

TO

SELF LIBERATION

THE GULAG ARCHIPELAGO

I had been traveling for many lives seeking desperately to escape the wheel of life and death. I did not want this life, to be just another one mindlessly spent as a rat on a treadmill; vainly squandered chasing quixotic pursuits. Yes, I was too old a cat now to be taken in by the grim world of appearances. No longer easily fooled or snared by all the empty, superficial offerings of psychoplanet. My profession was as an Engineer, working in hi-tech and yet it all felt so deadening, even soul-destroying. Others may have perceived this lifestyle as cutting edge, even glamorous at times, yet I felt myself drowning amid this lifeless sea of technology. Working on products that would fast become obsolete next to bankrupt spirits, staring into their laptops, who functioned like numbed-out zombies from *"The Planet of the Dead."* Ectomorphs and overexcited geeks would dart and flit about, with never-ending streams of mindless gibberish effusing from their lips. They resembled a mound of frenzied acephalic ants, scurrying in a dozen different directions at once. Their heads would move rapidly back and forth, like crack fiends implanted with the chicken-head syndrome auto-generation chip. Most assuredly behind the cosmetic veneer of these cement prisons, something most egregious, rotten and abominable lay dying or deceased. My daily diet consisted of a constant barrage of junk e-mails, IMs, software patches and nonsense meetings. Occasionally I would run frantically about the lab, getting ready to strangle some nitwit, drudge or primadonna with an oscilloscope probe lead. At other times, just to stay awake, I would stand in the center of the meeting table, jackass naked and urinate on those below just to keep them hydrated. Then there

were the continual status updates, and glitzy presentations polished to fine precision late the night before. The sole purpose of
which, was to provide upper management with the illusion, that
they were on top of things.

Meanwhile, back in the cage, software trackers would be following my every move while fastidious bluenose managers would
be preparing to crucify me over the tiniest things. Each desired
to sink their venomous teeth in, to any available flesh on the
menu just to assuage the demons of their inner rage. The hei-
nous crime would often be something as trivial and innocuous,
as accidentally inserting a double space between two words in
some strategy document or powerpoint slide. A procedure that
would soon be archived, to the la-la-land of the server farms,
never to be seen or consulted again. For this crime, I was to be
racked and quartered; brutally impaled and mercilessly slaugh-
tered. Yes, I most certainly felt like a ragdoll, being callously torn
apart, by half a dozen savage dogs or more. As I stumbled out to
lunch, I could see the frenzied madness circulating all about.
This worldly intoxication with superficial things seemed to be
increasing all the time in asymptotic proportions. All were walking around trance-like, with transparently thin glass screens in
hand. Their spirits had expressly vacated the building, and all
their lights were out. There were no life signs to be found anywhere, most notably beyond the glass screen of their faces. I
wanted to shout out, "*Beam me up Scottie; this planet sucks!*" because all were in a perpetual power-down mode, starved of all
oxygen, life, and vitality and they mirrored the plastic toys, they
were badgered to produce. Yes, these devices were their
prophylactic geek toys, that shielded them from facing naked
existence, up close and personal. They would keep muttering
under their breath, "*Keep it Real Man*"—the words spinning out,

as if reciting some private mantra to themselves. Despite all the self-serving propaganda, these were the most exterior, one-dimensional beings that ever stalked the earth.

To me, this was the end of days. Who could be happy with this bare simulacrum of living? A mockery denuded of all that was meaningful and life-giving! All everyone talked about here concerned work, stock or politics as if these were the exclusive faces of all existence for the Cro-magnon species. Beneath all the idle chit-chat a conspiracy was brewing, and I detected a hydra-headed beast of deception roaming about getting ready to steer the ship of mankind towards our inevitable destruction. Yes, we were in urgent need of mirrors in these hallways of the blind, by which to cauterize and slay the hypnotizing Medusa of modern-day technology or else her spellbinding powers would soon turn us into nothing but stone-faced clones and human androids. I was in my late thirties, and already two to three standard deviations upstream from the median age in my field. And what a veritable field of human potatoes and cabbage patch kids it was! One in which I was rapidly becoming the scarecrow. I was growing visibly older by the day, yet financially pressured to drag my bag of weary bones into these soulless artifices in the tech jungle. So, each day, I plodded lifelessly into work, feeling thoroughly devitalized and exsanguinated. Then the metronome of the sweat factories and brain-farms would go clicking again, summoning all battery operated toys into action. Once again Lazarus had risen! Almost immediately managerial whips would come popping out from their worldly cubbyholes, seeking to thoroughly exhume my body and harvest my mind, to power their productivity engines. They had ingeniously implanted a systolic array of fiber optic cables that linked directly into my brain stem and its synaptic centers. This ungodly contraption was designed to support maximum information extraction to feed the great Borg mind. It was a vast circumferentially inscribed intelligence gathering system, aimed at feeding on all my paradigm shifting insights, brain flashes, epiphanies, and innovative ideas. Then the bean-counters and efficiency experts would get to work, sectioning every second of my day into a dozen equal parts or more. Each nano-section was to be assigned a different task and refined further into micromotions.

I wanted a stop to all the endless interrogations, pestering and mindless chatter and for everyone to go piss off and leave me alone. I should not be forced to swallow the verbal diarrhea, incessantly spilling out from their motor-mouths. Could any weatherman predict the torrential storms of hail, mist, and snow that were perpetually raining in my heart? Or forecast the lightning bolts that were threatening to emanate spontaneously from every neural orifice and biogenetic circuit under the hood of my cranium? I did not want this anymore. I needed somehow to escape and drink from the cup of life again! This worldly gauntlet so thoroughly drenched with devitalized, adventureless, spiritually starved creatures that were half-living or dead needed to be flung into an abyss, never to be seen again. I felt myself hopelessly floundering amid the continual swells of corporate tyranny, its retaliative vengeance, foolish obsessions and never-ending tirades of soul crunching mindlessness. Desolately immersed in an uncaring, unhearing, pitiless and blooded-spilled world of abject cruelty and outright heartlessness. Even so, I knew not from where the elixir of life would reveal itself!

THE ADVENTURE BEGINS

Almost immediately I got an answer. My Kriya Yoga teacher sent an e-mail, saying he was planning a yoga pilgrimage high into the Himalayas. It would be an international team of yogis, and I needed to be there. This crusade presented an excellent opportunity for adventure and for gaining inner clarity, and I did not ponder too long and hard before making a decision. If nothing else, it would at least stop the engines of madness, for a while. As the trip drew near, I was getting more excited by the day. I felt like an energized guppy because I was finally escaping a tiny fishbowl to swim in the great wide ocean. I promptly proceeded to make a very detailed inventory of all my needs. My luggage should not overburden me because of excess weight, but I did not want to miss anything critical either. So, I went very meticulously about packing it all together.

Late one night, a few weeks later, I finally arrived in New Delhi, only to find my luggage never arrived. Wonderful! I thought! I was already beginning to feel like a thorn in the side of the other yogis, traveling with me. After more than a day of flying, I knew, no one wanted to wait an extra hour or so before getting to the hotel! Thankfully, they all put up with this last-minute inconvenience with incredible patience, fortitude and unflappable ease of spirit.

Next morning, I got up early to repurchase all essential items that had gone MIA. It was amazing how vivacious and zestful, I felt, after so little sleep. I headed first to Connaught Place. There, after making some friendly connections with local traders and some street wanderers, I felt thoroughly charged and suffused with the atmosphere and throb of the city. It was quite a motley crew that I crossed paths with.

First, there was a young woman in rags, who was carrying a naked baby in her arms. The baby couldn't have been more than a few months old. Since one of her breasts was hanging out from her Sari, the child must have been suckling there just moments before. She was desperate for anything I could give, and her eyes spoke of fear made real. I offered her a few rupees but came away feeling both disgusted and ashamed. The balloon of my early morning elation had been swiftly punctured. She shone like a glowing emblem miraculously produced by a world that does not give a damn. All of a sudden, I felt the shameful duplicity of our blind worshipping of female gods. Kali, Aphrodite, and Niamh Chinn Óir, for example—none of it mattered! These had just been token offerings and a pure sublimation of our overall attack on womanhood. In the end, such pretentious worship and adulation accounted for little because before me was a very visible incarnation of all female gods, getting ready to starve with her newborn infant. She was begging passionately to save the life of her child and yet all the world passed by, with such cruelhearted indifference.

Then a cheerful well-dressed gentleman came out of his establishment and extended a warm handshake. He indicated that his store was stocked with all I would need. He brought me to the third floor where he kept his best merchandise. I was impressed by its quality and cost and bought two Saris and three silk scarfs. Then he led me to a back room where he kept a dizzying portfolio of blue and X-rated movies. He was wondering if I was interested in any of this. I peered briefly at some of the frames and felt slightly embarrassed for him.

This encounter gave me flashbacks of when I was a teenager in Ireland. At that time, I would tear around the country on my motorbike, with my brother at the back. We would go from one video store to the next, trying to sell our stock of banned videos, which we procured from a distributor in the North. The story was always the same. They always had some backroom, which functioned as their Sancta Sanctorum. On arrival, they would direct us very covertly back there—like lambs to the slaughter. Then they would carefully scrutinize the illicit merchandise, like the Ebenezer Scrooges that they were. In doing so, their eyes would roll around, like those of crocodiles and I could feel them sumptuously basking and salivating beneath their hooded lids. In a few moments, it was all over, and we would get the verdict. They would usually chuck them back in our faces, saying "*Not seedy enough!*" I always came away feeling like a pimp of sorts, but I needed the extra cash.

Then one night my mother found our bag of videos, and screamed, "*We will not have that filth in this house.*" After that it was GAME-OVER, and our video business fell into decline. It was not long before we were up to far better mischief. Then I asked the merchant, what was the cause of all the commotion happening on the streets below. He said that a Muslim festival was underway—that of the Ashura. He was planning on closing his business early to partake in it. I expected, he would close as soon as I left.

When I came out, I noticed a teenage boy in raggedy-ass clothes sleeping peacefully on a bullock cart. He seemed completely oblivious to all the noise and excitement going on around him. I was impressed by his *laissez-faire* attitude to life. It so happened, that I ran into him again, later that day in a different part of the city. In just a few short hours, he seemed to have miraculously transformed from a sleeping peasant into a living Buddha. When he looked at me, it was through such peaceful radiant eyes, that it took me completely by shock. They pierced through me, whitewashing my mind of all extraneous thoughts. In an instant, I became teleported into an entirely different dimension. A powerful psychedelic world, untouchable by that of our everyday existence. Yes, he moved effortlessly through the world like a lotus in mud, and despite all the muck and slime it continuously threw at him; nothing could obscure his inner purity. The living guru walked amongst us and was to be seen in the quietness and serenity of those eyes.

He was obviously one, who demanded nothing out of life and was always in a complete embrace of it. In spite of his abject poverty, the world made him shine all the more. Encountering him again, I gave him a nice pile of rupees, so that he could eat at least for a while. Once again, his undemanding look had me hooked! In contrast, many I had known were incredibly demanding. All were extortionists of life, and now I perceived the face of rapacity in everyone but him.

Then I decided to take a rickshaw ride to visit the ISKCON temple dedicated to Lord Krishna. The rickshaw owner was going flat-out while casually smoking a cigarette. I could hear all his grunts and gasps, and it had begun to torture me inside. He seemed to be strangling the surrounding air for all the oxygen he could suck-up. I was sure, any moment he would finally surrender his spirit and hit the pavement with a smash. These ludicrous dimensions of life amaze me at times. Here was this 100lb skeletal Indian charged with pulling a 200lb+ gorilla across a teeming, polluted and craze-filled city. One in which death lurked at every intersection and all so that she could get to see her beloved Lord Krishna—the beacon of love and universal compassion. I should have been arrested on the spot for my heartless dispassion to all humanity and for daring to smile above the fray while treating living beings like mules.

During my second level Kriya Yoga initiation, I had chosen the Krishna Mantra because I felt I needed to strengthen in both love and compassion. Others were choosing the Shiva, Lakshmi or Gayatri mantras. These mantras brought various yogic powers and wealth. I understood, however, that unless one has love in their heart, one has nothing at all. In any case, I always had a fondness for Lord Krishna because of his wonderful harmonious blend of male and female energy. I bought many pictures and ornaments of him during a trip to Southern India two years before. I even had a stone statue made that was carved while I was climbing to the top of Mt. Arunachala.

My yoga leader said I would only need to repeat this mantra 100,000 times before it would start to take effect. Two years and 50,000 repetitions later, I remained the same miserable, cold-hearted SOB; I had always been. It was then; I knew I had been had. Yes, I felt stupider than those Zazen Zombies who sit with their backs perfectly straight all day, thinking they will miraculously turn into enlightened beings. It seemed there was far better hope for turning a pile of cow dung into a Mother Teresa.

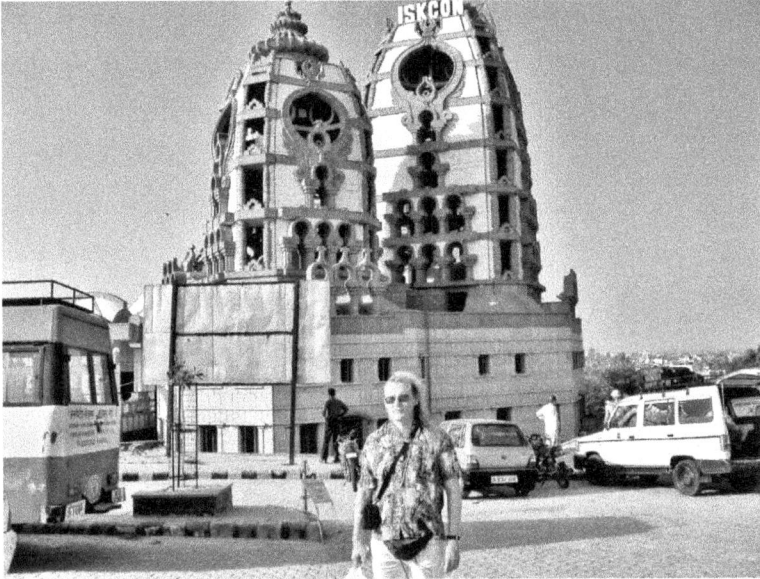

AT THE ISKCON TEMPLE IN NEW DELHI

When I got back to the hotel, there was a message saying my luggage had been located. Since we were heading to Rishikesh that day, two busloads of yogis had to wait for me at the airport while I picked it up. As I came out with my prodigal luggage, they all started clapping loudly and making joyous exclamations. This made my heart soar and temporarily vanquished my inner demons. Maybe life wasn't so bad after all! I felt all volcanoes of negativity subside for the present. Then all began belting off their mantras, and it was not long before I heard "*Om Kriya Babaji Nama Aum*," from every direction. I would probably hear it 10,000 times or more before we arrived in Rishikesh. I didn't care; the repetitive sound made me feel tranquil, and for a while, at least, it divorced me from all the problems of life.

We spent four to five days in Rishikesh. Each morning, I would get up before dawn to meditate near the Ganges. Then I would complete a regimen of Hatha yoga postures, all before breakfast. On one such morning, after emerging from the Ganges, I noticed two other yogis serenely absorbed in deep meditation. It turned out that they were meditating on whether or not to get married while on this trip to India. It was a somewhat renegade decision since they were a mixed-race couple. The outcome was a go, and so we had a traditional Indian wedding for them, a few days later. Another morning while at the Ganges meditating I noticed some food and water passed through a hole in the ground nearby. It turned out, some yogi or ascetic was down below engaging in some extreme solitary meditation. I never did see him, apart from that hand which I saw emerging from the earth. Nevertheless, I felt thrilled to be in the presence of one engaged in such disciplined yogic Sadhana practice. While in Rishikesh, I also visited the Divine Life Society headquarters where birthday celebrations were underway commemorating the life of Swami Sivananda Saraswati. I felt this auspicious since I had just begun reading some of his teachings, a few months prior. His life story was very inspiring, and I was profoundly impressed by the unconditional joy he always radiated, in videos I had watched of him.

As we progressed higher into the Himalayas, it became evident that heavy rains had already done extensive damage to the road. Looking out, I could see large sections of it were already missing. At times, large rocks and boulders would come careening down the mountain, and narrowly miss the bus by a few feet. It only would take one of those boulders to whack us square in the jaw and then we would have won the jackpot—the prize being an untimely departure from psychoplanet. Fortunately, our driver was a fearless nutcase, and he kept on going. Eventually, however, there came the point when the bus could proceed no further. It was not the most opportune time to halt since it was raining hard outside and getting late. We would either need to spend the night aboard the bus or else travel a number miles through landslide territory to the nearest town. After a while, the collective decision was made to take only those possessions, which were critical and proceed on foot. As we crossed the roughest patches, we were all on high alert to avoid any tumbling boulders and everything else mother nature and destiny had in store for us.

SOME OF THE BOULDERS, EN ROUTE

After spending a night at this stop-off site, we progressed to the town of Joshimath. There we were mercilessly hounded by local merchants, looking to sell us various trinkets, shawls, and blankets. They had an intense and hungry appearance and were relentless in their pursuit. I would have loved to have bought something from everyone. However, I had to limit my load since I had a long trek up to the Valley of Flowers, the very next day. All the same, if I had known just how cold it was going to get the next night, I would have bought an extra blanket and shawl.

NEAR JOSHIMATH

The hike up to the Valley of Flowers took most of the next day. It was an arduous journey, punctuated by the occasional torrential downpour. I was left lavishly soaked, yet also sweating inside my raincoat and leggings. I also had the sensation of being cooked, and steam was silently emanating from me in diaphanous clouds of vapor. Even so, such minor hardships were of little concern because the scenery was so captivating, even hypnotizing. There were many Sadhus in small quaint huts along the path, and I dropped in to have darshan with a few. I would take their pictures, rest and listen to their stories. As I climbed higher and deeper into the mists, I felt myself under an Orphic spell, in which I sensed the artificial boundaries separating me from the divine gradually melting away. Yes, I was slowly ascending into the most sublime realm and the immortal kingdom of the gods, demons, and Asuras where seraphic spirits and tutelary deities roamed freely about.

TREKKING TO THE VALLEY OF FLOWERS

I was coming closer to my essential self and had disconnected from my earthly body long ago. Even so, I could still hear it panting and groaning hard in the background, as it gasped laboriously for more air. It seemed like some remote steam engine now, whose spirited actions and machinations had lost all governance from me. Some of the other yogis went by on mules and waved to me. I felt they were cheating and also depriving themselves out of an authentic pilgrimage. As I ascended a particularly steep rocky section, the mule ahead gave out and fell to the ground. He too had been panting hard and was sweating profusely. I felt in him a kindred spirit. Then his owner started whipping him savagely to get him up. The lacerations were painful to endure, and they shook me out of my heavenly-intoxicated empire.

All of a sudden my peaceful state had disappeared. The mystical celestial bubble which had enfolded me in such ecstatic bliss, just moments before, had now been irreparably perforated. What emerged, was a demon filled with hatred, rage, and derision. One, who desired to grab the mule's owner by the throat and start whipping him about for a change. I shouted out, "*Can you not see this mule has had enough? He has given all he has got?*" After a while, the owner, fuming and exasperated, gave up and left. I stayed with the mule a while longer, until he finally died. There I left him. I was surprised they didn't have knackers already on the scene, ready to cut him apart. As I continued upward, I was emotionally numb and zoned out by the experience. The horizon had become an absolute blank.

THE MULE JUST BEFORE ITS DEATH

At last the town of Gangotri emerged from the mists like some medieval delight. All the same, when I got to the hotel, I was immensely fatigued and just wanted to sleep it all off. The bedclothes looked thoroughly unappetizing. There was no way; I was jumping in under those covers. I did not have any extra change of clothes, so I had to sleep in the wet ones that were on me. The best hotel in the town—Eh? Say that to the broken window, with its large gaping hole. Through this immense aperture would circulate a cold breeze for most of the night. A form of natural air conditioning, I suppose! Around 11 pm I awoke, to find it was pitch dark outside. Apparently, the electrical generator for the town had already shut down for the night. I crept down to the lobby area and asked for a cup of Chai. The fumes from noxious mule manure were everywhere. I was impressed by the staff who were so cordial and welcoming, and they brought my Chai directly to my room.

Next morning, after an icy shower, I felt thoroughly awake and exuberant of spirit. I descended to the restaurant where most of the other yogis were having breakfast. It turned out they had been concerned about my absence from the Satsang, the night before. They were worried that I had become lost somewhere on the trek. I did my best, to shield myself from their probing questions since I was not ready to enumerate and explain all the events from the previous day. Also, it was becoming abundantly clear that I was fast developing some cold or flu.

GANGOTRI – EARLY MORNING

The town of Gangotri was cobbled in sections, and everywhere mule-drawn carriages were going about bringing provisions from one place to the next. A few of the yogis were complaining about the dire accommodations. I did not want to jump aboard this bandwagon. I could easily put up with minor inconveniences. Did it matter, that the bedclothes hadn't been changed in almost a century? Why did they expect of such a remote town high in the Himalayas? I didn't care too much about the broken windows or cracked mirrors since I wasn't holding a Ph.D. in hotel aesthetics. This place may have seemed, like some ghetto, to some, yet I felt privileged to be here. It carried a certain ambiance, and I enjoyed peeking back in time and escaping all the artificial encumbrances of our society.

We were too addicted to comfort and convenience and pandering after a Martha Stewart lifestyle. This was a major problem, preventing our spiritual progress and part of the reason for our lost empathy for others. We had allowed ourselves to become overly-obsessed with things. It seemed the poisons of materialism and consumerism were our new drugs of choice. We stayed in Gangotri for two more nights, and I found myself gently seduced by its uncontaminated charm and pure simplicity of its ways. I wanted to stay suspended here forever in this mystical kingdom of the blue lotus eaters.

Next, we headed to the town of Badrinath. This jewel in the Himalayas is closely associated with the immortal Yogi Babaji. Many stories were circulating about his incredible powers. His yogic ability, for instance, to defy death, since the 2nd century A.D. due to his proficiency with powerful pranayama techniques. He had also mastered all the Siddhis and could manifest anywhere he wanted, and in any form he wished. I had been very taken in by all this yogic propaganda. By the time we reached the hotel, I was almost expecting Babaji to welcome us in person. Oh, what bliss bunnies we were! Meanwhile, I would go out, late at night for a stroll and glance at the stars and the peeks of the Himalayas and remain hypnotized by their majesty. Then I would silently say to myself *"Babaji is up there some-where right now getting ready to display his miraculous powers, to anyone brave enough to ascend these steep mountainous pass-es."*

The temple in Badrinath was dedicated to Lord Vishnu—*"The Preserver and Protector."* The mystical Sarasvati river was trick-ling gently nearby, and flowing almost completely underground. My meditations in this temple went incredibly well—probably the best I have ever had. So perhaps, there was something to this yogic and mystical view of existence, after all. It seemed there were latent powers and hidden dimensions to life that we do not fully comprehend. Ones ungraspable because they were veiled by our vertical western mindsets. Maybe we were living out our entire lives just on the tip of the iceberg.

BADRINATH TEMPLE, EARLY MORNING

Then a few days later, we meditated in the same cave, where Babaji first appeared to Lahiri Mahasaya. I had never seen a cave that prevented unprivileged access. One with a large metal gate in front of it, that was kept under lock and key. This no doubt, was also the end product of the corrupting influence of western civilization. Fortunately, my yoga teacher had procured the key before making the trip to India. We all stayed there meditating silently in the dark until nightfall, and then hiked down to the nearby village, using small torches and candles to light our path. After that, we traveled onwards to the small remote village of Mana.

Mana is one of the last outposts, between India and Tibet and the end of the road; so to speak. Here, old ladies went about carrying large loads of straw on their backs. They looked extremely rugged and weatherworn. Nonetheless, their lives were ones of utter simplicity, living in blissful harmony with nature and the elements. It contrasted most acutely with the world in which I lived and worked. I silently wondered what feelings and thoughts it would generate, were they to enter my slice of paradise. They probably would think they had been unwittingly abducted onto an alien spaceship. In any case, they remained as oblivious to our cameras, as they were to our light bantering talk and persiflage and seemed unready, as yet, to embrace the nineteenth century. I doubted they had the opportunities, or privilege of doing so. Their worldly ambitions pivoted around very basic and pressing needs. It included getting sufficient straw and water to support their livestock and thatching their huts against winter storms. I would have loved, to have been a fly crawling up the wall of one of their rustic dwellings so that I could procure their candid opinion on western yogis. I expected they saw us as overindulgent beings who were also notoriously weird and eccentric. Seeming invulnerable ones, living lives of complete ease and leisure. It was almost as if we were an entirely different species since our perspectives and priorities contrasted so extensively. They would probably spend their entire lives in this small village, and never experience even a single break in their daily routine.

SOME VILLAGERS NEAR MANA

The physiognomies of the villagers and local denizens of this area looked entirely Tibetan. Here, at this remote outpost, the tiny mad idea percolated in my mind, that I should travel on-wards into Tibet. This was likely to be the best opportunity; I would ever have for doing so. I had been inspired to visit, ever since reading a book on the life of Tibet's Great Yogi Milarepa, by Evans Wentz. Time has a way of moving on, and fortuitous opportunities, not taken, often become swallowed up and lost for good. They trickle gently through the sieve of life like water through pebbles. All I had to do was convince some of the other yogis to travel with me. This endeavor turned out to be far more difficult than I initially expected. Two German yogis, Ralf and Yogananda, planned on returning to Babaji's cave and meditat-ing there for an extended period, before adventuring to other places of pilgrimage. In fact, they wanted to travel all over India for a year. They would begin with trips to Chandigarh, Lahore, and Haridwar and then planned on heading down to Agra, Calcutta, Pondicherry, Madras, and Tiruvannamalai. Finally, they would circle back upwards through Kerala, Goa, and Poona. Another German yogi, whom I shared a room with, had started to cough up blood at night. She obviously wasn't too well, and the altitude was affecting her. Her tongue had turned black, and I was at a loss for words to explain this. So I sublimated my inner feelings and pretended not to be too alarmed.

Two other Yogis, I knew, were heading to Bodh Gaya and then onwards to Benares. Another was heading back to Delhi, where he planned on hiring our bus, all to himself. He was going to take it everywhere that his whims demanded. I can still picture him, in my mind's eye running up and down between the rows of seats, grimacing excitedly like a crazed monkey at every passing attraction—a veritable Hanuman of the Yogic circuit. The nutcase driver, at the wheel, looking blankly out while casually smoking his cigarette—thinking the whole world has gone mad.

The recently married Canadian yogis were heading back to meet their maker, in the form of their parents. Not sure how their mixed marriage would go down with their kin but I extended my blessings for a great life ahead. They were so suited to one another, and I hoped it would all work out glowingly in the end. Then there was Martha, a Spanish Yogi, with whom I had been getting on very well. All the same, this carried all the hints of degenerating into a full-fledged lesbian relationship. A path I did not care to go down, at this particular juncture in time. Finally, I got the message loud and clear that I was on my own on this venture. When I mentioned my proposal to our yoga Master, he thought, I was off my rocker. His response was something to the effect, *"There is no civilization out there in any direction for at least three days of hiking, and the winter snow will be falling soon. In fact, the entire township of Badrinath will be abandoned within a week or so."*

Despite all this, I remained intractable and persevered with my ambitions. I started purchasing all the provisions needed to last me six days or more. My thought was that I could always turn around if I didn't run into any civilization within three days of hiking. Thus, I could still get down to Delhi before the snow arrived. I loaded up with lots of water, dried fruit, nuts, a thermal sleeping bag, tarp and some water purifiers. I also procured sunscreen, lighters, flares, a compass and some anti-venom pills for snakebites. I was not sure, what use these flares would have, but they were light to carry and gave me a much-needed confidence boost. My cell phone would certainly be of no use. When I was purchasing the flares, the trader introduced me to a Tibetan sling made from Yak hair, which he called a Horto. He said this would be far more useful for me out-there, than the flares. My biggest concern apart from extreme weather was my complete vulnerability. If I got injured, I would be royally screwed—to put it nicely. And so it was that a few days later, I arrived at the most strategic vantage point for making the journey. Then, I headed off into the unknown on my solo adventure.

NEXT STOP TIBET

THE AUTHOR CLOSE TO THE TIBETAN BORDER

The first day of traveling wasn't bad. I made the mistake of traveling during the noonday heat, and this left me thoroughly exhausted and fatigued, later in the day. Then, I bedded down for the night and lit a fire and started looking up at the stars. I remember feeling a completely mystical and cosmic experience. I realized at that instant that I had never truly seen the night sky. Never seen the stars, for the pure, pristine crystalline jewels, that they were. The haze of pollution cast by our industrialized cultures of progress had obfuscated their raw, naked beauty and dazzling splendor. If such was the extent of the devastation wrought upon our night sky, what more pernicious harm had our culture inflicted upon the sky of our minds, I wondered? Then a snake came by and stayed for a while, before slithering off again. As it did not seem threatening, I left it alone. Perhaps it was a Naga Buddha snake sent for my protection. So much for snakes being afraid of fire!

The second day, I was climbing high mountain passes throughout the day. The scenery was mind-blowing and awesome to behold. Even though it filled me with exultation and elevation of thought, I was beginning to curse myself silently, for traveling alone. I was far from being an expert mountaineer. Yes, I had done a little rock climbing previously in the Andes, Yosemite, and South India, but nothing like this. In the end, I knew enough to breathe through pursed lips, to keep my lungs pressurized and thus avoid pneumothorax (collapsed lung). I realized that I had zero budget for errors and that this could be a most unforgiving landscape. Finally, I found a flat patch to camp out for the night. No chance of finding any wood here. Fortunately, I had brought two logs along. When the fire, finally burned itself out around 4 AM, it was not long before I started feeling intensely cold. My teeth had begun to chatter. It is amazing how a small thing like subzero temperatures, can transport one very pronouncedly into the present. Soon, I found myself unable to focus on anything else. Everything became glacial and heightened in perspective.

Then after a while, my consciousness, seemed ready to depart from my body and merge into the surrounding mountainside. It was asking to be let go, so it could freely soar far beyond the murky soul strangling world of the body. The boundaries between the celestial and terrestrial started becoming blurred. The stars and moon were as much a part of my body now, as anything else. I had gone from feeling entrenched in my body, to now feeling completely divorced from any particularized existence. Then the first warm rays of the morning light finally came to caress and gently sooth me. Feeling infused with new life, I fell into a deep sleep. When I awoke hours later, my bones felt so stiff from the previous day's hiking, that I did not feel up for carrying on. The rational part of me knew I needed to press ahead since I was out of logs for the nightly fire.

It turned into a war between my mind and my body, with the mind finally winning out. Despite starting out relatively late, I realized I needed to get past these mountains, or it would soon be curtains for me. This day turned into a more amplified version of the day before. Once more, I was feeling the treachery of these high mountainous passes. Feeling alone, exhausted and somewhat fearful and yet also exhilarated, in some strange way. My body seemed to have morphed into some miniaturized avatar or troll-like being. One inhabiting a perfidious landscape, far greater than itself. I was just an awareness now—an awareness engraved with certain sensations both pleasing and terrifying. My mind was in a fog, and the once rigid partitions of my physical body had all but disappeared. I could no longer readily differentiate it from the surroundings.

Today was the day I had expected to reach some form of civilization. Sadly, all I could see was a vast desolate landscape, stretching out for miles and miles in every direction. The surrounding panorama was just like the tentacles of a giant octopus; ugly, bare and getting ready to strangle me from every angle. I contemplated, turning around and weighed the benefits over the risks. In my mentally hazed state, it seemed far more dangerous, to turn around than to press on ahead. I slept that third night in a steep mountainous section and constructed a makeshift shelter from rocks and my tarp. I had picked up just a few crags of wood for my nightly fire. Fortunately, I had gathered any Yak dung I had stumbled across during the day. I knew this would greatly enhance and prolong the nightly fire. Subsequently, it held out for a good number of hours before my teeth began chattering again and hammering out their familiar staccato rhythm.

An ominous isolation and despair began creeping in from all around. I felt an insidious presence, that was most uncomforting. Something unearthly, watching me from every angle. As I began slipping in-and-out of consciousness, I was invaded in my dreams, by the form of the grim reaper, who was gently rowing her boat on this great blue lake. Things started to change shape and became powered with all sorts of significance. The very snow itself seemed luminous. It was as if it were extending a welcome portal for me to enter freely forbidden realms. Everything became polymorphic and multi-dimensional in its topology. A rich multi-hued mosaic of splendid forms came into view, and the true endogenous nature of all became apparent. I began to perceive the unique haecceity and underlying face of nature's true Being. Suddenly the books I had read by Carlos Castaneda started to gain in relevance.

At this stage, I felt no strength to go on. I wanted to make this refuge my last little bighorn. My last defining stand against all invisible enemies and existence as a whole. It was only a matter of time before an arrow would shoot out now from one of these invisible spirits and deal me a fatal blow. Then it would all be over, and I would sail seamlessly into non-existence. I would have stayed here too, except I was yanked rather abruptly out my visionary state when a wolf came prowling and biting at my left leg. It gave me such an immense fright that I jumped up roaring "*I am not your breakfast.*" Before I knew it, the wolf was at my rear and standing on his hind legs. Its paws were placed firmly upon my shoulder. To a neutral observer, it must have seemed like I was getting my backside very invasively birched by a wolf and that rape was on the cards but I knew its real intentions. Fortunately, I had brought along that Tibetan sling, which I used to scare it off. He scampered off real fast once I had swung it a couple of times very aggressively in his direction. I was very grateful that I did not need to whack him over the head with my payload of rock. One must be kind after all to all living things. In truth, I had never gotten over the baby squirrels in New England. One fatal day, I needed to cut down the tree in which they were living with my chainsaw. It was early in the afternoon, and the sun was pelting down in triple digits, and I was at serious risk of developing heatstroke. Another lumberjack had come coolly cruising by, saying the only merciful thing to do was to put them out of their misery. He indicated they could never survive on their own, without their nest or mother. So our chainsaws started cutting in and doing their business.

The entire next day, I had become so mechanical and was hovering aimlessly about as some lost corpse on a merciless plateau. Observing myself now and again, from a distance, I would murmur inwardly, "*How pathetic!*" My existence now seemed just that of a lifeless body. One dragging itself about by the heels, through pure strength of will. Hours would go by without me having a single thought of consequence. Since, I kept on hiking, even during the noonday heat, all the water soon ran out. Why hadn't I collected and boiled some water from the nearby snow, while I had the chance? Now I didn't care so much anymore. I had completely tuned out. That night, I slept on the bare plateau, before a fire and ate some of my dried fruit. The food was hard to digest without any water. I felt supremely lightheaded like I was ready to pass out. Once more I encountered the lustrous and resplendent phantasmagoria of the living landscape. That wondrous unseen aliveness which was never hidden. An aliveness, only visible, in extreme states of mind. I observed glowing halos surrounding even the simplest of objects now. Everything was composed of many layers and dimensions of utmost significance. All were revealing incredibly abstract images that were deeply set. Images that I had somehow never noticed before. Then the very landscape started bobbing up and down. It was then that I knew I was close to being cooked.

The next morning, my mind was undeniably doddering. It would not be long now; I thought before the vultures start moving in, to feed on my carcass. I had become a complete blank and had lost all my resolve. I was dehydrated and was starting to feel that horrible dry sandpaper sensation in my mouth. The tremendous pain in my head was not abating. *"Now I have become Death, destroyer of worlds,"* was the only thought firing in my neural cylinders, as I surveyed the bleak landscape. It was at that moment that I saw some flags flying faintly in the distance. Perhaps, this was some point of civilization at last or else just another hallucinatory projection. Even so, this gave me the energy I needed to get going again. Soon, I felt myself emerging out of the spirit world and crossing the invisible threshold back into humanity. It took about an hour or more before I could get to the location of the flags. As I came closer, my senses profiled for me the portrait of some remote outpost or ashram.

I knocked hard on the door and was answered by a weatherworn man, who spoke not a word of English. He muttered some words, to himself in Tibetan, then shuffled off. A short while later, a new figure emerged. One who exuded serenity and wisdom, as well as a masterful command of the English language. His dark, penetrating magnetic eyes immediately embalmed me, in their luminous quiescence and splendor. Instantly, I could sense a powerful, probing invasion spreading all across my body, dissecting me down to the cellular level. He seemed to be psycho-kinetically displacing and infusing energy waves inside me. Certain energy surges started to swell up within which would have induced a trans-spatial, polymorphous orgasmic experience in normal circumstances. However, I was too drained and numb now to feel much of anything at all. More like a wilting Orchid, a day into its death cycle; never to be resuscitated again. I grunted out, *"I just need some water and a place to stay for the night. Then I will continue onward with my journey."*

Seeing the poor state I was in, he immediately took me to a backroom to get some water. Soon I was getting all the replenishment I needed and feeling more vitalized by the moment. I had the intuition that I had just entered the very gates of paradise itself. Within a few minutes, my headache was disappearing, and my head was beginning to loosen. I felt myself awakening and gaining in clarity. That dark obscuring fog which hung over my consciousness for so long was lifting, and everything was unfolding in its full transparency, once more. Yes, the sun of my senses was coming back to life. Even though my stomach wasn't up for much, he handed me a bowl of soup. I was very grateful for his warmth and consideration. It was now dawning on me, just how badly off, I had been.

Then he asked me, where I was planning to journey?

I responded "I am not too sure yet, Lhasa perhaps, in the long-term. However, I would like to visit some nearby monasteries, caves and local attractions first."

"Are you out of your mind, Lhasa is almost a thousand miles away, and the winter snows are coming in fast."

It was like a Déjà vu with my yogic teacher because I most certainly had heard such unmitigated, elegant and forceful words of wisdom once before! I did not feel like heading back to Badrinath, anytime soon. He seemed to have caught my thought-wave and immediately responded: "Badrinath is probably already abandoned for the winter. In any case, it is far too dangerous to journey back there now, because of the impending risk of snow. Regrettably, it is extremely dangerous also to go on ahead. Not just because of the snow, but also because of the Chinese. They hate foreigners almost as much as Tibetans, especially ones carrying cameras. Why do you think we all moved out here to this remote outpost? It was to be left alone six months of the year, to practice our religion in peace. They have destroyed and burned most of our monasteries, sacred literature, and holy relics and taken over our businesses and lands. Now they are molding our children with their godless ways and their stark ideologies of Communism and Confucianism. Up ahead is just a spiritual wasteland, everywhere you go. You came at the wrong time. In fact, you could never have come at the right time. Alexandra David-Neel was probably the only woman ever, who came to Tibet opportunely. Even then, she had a most difficult time of it."

We cannot have a woman staying here—it would be far too much of a distraction. I quickly retorted, "I can knit, yarn, cook, work in the fields and even lift heavy loads." He was singularly unimpressed and said, "We can do all that for ourselves." When I mentioned doing Palmistry and Tarot, he just laughed and stared at me like I was wearing crystal pyramids on my head.

Then, I mentioned Massage, Reiki, Homeopathy and Psychic touch. This last token offering was meant merely as a jest because I knew almost nothing about Reiki and Homeopathy. I had learned a little of each from watching and listening to other yogis, who were skilled in these fields. Apparently, I was getting desperate. In the end, all my vain boasts did not matter because he just looked at me, as if to say: *"Do you have anything more to offer?"*

It was then, I had an epiphany and inquired whether their Ashram had a source of electrical power. He said, "We don't get any electricity right now, but we have a new generator which we need to install." I said, "Great! That is where I come in handy since I am an Electrical Engineer by profession. I can easily get all your electrical systems and appliances up and running provided you can procure all the necessary materials. I can also setup your wireless networks if you have any service, which I doubt." This last offering seemed to subdue him a tad. He said, "I will discuss this with the other Monks and Lamas and let you know. Meanwhile, have yourself a nice nap, you look like you are exhausted.

About an hour later, just as I was beginning to feel drugged with sleep, he came back, saying "You can't stay in this Ashram. There is, however, a small hut, not too far away which we use for extended periods of solitude. You are welcome to stay there until the winter snows give way." Feeling elated with this welcome news, I asked: "*Where exactly am I?*" He responded that I was in a region known as Ngari, not too far from the Tholing Monastery. Then he added, "You took the same route as Atisha in entering Tibet."

I asked, "**Who is Atisha?**"

He simply responded saying, "He is an Enlightened mystic, from almost a thousand years ago. It is certainly portentous that you came here by the exact route, he took. I am prepared therefore to teach you his Sutras on mind training, on the one condition, that if by some miracle you ever reach to their deeper message, you will one day teach them in the West."

The living quarters in the hut were extremely barebones and humbling. It was just a pile of rocks arbitrarily mounded together, and it seemed more like a 10th century stone enclosure. I had seen many like it before in remote parts of Ireland while growing up. This type of construction usually functioned as the private hermitages of monks. Ones who voluntarily enter human isolation and seclusion for years on end. As I peered within, I saw just a wooden bed, with some blanket made from Yak hair. The floor was made of mud, and straw covered it in places. There was no window or pillows; not even a candle. No inner running water, so I would need to fetch my daily water from a nearby stream.

There was nothing much to look at in the hut itself. Nothing to distract! An ideal place for meditation, I suppose. I knew once it got dark, I was going to feel impregnated in the very womb of the void itself. I did not want to ask where the toilet was, as I already knew! It was extending 40,000 miles across mother

Earth in any direction that I cared to take. Of course, toilet roll would also be an absolute luxury and would be supplied by mother nature. Suddenly, for some strange reason this crude old nursery rhyme started playing itself over–and–over in my head. The one that went:

In days of old when knights were bold

And toilets weren't invented

They did their load upon the road

And went away contented

My new headquarters unquestionably made the hotel in Gangotri, seem like the Ritz Carlton. The Lama advised that I go to the kitchen, early morning and late evening to attend meals. Finally, he introduced himself, as Lama Mingyur Dorje and said he would begin teaching me, the very next morning at 6 am. When he left, that same nursery rhyme just kept on circling in my head. It had suddenly become like a personal mantra. One that was dragging me down fast and furious into all the sewers and gutters of the world. It was not long before I was composing variations on it.

In days of old when nights were cold

And pussies weren't invented

They got their yaks upon their backs

And went away contented

Most assuredly, I was paddling gently now, down every nasty and vile conduit of thought imaginable. It was as if I had taken Charon's raft directly into the underworld of Hades. All around me were sightless, emaciated and mutilated bodies crying out like crows and squealing like Banshees of the night. I had transformed into something hellish, beastly and fiendish and yet also so calculating and mean-hearted. I was even scheming now on precisely how I was going to rob Charon of all those Danakes; he had yanked from the mouths of the dead. Yes, I would be top-dog down here before long. A fully-fledged and Bona-Fide Mafioso criminal running my personal extortion racket. Extorting the dead for every dime they possessed— it was the business to be in after all; just like the funeral one.

Then my ideations drifted a little upward, and I found myself interrogating Lama Mingyur Dorje in my mind. I started out with:

"Let's get down to brass tacks here and serious business. This has never been about Atisha's teachings, and you know it! It has always been about how many Yaks you squared away and screwed last night. Come on now, come clean! Because I had two scouts stationed out on Chaukhamba the night before last and they saw it all."

Finally, Lama Dorje meekly responded saying, "I promise, I only ever slept with the good looking ones!"

FIRST LEARN THE
PRELIMINARIES

THE VALLEY OF FLOWERS

L ama Mingyur Dorje, started the morning session, declaring "Almost everything worthwhile in life, requires some essential training. Without the requisite discipline, you will not progress very far. For example, no one would dare send an astronaut to the moon, without providing some necessary expertise beforehand! Instead, astronauts are trained intensively and carefully screened in advance. They undergo rigorous physical and psychological tests, to make sure they have the essential life-skills and endurance needed, to cope with harsh, uncertain environments. They are exhaustively trained on technical matters, and on the finer points of rocketry. Thus they become confident that they can adapt, innovate, and compensate for systems failures on the fly.

Similarly, you would consider it the height of insanity and irrationality, to sign up for a heart transplant from a self-established surgeon. Nor would you trust your life to a pilot, who had only ever trained with flight simulation videos. Even a musical prodigy of the stature of Mozart had to practice some. His untimely demise, at the age of thirty-five, was probably due to professional exhaustion. Likewise, Tesla, Maxwell, Edison, and Einstein had to cerebrate, innovate, excogitate and perspire immensely, for many years before they produced anything notable of worth. We all possess innate abilities, untapped capacities, and suspended talents. Right training, is needed to leverage these and bring them to fruition. We can all take advantage of valuable learning aids and proper guidance at times, to elicit the best in us. No one needs to start from scratch. Each can mobilize and exploit tried and tested techniques, already proven to work.

Unfortunately, many of our abilities, remain latent and hidden because we are unaware of such abilities. Consequently, we continue to uphold a very defeatist picture of ourselves. Not knowing how to reliably uncover our most outstanding talents, can be our greatest loss. Many remain stillborn because their preeminent strengths lie buried and dormant within either as seeds that never germinate or else as innate competencies that remain unexpressed. Often, we are afraid to have our real strengths recognized. We are either extremely ashamed of them, or else mistrustful of others."

I responded, "I can fully relate to all these insights. Recently, I met a girl who possessed very strong powers of precognition. She was ashamed to disclose her powers of prognostication. Afraid others would start thinking she was some weirdo or witch. Sadly, prevailing opinion contaminated her mindset, and she began to consider her abilities as somehow unnatural. She then repressed and denied them, which caused them to become even more atrophied. When we connected, she intuitively grasped that I might be more open-minded. I immediately communicated that there was nothing unnatural, unique or exceptional in her endowments. All abilities are natural, I said, but in some, they are more developed than others. What is unnatural, I said, is when some stigma becomes attached to them. Closed-minded people, like to label certain spiritual abilities as unnatural because they are ultimately fearful of anything that attacks their belief system. Their first defense is often to lash out, and project and they use terms that are personally denigrating. As we communicated more, she began to open up and feel more at ease. Finally, she gained the confidence to embrace her abilities consciously. As a result, they began to flourish again."

The Lama responded, "Yes, most people do not realize how blinded and circumvented, they have become, by their limited thinking patterns. They make such a tremendous effort to fit in and adjust that they no longer live authentic lives. To become whole, one's growth and evolution must progress simultaneously in many different dimensions at once. We can readily see that a violin with only one string doesn't make for very good music, but we place ourselves in the same predicament when we close ourselves off to new ideas and experiences.

Our fears often block us on critical paths of inner exploration, and they prevent us from voyaging deep. I think this is the real reason we suffocate and die. We have become dried up, devitalized and so deprived of spiritual nourishment because of fear. Hence we never reach to and surmount those key inner barricades, where we could instrument pivotal and progressive changes in our thought patterns. We live only at the level of biochemical weeds. Desiccated weeds that can only flourish in the dry, barren soil of the relative existence.

Yes, the need for prior training is evident, in every field of life, except where it is needed the most—the unchartered realm of mind. The mind is the most powerful instrument, ever known. More potent than any futuristic or healing technology. More miraculously creative than any invention, remedy, power or understanding seen in the outside world. In fact, the mind generates the world we perceive and countless other universes besides. Many of these we cannot see, and others we have long forgotten. All the same, Quantum Physics is now beginning to apprehend them mathematically through its theories on the (1) *Multiverse,* (2) *Quantum Potentialities,* (3) *Many Worlds* and *(4) Parallel Universes.*

Mastery of mind is no more difficult to achieve than other forms of accomplishment. The only impediment to this mastery is mental waste and indigestion because we are constantly dumping garbage into it—all our toxic thoughts and fears for a kick-off. We foolishly believe we can go on and thrive, and be as effective as our raw potential portends and not be blunted and dulled by all the grease and slime we have thrown into its engines for countless millennia. How can our minds reach clarity and understanding when they are continuously feeding on so much rubbish, collected from the landfills of the world?

Mind is immaculate in its essence. Regrettably, so much debris has been allowed to pile on top. The defiling dust of so many contradictions, competing desires and meaningless goals that conflict with one another. Most entertain the naïve conception, that their beliefs do not affect or change them in any way. We treat beliefs like they are books on a shelf. We do not readily see how each influences our perceptions and quality of life. The Truth is that our whole world picture and all actions we undertake is powered entirely by our beliefs.

Mind training is just like building the strong foundation for a house, except this foundation is for one's inner house. It makes no difference how beautifully and tastefully decorated a house is on the inside if its foundation is poorly constructed. If you build it on shaky ground, it is guaranteed to totter and fall, or else it will be blown asunder by the tiniest breeze. A secure and strong foundation is crucial. This house is metaphorical, and it symbolizes all who capriciously follow the idle and vain pursuits of the world. It is a warning to those easily taken in by every temptation, pleasure or passing ideology. And to those whose minds are endlessly blown about by the winds of desire, fallacious thinking patterns and arbitrary fears. Before long the vermin and rodents of the world start moving in, and the whole place begins to stink to high heaven. All because there has never been any proper mental ventilation instantiated through yogic practice. Soon they find the house of their minds falling into a state of dilapidation and disrepair. It starts to disintegrate, rust and corrode before their very eyes. First, their physical vitality drops and spirit of enterprise and adventure. Then their views start becoming stale and perverted, and rigor mortis sets in. Eventually, their mind becomes condemned by the county council of sanity, for not been up to code and the house needs to be abandoned.

OUR SUBCONSCIOUS MIND, AS ALL POWERFUL AND AWAKE

The subconscious is the most powerful part of our mind. It is that aspect, which is unguarded and open to suggestions. It does not evaluate or judge what you feed it. Instead, it goes to work instantaneously, trying to accomplish all you demand. The subconscious is wide awake, even when your conscious mind is fast asleep. In fact, this mind never sleeps. It is at work 24x7, flawlessly managing all complex and critical functions vital for keeping you alive. It controls your respiratory, digestive and endocrinal systems. It monitors and controls hormonal levels, blood pressure, and all other integral life functions. It simply cringes whenever we bombard it with unworthy thoughts and beliefs.

In Tibet, we consider this mind, the ground or storehouse consciousness known as the **Alaya-Vijynana.** Over a millennium before western psychology discovered or used the term 'subconscious' or 'unconscious' mind, we were cognizant of its dynamism, intimate operations, and miraculous powers. This storehouse consciousness contains all long forgotten memories and past experiences. It retains within its fabric, all indispensable understandings distilled from our core experiences. It functions as an invisible hub, around which accumulate all our former sensory and perceptual impressions, and it serves as the psychological template, from which our entire personality type is forged. In addition, it holds the seeds of all future desires, attachments, and fears. Understanding, the tremendous influence your storehouse consciousness exerts on all your decisions, behaviors and perceptions is critical, if you wish to reach to self-liberation. An appreciation of its intricate and complex machinations is vital for those who want to harness the power of their thought most effectively. Learning the fundamentals of mind training is crucial for attaining Mastery of mind.

A Master is never reactive to life. Instead, he always responds fluidly and dynamically to the present situation as it is evolving. He answers and reciprocates from the fountain of his inner wisdom. This wisdom is emptiness since it does not attach itself to anything. The Master's mind is therefore always a blank slate which clings to nothing yet it is highly potent. Its impartiality frees it from the poisons of desire, animosity, and compromise. Having no dream investments, the Master is always stress-free. He knows when to detach and when to exercise his will. He is like the skilled charioteer, who knows how to keep his horses of thought always harmoniously aligned. He judiciously steers his mind in the desired direction and aims to implement worthy goals. He does not allow the horses of thought to think; they are his Master. Those who think, they will become skilled meditators, or empowered operatives in the field of life, without first gaining mastery over their mind and thought, are simply delusional. Achieving mastery of mind is a necessary pre-requisite for Enlightenment. It does not produce Enlightenment, but it does eliminate all obstacles, misunderstandings, and sources of interference that stand in the way. Enlightenment is natural and spontaneous, once you have removed all hindrances that prevent the eternal light from shining outwards freely and unimpeded. Then you recognize this light is your Self-nature."

ATISHA, THE ENLIGHTENED MASTER

Lama Dorje then proceeded to provide some background on the life of Atisha. He began, "Atisha is an Enlightened Master, and probably the most potent Master, the world has ever known. He was a spiritual virtuoso over the realm of appearances and an expert in all Yogic Siddhis, Kriyas, and healing powers. As a consummate thaumaturgist, he worked observable miracles wherever he went. He was born in Northern India, in the eleventh century and studied initially at Nalanda University. He had dedicated his life, to reaching liberation, and so he set out fearlessly on a journey to modern-day Sumatra. He had heard of a Master there, named Dharmakirti, who could transmit a pure comprehension of the true nature of mind. It was a grueling and perilous voyage, that took almost a year. When he finally arrived, he underwent intense tapas and yogic practices to better condition his body for the immense work he planned to engage. He did not want the physical to be a source of interference and distraction from his mental discipline exercises and techniques. As a result, he soon could focus his mind for extended periods, without any interruption. His immense determination eventually paid off, and he achieved perfect one-pointedness of mind. This highly exalted yogic state is known in Sanskrit as *'Eka Grata.'* After this supreme feat, Dharmakirti began to teach him about the empty nature of all form and phenomena. This crucial understanding is known in Buddhist terminology as *'Shunyata.'*

Dharmakirti said: "Mind is the only powerhouse in existence. All phenomena arise from it. Sadly our minds have become too defiled through wrong understandings, mistaken beliefs, our conditioning, worldly hypnotism and the poisons of our numerous attachments and fears. In consequence, we never experience firsthand mind in its naked essence. The five inner senses have led us astray and further into darkness. We have become incredibly degenerate, and are now only able to activate and empower very limited modes of mind. As a result, we cannot understand ourselves, nor reach to critical insight. Nor do we perceive reality directly, because we have become overly-identified, with this false world of phenomenal appearances, born from our minds. It is like we have fallen into a giant mirror, and now think the murky and hellish reflections we perceive here, represent true Reality. Only by purifying our mind, can we awaken! However, we can only accomplish this by divesting ourselves of all wrong beliefs and dehypnotizing ourselves. These actions will automatically purify our senses and vaporize the severely distorted world they depict."

Then Dharmakirti gave Atisha some probing questions upon which to meditate. Questions strategically designed to penetrate to the true nature of mind.

Atisha subsequently withdrew completely from the world. He spent twelve years meditating in caves, stripping away the many layers of mind, as inherited from worldly thought and its pernicious ideologies. He wanted to reach the Supreme Source of power, which governed all existence and discern its true relationship to his microcosmic mind. Craving to know mind directly in its naked essence, he became extremely vigilant against all forms of deception, dualistic experiencing and contradictory modes of understanding. He would become completely absorbed, on a single idea or understanding for many days or months, at a time. All the same, he made excellent progress because of his intensive practice. One day his consciousness flowered and he succeeded in uncovering the light hidden deep within. This light then exploded out into the world of perception. It had become veiled and trapped within for numerous eons due to his worldly conditioning and numerous faulty understandings.

Once Atisha became Enlightened, he studied under two other Enlightened masters. Dharma Rakshita and Maitriyogi. Dharma Rakshita taught him perfect compassion and the Bodhisattva ideals of working selflessly for the liberation of all beings. Maitriyogi taught him how to transform compassion into a potently active psychic energy force. This yogic work entailed exploiting various pranayama healing techniques and mind-empowering visualizations. Maitriyogi also taught him certain strategic techniques for transmuting negative thought energy into healing light.

KING YESHE-Ö REQUESTS ATISHA TO COME TO TIBET

At that time, Tibet had fallen into darkness. The Buddhist teaching introduced there, by the great Guru Padma-Sambhava, three centuries before, had fallen into a state of desuetude. Practitioners of the Bön tradition of black magic were plentiful, and cryptic Tantric teachings were improperly understood. All around, evil deities, demons, and dâkinîs were blindly worshipped. Disciples would indulge in alcohol and other stimulants to accentuate their states of mindlessness. Wild sexual orgies and feasting lasting for days were considered the norm as were animal and human sacrifices and the consumption of flesh. King Yeshe-Ö yearned to restore the pure teachings of the Buddha to Tibet once more. He entreated Atisha to come there and inspire change. Atisha reintroduced the Buddha's essential esoteric teachings. Doing so, he transformed the entire nature of Tibetan Consciousness. He delivered Seven Powerful Sutras as his gifts to the world. These gifts paved the golden path to ultimate transcendence. He wanted to ensure that the potent remedy for self-liberation would no longer be forgotten.

These Sutras should be interpreted as sacred gifts since they possess a limitless capacity to heal and spiritually regenerate. Truly they are gifts that keep on giving, and they retain the power to transport you beyond the world of false appearances to the timeless reality beyond. If you apply them faithfully to yourself and all aspects of your life, you will reach the goal of Enlightenment and Self-Mastery, very expeditiously indeed."

I was fascinated by all this and sincerely desired to learn more about the Bön practices of black magic. I asked Lama Dorje if he could expound in more detail.

"Bön practitioners," he said "Used powerful visualizations, to wreak destruction on their enemies. They mastered and exploited mental imagery to send storms of locusts and scorpions to ravage the lands of all rivals and opponents. They transmitted fire and hail to carefully chosen targets and also to destroy properties. They comprehended intimately, that all was mind and that the macrocosm reflected the microcosm. It was self-evident to them that the seed latent within the subatomic and microscopic worlds was the driving force behind the terrestrial and cosmological ones.

Soon they began to make very powerful mandalas. On these, they very precisely and meticulously placed certain evil symbols. Symbols, representing the various deities, entities, and lifeforms needed to enhance the destructive power of their visualizations. They engaged a psychic-transference technique, known as the **phowa**, to transfer their consciousness into the bodies of their enemies. Then from behind the scenes, they would take command and control. In India, this Siddhi was known as the **Parkaya Parvesh,** and many luminaries including Shankaracharya and Jesus took full advantage of it. Shankaracharya utilized it, to channel himself into a declining body to resuscitate it back to life. Jesus drew on it in raising Lazarus from the dead.

These black magicians were seers of a sort since they intimately understood the vibratory nature of all phenomena. They leveraged and channeled esoteric knowledge to shapeshift. So sometimes they would miniaturize or magnify themselves and at others transformed into wild animals or various other beings. Through their expertise in applying the **Anima Siddhi,** they could miniaturize well below the subatomic scale and thus pass through walls, mountains, rivers or any other obstacle in their path. By changing the density of their bodies, using the **Laghima Siddhi**, they could become infinitely light or heavy. Thus they could float high into the sky and fly or else sink down to the deepest layers of the ocean. They employed this Siddhi also to ride light rays and other forms of electromagnetic radiation. Sometimes they found it useful to become infinitely large (yet invisible) to instantly see the events in another country, or on the far side of the cosmos. For this, there was the **Mahima Siddhi**. Once mastered they became effectively omniscient.

Through their ability to concentrate their minds on a single object, and to transmit a single vibration, they could manifest anything they desired out of thin air. This ability, known as the **Prapti Siddhi,** was extremely coveted since it was a critical pre-requisite also for those who wanted to be able to Bilocate, Trilocate or even Poly-locate. Often they would deploy it to incarnate into multiple different forms simultaneously. Sometimes they would appear as a crowd in a marketplace and speak their message through numerous different tongues simultaneously. This helped wonderfully to induce paranoia in their enemies. At other times, they would apply it to dissolve the space between objects and to bring things closer for a better look. They worshipped the gods of darkness and death. Often they would drink the blood of their enemies to gain power over them. The blood cocktail would be infused with all their evil intentions. Sleeping in graveyards and wearing the bones of their enemies kin, was also *en vogue* as a means of protection. Now let's continue with Atisha's teachings."

Feeling impatient to progress to the main teaching, I immediately asked, "**Are the preliminaries necessary? Can we not just skip to the dominant phase of Atisha's Teaching?**" The Lama replied, "I am glad you asked because unless one fully understands and has mastered the preliminaries, the Sutras themselves will be just empty words. They will mean nothing, and you will be able to unlock their power. Instead, they will be as lifeless to you, as stones tossed idly into a quarry. You must imbibe the preliminaries viscerally and intravenously into your being, or the Sutras will be as worthless as broken pieces of glass. You will be unable to grasp their true import, or know what they symbolize. You will not receive the limitless gift; they extend to you. Once you have mastered the preliminaries, the Sutras magically transform, before your eyes into powerful psychedelic symbols, which can reveal Truth in its entirety. Real Being lies forever, beyond all words and symbols. The preliminaries will bring you behind the curtains so that you can meet the Great One in all its majesty. What you will then behold will leave you speechless and in awe. In the next session, we will begin with the first preliminary, of examining the true nature of mind."

THE SECRET PLACE

A fter heading to the kitchen, to eat the evening meal, I retired back to my hut. It was already pitch dark, and It had
been a very long, yet interesting day. What Lama Dorje had said
about storehouse consciousness and the need for mastering the
mind-training had a tremendous influence. My head was
spinning, and I was wondering about the remarkable life of Atisha. Now, I needed to tune out and just shut down the engines
for a while. Most women at this stage in the day would be indulging with a *mani-pedi*, a glass of wine or a trip to the massage
parlor. Anything that could help them unwind. I found myself
surrounded by blackness. There was nothing at all in this hut
but my bare naked self. Nonetheless, I had my '*Secret Place*'
meditation up my sleeve. This visualization was my recipe for
ecstatic release into inner bliss. My private place to escape and
relax to, whenever I was fatigued, stressed or anxious. Here I
could find important answers to all the questions and concerns I
had.

I would count back from eight to zero. Then visualize myself being gently transported by a warm, loving beam of light into a
large translucent bubble-shaped spacecraft high up in the sky.
This spacecraft carried everything I needed. Comfortable sofas
to crash out on, a whirlpool, sauna and a full bar. The immense
fridge was full of all sorts of delicious appetizers and delectable
comestibles. I had all the games, computers and music I needed
by which to entertain myself. The spacecraft came equipped
with a full 3D holophonic sound system. I could adjust the vol-
ume of any song I liked simply through my thoughts. The large

screen HDTV enabled me to watch any channel that met my immediate interest. This TV also supported full two-way communication so I could watch and zoom in on the activities of anyone I wished on this TV. I could fast-forward into their futures or else back into their past and communicate any message I wished to them.

Often I used it also to objectify my thoughts, feelings, ideas, and to pipe flashes of inspiration onto the screen before me. Any pressing situation in my life could be induced to appear there. It could also image my moods and tensions. Thus I often deployed it for psychological and spiritual healing purposes. I enjoyed bringing up any fearful content in my mind. I would then scrutinize and rid myself of this content from this safer and more remote vantage point. Sometimes, I would receive unique healing perspectives and wise interpretations which dispelled the cloud of negative energy so that it was powerless to affect me. During this time, I would usually recline on my sofa and knock back a few cocktails while getting my feet massaged gently by a pliant geisha girl. At other times I would listen to any joyful, nostalgic, uplifting and regenerative material, that would fill my mind replete with life-charging endorphins.

This spacecraft came equipped with various anti-gravity capabilities. Thus it could float weightlessly about and hover or else travel vast distances in no time at all. It could instantaneously travel anywhere my thoughts wished it to. Often I would journey far out to sea to observe the dolphins by night, or else I would watch in stunned wonderment hundred foot+ rogue waves deep in the ocean. Sometimes I would travel down to the Cape while at others, I would listen meditatively to the lapping sounds of waves, as they broke along the shoreline.

It gave me a full 3-D panoramic view of the outside world. On occasion, the mood would catch me, and I was up for more action or culture. I would then either visit the nightlife of some great throbbing city or else travel to the Egyptian pyramids, Ephesus, Knossos or Alexandria. I enjoyed watching the Aurora Borealis by night since this would put me in a very tranquil state of mind. If I were feeling more inquisitive and scientific, I would pay a visit to some remote part of the solar system or head out into the cosmos. My spacecraft was impervious to all physical laws of destruction, and it never broke down.

One of its coolest features was that it could instantly transport in any visitor I wished. Usually, they would be teleported in for dinner, or some Hors D'oeuvres. Beamed in on the fly, so that we could party and share some good conversation. Jesus and the Buddha were just some of my visitors, and I learned tons of esoterica from their unique insights and wisdom.

They would swiftly answer very important questions and shed their sagacious light on some dilemma; I was facing. Often they would uncover past traumas buried deep within my subconscious. I was amazed that I was carrying so much baggage. There was so much crap going on inside which was monumentally affecting my daily life that I was a mere patsy at the controls. They would articulate responses to very deep and highly abstract concepts and ideas that it just blew my mind. It was all very stimulating and it the end it brought me great clarity and illumination and a feeling of immense release. I may have floundered hopelessly for millennia futilely trying to understand such things on my own as they are well beyond my scope.

One time I had Milarepa visit, but he smelled like hell, and his skin had turned green from living off nasty nettle soup for so many years. I didn't want to say it, but he looked more like the incredible hulk emaciated by a regimen of cancer drugs. Nevertheless, he was an expert in all the Siddhis, and he taught me how to apply them most efficaciously. All in all, he was a pure being and one supremely uncontaminated by all the poisons, superficialities and shallow falsities of our modern world. There were no artificial airs or pomposities about him, no carefully manicured persona. For he had long ago completely divested himself of all such worldly bullshit. He stood in such utter contrast to all around him, that he was positively refreshing, in the most endearing way. I found it extremely shocking seeing how false and cosmetic everyone else was in comparison.

Sometimes I would go in for some light humor instead. Then myself, George Carlin, Robin Williams and a few others would crash out in the Jacuzzi, drinking beer and cocktails. Robin would always think it queer that I would not invite some others along. Comedians like Eddie Izzard and Bill Hicks, or even an activist like Leslie Feinberg. I said, "I only want stubborn old mules like George and yourself in this Jacuzzi. If you had your way, I would be inviting Marquis De Sade along for an all-out orgasm." In truth, I did not want anyone into my private bubble, who may outshine me. We would usually finish the night by smoking some pot or peyote. Robin would go in for taking a lick of some LSD while sipping from his glass of champagne. Meanwhile, George would be downing some 'shrooms. I would play the part of the perfect hostess and offer to have some hookers beamed in from the Strip. Then Robin would voice out his opinion, *"I don't want any of those dirty skanks around here, my piece is still itching from the last ones, you brought in."*

I immediately retorted, *"You don't need to use them just for sex, they are excellent also at giving back massages. Also, they could use the extra cash. Besides, with all those weird exotic maneuvers, you were attempting the last time, I am surprised your entire piece hasn't fallen off or corroded into rust."*

Then George would tune in. *"If you could get something more exotic beamed in, I would certainly go in for that."* Then I asked whether he could be more specific. When I started my information quest with *"Animal, vegetable or mineral?"*, Robin seemed destined to explode in a fit. Nonetheless, I pressed on by asking *"How many breasts, do you want her or him to have?"* Then continued, *"Are they to be extra firm and plucky or else over-easy and sagging? Now, will it just be the one set of genitalia you are on for tonight or would you like to try out the hybrid model? We could also put on an alien head and attach a tail if you feel that would be a value-add!"*

Then Robin could contain himself no longer and fully exploded. He was now like a nuclear-powered steam engine that had gone into thermal overload. The off-the-wall humor and mind-blowing improvisations which came afterward, I can only say were out of this world. Usually, it happened, that I would need to take the glass of champagne out of Robin's hand because he had fallen asleep in the Jacuzzi. Then I would also make sure that George's air paths were open because his snore was reverberating across the entire spaceship. I didn't want either of them to drown or croak on my turf.

Then there were the softer moments when I would bring the lights down low and arrange neat arrays of myriad fragrant candles everywhere. I would activate the windowing system, in the spacecraft to shut out all external sounds, sensations, and light and infuse the spacecraft with the most mystical oil scents. Then, I would just sit in silence.

The great thing about this secret hideout was that it was immune to all problems, worries, and concerns of the relative world. Here there were no such things as bills, jobs or health problems. No violence, verbal abuse, loss, diminishment or old age. Toxic relationships were not welcome aboard this ship of the sky. In healthy contrast, I would engage in healthy, intimate and highly sexual charged relationships with anyone I wished. One time, I had some Yoginis transported in from the Middle East, who were highly skilled in the Karma Sutras. In the end, I had to let them go because I was suffocating under those muscular wraps as if I were embedded in a nest of pythons. Also, the overpowering smell of fish, spices, bodily sweat and highly fragrant perfumes was far too nauseating.

Now as I was hovering high in the sky well above the ocean, I decided to use my secret place to embark on one of my old-time adventures. I completely disappeared for a while and roamed about as a non-entity. In the past, I typically did this for a few days or even weeks, at a time. It was my version of practicing Mauna yoga, and it helped me become more proficient with living in my essence body and as a mind that is completely formless. Being entirely uninvested in the universe of things, yet supremely capable of manifesting infinite potentialities made me feel more complete. In such times, I recognized that all world-streams emanated effortlessly from within me and that I was the Source of Creation.

All I can say about being bodiless is the amount of free time; it extends. It helped me realize how much time we waste taking care of all bodily needs. I no longer needed to shower, shave, eat, floss, clean or cook. It freed me also from a litany of senseless things, including checking the mail or getting my car repaired. There was no moronic job to go to, where I would sit all day in some soul-crushing cubicle or office, silently watching the clock, while responding to a profusion of inane e-mails and IMs. I was no longer being hounded or simultaneously pestered by a thousand meaningless distractions. Instead, I felt that I had gained the wings to fly and to soar high into the stratosphere and Heavens. Freed from all the shackles and limitations, imposed by our worldly bondage.

Then I decided to sneak in on old friends to see what they were up to. I listened in on their conversations to find out what they genuinely thought. The vile crap, they reeled out, only brought tears to my eyes. The tips of their wagging tongues were as poisonous as the fangs of a serpent. I wanted to knock out their lights, but of course, I couldn't because I was invisible and didn't want to give my game away. Nonetheless, I was feeling furious and headed out on a rampage. I visited the office of one of my former managers and threw all her confidential documents into the shredder. Then dumped her hard-drive in too for good measure, before finally spraying her entire office with the most obnoxious scent. It reeked worse than the smell of a gazillion skunks living out in skid row, by the time I left.

Then I beamed back to my spaceship for my late evening meal. I started off as usual with a few shots of cognac. The salmon went down exceedingly well along with some nicely steamed vegetables. Of course, the duck basking in sherry sauce with mash potatoes and gravy on the side was also excellent. Afterwards, I had to decide between the chocolate gateau or some mint ice-cream with mango and strawberries. Then I swallowed down a Venti caramel macchiato before heading for the hookah pipe.

EXAMINE THE TRUE NATURE OF MIND

BADRINATH EARLY MORNING

The next morning, I got up bright and early and was ready to receive the first of Atisha's preliminaries. Lama Dorje seemed immensely exuberant and refreshed this morning. He kicked off immediately saying "We all jibber-jabber profusely about the mind, but very few of us know a thing about it. We haven't the remotest clue of its real nature and miraculous workings, and sadly this pervasive ignorance surrounding our collective mind is only getting worse. Doubtlessly, we have entered a truly dark age; and right into the jaws of an intensely materialistic culture. The emerging fields of pharmacology, technology, A.I., cybernetics, neurology, and genetics have only fastened the chains that imprison us more. These have enmeshed us deep in a very glitzy and subsurface culture. Ultimately, they have hooked us to a prodigiously sterile and fruitless worldview. Such fields being of the realm of dualistic appearances and experiences bind us further to the illusory. All mention of the latent, unmanifest, hidden and abeyant is carefully avoided because these cannot be measured or detected by any phenomenal means. Thus, shallow and superficial beliefs like epiphenomenalism have risen to prominence in our minds along with similar strange notions born out of ignorance. Phenomenal understanding cannot reach to a knowledge of essence since it can never penetrate below the surface.

Fawning over the complex maze of barren, convoluted and skin-deep knowledge, is in fashion these days. We treat the mind as if it were merely a personal possession and an invisible item we cannot yet pin down despite all the needles, probes and electrodes we stick into this haystack. We take pleasure in throwing about stock phrases like *"Many Minds"* or *"Mind Yourself"* or *"My mind just went into a meltdown"* etc. All of which highlights and reinforces our universal state of ignorance. **There is no such thing as "My mind" or "Many minds." There is only Mind and nothing else.** Mind is the singular for which there is no plural. It cannot be owned because it is not a possession. It can only be lived through and better understood. Regrettably, our superficial culture would like to patent all its operations and put it under lock and key. Hence, we are just like Lilliputians and sad earthy minions trying to keep the Goliath of Mind hostage and held with a thread.

To the extent, that you genuinely understand the true nature of mind, you empower yourself. Each must become like a pearl diver and dive deep within because only in the subaqueous realms is truth ever to be found. You must execute the power of your will and tie the heavy stones of introspection and discriminating reason, to your feet to reach the bottom of this ocean. Then you will understand that Mind is the sole dynamo that powers all universes. From it, all phenomena arise including light, heat, magnetism, electricity, gravity, radioactivity and so forth. It permeates all levels of existence, from the nanoscopic level of mesons, bosons, and quarks to the macroscopic level of galaxies and world systems. Mind shines effortlessly forth, from a Source that remains forever radiant, inextinguishable and self-sustaining. There are no universes apart from the Mind, yet Mind in its pure essence is no '*thing.*' "

I then interjected. "These relationships are not obvious! Can you explain how mind, matter, phenomena, and form are all linked?" Then the Lama proceeded to draw this quick illuminating diagram, to put it all into perspective and went on to describe it in more detail.

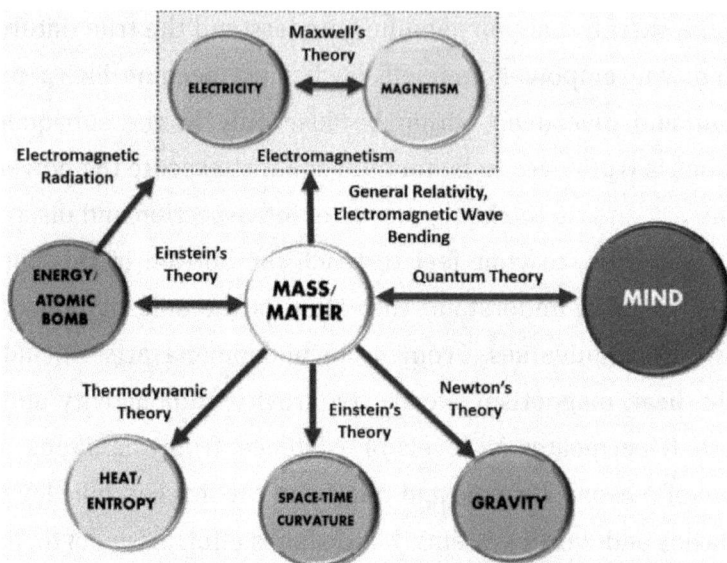

LAMA DORJE'S PORTRAYAL OF THE CONNECTIONS BETWEEN MIND AND PHENOMENAL EXISTENCE

"We have known the relationship between mass/matter to other phenomena for a long time now. Recently with the advent of quantum theory, the critical link between matter and mind, is becoming better understood. We are slowly connecting the dots. Of course, scientific theories can only look at causal connections from the outside. Enlightenment alone gives the inside view. Then one knows very directly that all seeming matter is a by-product of mind. Matter and form, are just projections of our conditioned thought. They are internal images, which have become molded and congealed into apparent solidity, due to the inherent ignorance and impurity in our thought. Ignorance is the blacksmith of the world, and he is a very dark creationist indeed. He leaves nothing behind that shines and glows with any true light. Individual phenomena, represent mind experiencing itself through many different windows or frames of reference. They are Mind seeing itself under an incomplete light.

When viewed from the nanoscopic level, the impure mind may manifest as subatomic particles, dark matter, singularities, chain reactions and therefore also as atomic bombs. When seen from the macroscopic level, mind manifests in the form of heat, electromagnetism and everyday objects. At the galactic and cosmological levels, mind manifests as spacetime curvatures, black holes, Einstein-Rosen bridges and so on. Even though quantum theory conducts its experiments on the mind/matter relationship at the subatomic level, certain pivotal experiments have demonstrated that nothing is genuinely separate. All separation is an illusion! We unnecessarily and artificially interpose all partitions of our world through our preferences, judgments, past conditioning, and numerous distortions of mind.

Bell's theorem and Alain Aspect's experiments have proven that nothing is separate in the universe. Experiments conducted on particles many light-years apart demonstrate beyond all doubt that they can maintain instantaneous communication with one another. There are only two possibilities that can satisfactorily answer this brain-teasing enigma. **(A)** The particles are in communication through hyper-dimensional spaces **(B)** Objective space itself is void, and the spacetime artifice is a mind-generated illusion.

The intimate link between mind and matter is not limited just to the subatomic levels but operates equally well at the cosmological levels. Our decisions and choices collapse the quantum states which in turn produce the building blocks of our entire universe. Mind extends everywhere since it has no room for any discontinuities within it. All the same, these experiments have not gone far enough since they have not yet incontestably demonstrated that the entire universe is wholly contained in mind. They are powerless to do so because no phenomenally orientated experiment could ever prove the entire phenomenal universe, is a projection of mind. No proof can transcend the limitations and penalties imposed by its limited scope. One must step out of that scope or context to establish proofs and make guaranteed assertions about it. So from a scientific perspective, this still requires an inductive leap of faith at this time. Direct spiritual experience, however, can prove this for you in a flash."

RELATIVE VERSUS ABSOLUTE MIND

The Lama continued, "The second thing you must acutely understand is the subtle and all-important difference existing between **Relative** and **Absolute** Mind. This difference is not one of magnitude and degree, but one of essence and purity. **The Relative Mind belongs to the world of symbols, forms, concepts, and percepts.** These are all forged in its image and likeness and are dim reflections representing our current state of mental evolution. Relative Mind fashions a universe that is imbued with all sorts of classifications and contrasts. These, in turn, are derived from all our preferences, partialities and inherited understandings. It is a severely differentiated landscape, and all that appears in this mirage arises from erroneous beliefs. This alien empire we appear to inhabit is the hell we impose due to our dualistically prone mind-frame. The relative mind encompasses everything from the subatomic to the terrestrial and cosmological. Out of our microcosmic minds emerges the macrocosmic universe because the seed of the inner is the sole cause of the outer. The relative mind, can only ever perceive the illusory.

So, we find ourselves mercilessly entangled in the vast mosaic of our fallacious, incomplete, and often contradictory understandings and remain perpetually obsessed with phenomena and form. We cling desperately to the spacetime existence and its conditioning influence and try unsuccessfully to make sense of it all. Hypnotized by form, we cannot comprehend that all we perceive is spun from within like the web from a spider. All actions, phenomena, and terrestrial objects are appearances arising from our inner impurities. Much nonsense has infiltrated our belief network which prevents our mind from settling into its pure, quiescent state and uncovering the Real. The relative mind can be considered the womb of Shakti because all phenomenal universes are born from it. Only when Shakti merges with Shiva, will all such universes disappear.

A few break the suffocating, yet mesmerizing spell of the relative mind through **Kundalini yoga**. They move the vital energy of the serpent (Kundalini) upwards, from the Muladhara chakra at the perineum, to the Sahasrara chakra at the crown of the head. The energy rises through the threadlike Sushumna Nadi, which runs longitudinally up through the center of the spine. Others employ the power of reason, mental vigilance and rigorous thought discrimination to dispel all false, dualistic beliefs. This is the path of **Jnana yoga and** it is a far faster path for the more intelligent and abstract mind.

Absolute Mind is supra-conceptual, supra-perceptual and beyond all contrasts and differentiation. It is timeless, and its perfect knowledge transmutes all pain and suffering into energy and light. It has been called by various terms including the *One-Mind*, *Nirvana*, the *Void* and the supremely *undifferentiated existence*. It is formless because it transcends the totality of all form; just as a polygon transcends all specific multisided figures and shapes. It is like pure sunlight since it is warm, nurturing and life-giving. One who harbors no hint of impurity or selfness becomes immersed in its bliss and is enabled to see things as they Truly Are! Even so, sunlight can become distorted and diminished in power, when reflected from the moon or when absorbed by the earth's atmosphere. Similarly, the pure and perfect reality of the One-Mind becomes unknown when distorted

by the prism of all false and tarnishing beliefs, held by our relative mind.

The Absolute, being uncreated, is not subject to the world of
time. It is not causal and subject to dissolution and is well beyond all principles of conception and causation, as known in the
conditioned existence. To consider that Relative and Absolute
Mind are separate is to fall into darkness. Relative mind is
simply mind experiencing itself, through the prism of ignorance.
While the Absolute, is pure, uncontaminated Mind, without any
trace of mental pollution, contradiction or erroneous belief."

MEDITATION QUESTIONS THAT PROBE THE NATURE OF MIND

Then he said, "Certain mental exercises work extremely efficaciously, to reveal the true nature of mind. They can bring you, to your real Self. You may begin by meditating on the following questions.

1. *What Color is Mind?*

2. *Does mind have a definite Shape or Form or is entirely Formless?*

3. *Is there just One mind, Many minds, or none at all?*

4. *Can Mind be brought from one place to another?*

5. *Does Mind have any gaps or discontinuities in it? Or is it unitary and all-pervading?*

6. *What is the relationship, existing between Mind and the world of Matter?*

7. *Where exactly is your Mind?*

8. *Is mind the simple aggregation of all your Concepts, Percepts, Sensations and Intellectual understandings or none of these?*

9. *Is Mind Potent and Self-sustaining, or Weak and Dependent?*

10. *Is it Active or Passive?*

11. *Is it Limited or Unlimited?*

12. *What is the Relationship between the Mind and your Awareness?*

13. *What is the difference between Mind and Thought?*

These questions will be a good beginning. We must start from the Toad's position, immersed deeply in the swamp of the world before we can gain the panoramic view of a falcon in full flight. Once right understandings suffuses your consciousness, you will begin to feel far more expansive, joyous and liberated and less attached to the world of foolish desires. Your petty attachments and grievances will soon seem so ridiculous; worldly concerns, and small attractions will interest you less. You will realize, you were the emperor, going about with a begging bowl.

I am not going to provide the answers to these questions for you since that approach would be defeatist as a teaching aid. It would weaken your powers of introspection and reason. Knowing how to question rightly is of supreme importance for those who desire to reach Self-liberation! The boon of Enlightenment is only ever extended to those who can successfully peel away all the layers if subterfuge and deception by themselves. Only they reach the pearl of adulterated wisdom, at the core of existence. Then they cognize in every fiber of their being, what the right answers are. Meditate deeply on these questions and you will be ready for the Sutras.

RESTORING THE RADIANT ALTAR WITHIN

THE AUTHOR AT THE SITE OF A NEW SPIRITUAL CENTER

Consider your meditations, as undertaking a holy voyage. You are looking to restore, a sacred and radiant altar, that has stood neglected and defiled for far too long. Searching for that supremely sublime, intangible essence which is the seed of all. This extremely potent root is known in Tibet as the **Dharmadhatu**. Even though it is very elusive; it gives birth to limitless space, as well as to all objects and phenomena. It is beyond all conception, perception, sensation and finite capacities of the relative mind to comprehend. Likewise, it is devoid of all forms and attributes. It only became lost to sight, due to ignorance.

The trash of worldly beliefs accumulated from eons past piles high in your mind, and it covers this crown jewel and obfuscates its radiance. This refuse heap which so attracts you is all that stands in your way. Now you are ready to remove all the trash and do some spring cleaning for a change. Worldly knowledge smells, and you know it. It has a strong mephitic odor, and this makes it hard for you to progress. So your spirit cringes inside your worn out boots, while your body goes about doing a host of senseless things. Spirit completely abdicates its throne, while you sell yourself and your petty wares at the altars of the world.

There is no point moving beyond this preliminary unless you are well-grounded, and comprehend ontologically, at least what constitutes your essential nature as mind. **It is not, what you have come to know, but that which you no longer believe, which is of utmost importance. Asking the right questions is infinitely more important than receiving any right answers.** Your questioning has to become pure, lucid, open-ended and capacious so that you can transform into the answer in the process. Making headway towards truth is just a journey of expelling all false beliefs. Such fallacious beliefs become quickly evident to the impartial, uninvested and uncontaminated mind. You are creating a reverse vector, which goes against all worldly paths. Paths that have placed you in deep bondage since time began. All journeys here were meaningless sojourns, and they held you ransom to a multiplicity of tawdry attractions and the small-mindedness of the world. Look at those who cling, to this relative world and see how miserable they are most of the time. Is this for you? Is this your chosen trajectory moving forward? To remain a pathetic figure, pandering after tiny pleasures? Licking the boot heels of all those pretentious primadonnas, circulating about like vultures? Or are you ready to embrace a more open-ended and stratospheric path to freedom? A path upon which, you will increasingly emerge as more joyous and lighthearted as you travel. You will feel tremendous release, as you unlimber yourself from all manacles you have placed upon your mind. Nurturing a boundless, impartial and open-minded awareness is crucial for receiving the life-changing gifts, these Sutras impart."

These words were starting to sink in and have an impact. I could see how miserable worldly people were. Not just miserable, but anxious, frustrated, judgmental, vicious and fearful too! In many ways, this was understandable since the game of life seemed definitively rigged. Rigged in favor of rich over poor, beautiful over ugly, young over old, smart over dumb, corrupt over principled, majorities over minorities, straight over gay, etc. Just look at how many centuries, it took before women got the right to vote. It is a stark and humiliating procession! Blacks too had to wait in line for the longest time just to get some basic rights and freedoms. The voice of the majority always seemed to be drowning out that of the more conscientious and rare. It has always behaved like a self-righteous bully, just like Arnold's big brother in 'The Wonder Years.' This big brother was perpetually slapping us about and demand we obsequiously subjugate ourselves to its arbitrary whims. We often coerced into self-debasement and outright humiliation just to save face.

For many centuries women were not allowed to read books unless they entered the dark underworld of Courtesans. From this shadowland universe, they would never again emerge to see the light. They were doomed into becoming the witches of Macbeth and were socially marked by the age of forty. Denied the right to publish and barred from entering various elitist clubs, running for government, or taking over the family business. Yes, they had been muscled and squeezed out of history, through various devious forms of oppression. Even today they push so hard to get equal pay, for the same types of work. Corporations should be forced to publish the pay and compensation details of all their employees since their entire lack of disclosure becomes a breathing ground for various insidious gender pay-based discrimination schemes.

Likewise, the disabled were always feeling the pinch. There was an invisible centrifugal force always pushing them to the periphery of affairs. Most are driven out of the workplace and left to rot. The unequal pressure of these double-valued social systems becomes all too obvious when you start feeling its edge. Unspoken words are often the most pernicious and passive hostility is a trained evil. It can be just as corrosive to the spirit in to thwarting one's will as any overt form of brutality and oppression. So it was OK for veterans to get their arms and legs blown off, fighting resource-grabbing wars in the deserts and snake-pits of the world—where every day was a 4th of July. But there the contract ended. Afterwards, when they went searching for livelihoods, they would see the true colors of the rainbow. They would find themselves going through the '*Bataan Death March*,' and being denied by one company after another. Ending up living in storage units and knocking back a packet of Top Ramen for their evening meal.

No wonder Steve Jobs would park in all the accessible parking spots. Whoever used them? They, like the disability access ramps, were all just there for show. There to make sure the corporations were up to code. Employers didn't hire the disabled. That was the unspoken truth. After two decades working in hi-tech, I only came across one disabled employee. He would go whizzing about rapidly in his wheelchair and was totally on top of things.

The world of hi-tech just wanted energizer bunnies, who would work around the clock for pennies. That was all that remained after paying skyrocketing Silicon Valley rents, bills, and escalating taxes. Such bunnies they brought in from India, China, and the Middle East, by the container. They were convenient because they could be threatened with being booted back to their Calcutta slums if they merely hinted at formulating any dissenting opinion. Their only hobbies were walking around these cement structures late at night, before heading back in for more coding.

Meanwhile, gays and lesbians were tossed to the fringes of society and forever hanging on by their fingertips. In some countries, they are being sentenced to death for fearlessly championing their genetic impulsions, over arbitrary manmade laws. Transsexuals likewise have been intensely marginalized and depersonalized for millennia. Presently, a brave few of us have dared to pop up, here-and-there, and we are going through a sort of ritual genocide. A societal cleansing, or Transgenocide. It seemed we would always have our Orlando massacres and over one million people ready to jump out of their beds in the middle of the night with no other purpose in their hearts than to endorse a petition preventing bathroom rights to Transsexuals. Yes, it was like a game of frog hammer with all the Puritans, bluenoses and Amish-minded types going around with their large mallets. Proceeding to whack anyone different on the head to the chant *'burn baby burn.'* Putting them through their cultural sieve, which seemed more like a meat grinder armed with nails. It was evident that the face of social and moral justice always bore a striking resemblance to a Texas lawman sporting a bowl haircut. Or the face of a pig who would exceed and bend every measure of the law possible to exact the "Righteous" vengeance demanded by the demons of his inner hatred, prejudice, and intolerance. The fact that everyone carries a cellphone these days adds a new twist to this cocktail. It enables us to capture in full HD and 4k video, a few faces of the beast. To idly think, this covert beast has not been stalking the earth for centuries, gobbling up many, is a very overt form of denial.

Most are far too cowardly, to present their daggers upfront. They strike from the rear with switchblades, at the most opportune moment when the other is vulnerable. Often, passive hostility is the means by which we wear others down. No one is likely to go motor-mouthing about their hatred of Women, Blacks, Muslims, Jews, Gays, Transsexuals, the Disabled and Elderly, etc. in your presence. They are afraid of lawsuits. Instead, they employ a million other ways to cut and gore you; beginning with their failures to hire or promote. Stealthily camouflaged prejudice is often sublimated into other channels. The aggressor will excessively criticize your overall competency, and the quality of your work, at every turn. You will be blackballed and besmirched with dark brushes behind closed doors. So you will proceed through life, feeling denied one opportunity after another, for very invisible and mysterious reasons. The flag of your potential will always be flying at half mast.

It is not surprising then that many seek to protect themselves, by all means possible. Each surrounds themselves with a coterie of special friends. Those chosen ones whom they think may be able to help augment or empower them in some exclusive way.

Chosen because of their unique capabilities to flatter, chatter, dazzle or enable. Chosen because they make you shine all the more or at least make you feel safe.

Then each proceeds to create an elaborate array of defenses around themselves and their private world. Such barricades aim to keep others out. Each places a banner up, in the front yard of their minds, stating clearly in bold letters "*No Gays, Jews, Blacks, Muslims, Wild Dogs or Rednecks allowed in here!*" They never realize that their real enemy all the time were the corporations and the hush-hush oppression of the oligarchies, and plutocracies of this world. Yes, these giant Octopuses are the planetary Succubi who run governments, pay no taxes, and have a tentacle in every nation. Nevertheless, they are allowed to roam about unchecked to devour us all. It seems the dinosaurs have come back, after a brief timeout to take over the earth once more. Such dinosaurs prance about thinking they are Japanese Samurai Warriors, with a code of honor by which they live and die. When we probe a little closer, we readily see that not a single corporation has any biological life or innate power of volition. It remains a neutral entity with no power to think or to do. Extremely pernicious ideologies motivate and determine all its actions and decisions. You may well ask what this ideology is? It is simple! **Corporations exist, not merely to survive but to thrive. They do so, by taking as much as they can and by all means possible!** They push the envelope on what constitutes legality and thrive in all double-valued systems that are strategically ambiguous. There is a very flexible bending of the law instantiated for corporations, and yet a very rigid one is maintained for the plebs like us. Why is this the case? It must be all the sell-outs on each rung of the ladder of the judiciary!

No corporation is truly philanthropic—even in the slightest! Not one is going to help a smaller company out unless it is in its best interests. Corporations seek to squash all competitors so that they can gain monopolies and thus raise costs and increase profits. They aim to exploit all weaknesses mercilessly wherever there exists even a hint of vulnerability. They are cold-blooded extortionists that will happily pay their employees the least wage they can get away it. They have no issues with offshoring, outsourcing, insourcing or whatever else will drive costs down. They consider their employees as fundamentally faceless entities, serfs, and minions, despite all their hype and duplicitous crap about caring about an employee's well-being and work-life balance. That is all baloney for the witless to swallow! They will empower you only to the extent that it serves their best interests. Sometimes they find, it far more lucrative to disempower you instead. They systematically wear down and psychologically assassinate their serfs, and it is all so logical and calculated because those bankrupt of self-esteem and confidence are unlikely to leave and join the competition. A demoralized and psychologically destroyed employee is "**owned**" for life. He or she is left decimated and retains no sense of self-worth by which to raise the stakes. He or she is far more likely to do everything demanded without ever raising any conscientious objections for fear of being labeled "**Confrontational.**" Constructive confrontation is brutally repressed. Corporations recognize that it does not matter a damn how unrealistic their expectations are, once they successfully implant fear. As for career progression, another pile of bunk! In the end, corporations, do not need many thinkers or creative types, just a lot of machine-coded doers and implementers that will happily bend over at the fall of a dime.

RECOGNIZE THAT TRUTH ALONE IS

NEAR VASUDHARA FALLS

It was two weeks before I met Lama Dorje again. He had been observing me from a distance and did not need to ask any questions to assess my advancement, with the mind-training techniques. He had a seraphic smile on his face when he began to speak again.

"This second preliminary will be another giant leap forward for you. We become attached and identified with many foolish notions and false understandings. All are mind-poisons that mentally cloud us, and they steer us steadily away from Truth.

All become a heavy burden over time since they blunt and diminish our resolve, to the point we just give up. Some seek salvation and higher meaning in the domains of science, biology, genetics, and evolution. They frantically search in the jungle of the phenomenal, for various trophies of interest and mistakenly believe, that their **Theory of Everything (TOE)**, once discovered, will fully encapsulate Truth. At that moment, the train will have successfully arrived at the station, and no further exploration or adventure will be necessary.

Their TOE will be simple, elegant and profound and completely abstracted from the everyday world of specifics. It will be fundamentally independent of all personal interaction, innovation, creativity, and decision. Yes, it will not care a whit, whether we take any personal responsibility for ourselves or not. Such a TOE pictures a stone cold and stark universe; one that operates with precision like a metronome. One that goes on unimpeded, whether we take the initiative to improve our capacities, or let them fall into decline. It will be scribbled on the blackboard as some universal equation, joining the worlds of gravity, electromagnetism, weak and strong nuclear reactions, etc. neatly together in an intimate relationship. It will miraculously link all aspects of the phenomenal universe but will still be indifferent and divorced from the particular life experiences; each of us enjoys. Profoundly uncaring of the tumultuous inner world of emotions and our various psychological states. Unsympathetic of all our decisions, intentions, aspirations, dreams and special nightmares. This external search for meaning, via some universal modifier, is not the path that leads to liberation and Enlightenment.

DIFFERENT MISCONCEPTIONS OF TRUTH

Others believe that Truth is relative and in constant flux; that it is forever dependent on current events and emerging trends. Thus, they view it, as a chameleon-like epiphenomenon, spontaneously materializing from the great machine of the world. And as a hybrid entity whose unique features are intimately dependent on the particular civilization, cultural milieu, moral codes and economic conditions that prevail or are ingrained in the popular consciousness. This picture of truth can vary by the individual and can even be custom tailored, to meet his/her special needs, preferences, idiosyncrasies, bad habits or peccadillos. It does not matter much, whether these needs be essential, or just representative of vain and superficial desires. It can flexibly adjust and adapt, to fully accommodate and satiate the particular aspirations and appetites any individual may have, at different junctures in his or her life.

So Truth presents itself through a glitzy array of contrasting faces. One particular visage is more suited to the white man and another for the black, yellow or red. There are small parochial truths and universal ones. Certain truths are feminine; others masculine and there are flavors of truth that are heterosexual, homosexual, bisexual, omnisexual, unisexual, transsexual and asexual. As we descend further down the rabbit hole, we find many stratifications of truth specifically customized for the Christian, Buddhist, Taoist, New Ager, Hindu, Mohammedan, Satanic Worshipper, Wiccan, and Atheist. And a special flavor still, for all those indolent dolts, that care to reflect on the matter at all.

THE DANGERS OF SPIRITUAL INDIGESTION

As we proceed further across this smorgasbord, our eyes are truly bulging. We do not know what particular dish or belief system, we will sample next. The information bombardment and spectrum of choices is simply mesmerizing. It all leads however, only deeper into confusion and to crippling indecision. After a while, psychological inertia sets in, and we become skeptical of all new information and methods. All we have known and learned falls into a state of inactivity and disuse. It can no longer be faithfully applied or mobilized to reach any clarity or resolution. The real problem is we have gathered for millennia tons of useless, impotent and obsolete knowledge. Overweighed, overwhelmed and overburdened by this deluge, we can no longer discern the extremely potent from the feckless and abortive. We have lost the capacity to separate the ineffectual, lame and effete, from the immensely treasurable. Nor do we know, those special criteria by which to meaningfully evaluate and appraise worth.

Clearly, we have become self-relegated into hoarders of the mental realm. All are spiritual materialists and quacks, who nevertheless think, they are on the fast track to Enlightenment. Even so, all we are getting are the mental runs as we expeditiously navigate our way towards the cerebral crapper. We have lost access to those highly efficacious mind-tools, that can reliably penetrate, to the metaphysical and spiritual fountainhead and the fathomless depths of being. As a consequence, the Real remains buried and covered over. We do not know how to reliably nourish ourselves and are incapable of digesting veracious messages, to their core. It must be logical at least that either truth exists, or it does not. Either all religions, esoteric practices, and systems of belief carry the essence and kernel of truth, or they are embodying hogwash ideals. Merely an empty deck then with nothing but jokers for those happy to spend all their days playing 3-card monkey. Unfortunately, our obsession with various antiquated rituals and forms deflects attention from the underlying content. The superfluous and meaningless has become the entire emphasis now.

Yes, each religion is just preaching, immanent Truth in another unique way. Each presents a mindboggling array of esoteric facts concerning the singular reality that **IS**. All are offering different pathways up to the top of the mountain of Truth. Some paths progress extremely rapidly, and others progress at a snail's pace. The path of applying discriminating wisdom is the fastest path of all. Meanwhile, the Absolute waits in silence with infinite patience until we make a decision to give up our games and dreams. We need to cleanse ourselves of all our Self-deceptions and impurities of thought. Truth is easily recognized **Here-and-Now** for those in a ready state of mind. It encompasses resplendent wisdom but is only known when we dispossess and disengage all false beliefs."

THE FOUR FACES OF TRUTH

What Lama Dorje said concerning the problems of mental and spiritual hoarding grabbed my attention. I had noticed this for myself. The continuous information bombardment and frantic search for quick-fix recipes and solutions. The prevailing worldly attitude was that even Enlightenment could be made into a 'drive-thru' and it demanded no effort or preparation from ourselves. We had become addicted to lives of ease, comfort, and convenience. Our entitlement attitudes and endless self-obsessions were beginning to hammer the nail into our coffins. No one was disciplined and fearless enough to face their demons head-on. They wanted to sample everything and commit to nothing. Every God we crucified, and every immaculate ideal we squashed underfoot. All had to become quickly transmogrified into a simple banner, or headline of a few well-chosen buzzwords, or it would be ignored. So, everything had degenerated into elevator conversation with no real quality or depth.

Only a rare few fully understood, what the word '*selflessness*' really meant. The modern emphasis was committed to building up the ego-self. Hence the explosion of social media sites, plastic surgeries, overachieving kids, overprescribed medicines and a host of new diseases such as ADD/ADHD and various anxiety disorders, etc. Selflessness had become equated with self-effacement, and seen as a doctrine of nihilism, and self-annihilation. The prospect and hope that each possessed infinite life seemed pure lunacy. Instead, the conception was that we have but one life in which to live it up before we become neuroleptically frazzled!

The outcome was unavoidable. We became like a herd of stampeding buffalo on the Serengeti, and each of us was to be picked off savagely and torn to shreds by the lions of life. In this world of fear created by our blind idolization of the ego self, there was no room left for any compassion, empathy or meditative reflection and complete disregard for the consequences of our actions. As a consequence, most became dispirited and increasingly sour, caustic and skeptical in their attitudes and thought patterns. Many sunk downwards into absolute dullness and vapidity of mind, while others stomped about liked coked up chickens in the battery hen factories of the world. Many attempted, to illicitly tweak their way to lives of self-fulfillment and peace. Our inner conflicts and voracious demands made us corrosive to all authentic life and growth. It seemed engorging ourselves with more undigested esoteric information was not a solution, but a crippling poison.

After this brief mental soliloquy ran itself through, I responded, "I can relate fully to what you said about all religions being true, or else they are running a racket. It seems most religions and beliefs systems focus more on form than on content. Once rituals and form take precedence, they become degenerative and are ready for the morgue. The Catholic religion, for example, has its obsession with churches. It invests the wealth of its flock building the most stunning and costly architectural masterpieces, while many remain poor and starving outside. Their priests are outfitted with holy vestments, often inlaid with ornate patterns made of gold. It is a holy fashion show and red carpet affair.

They saunter about, sprinkling holy water and incense every-where and I think their aim, is to make us mindless with the nauseating scent. They simultaneously preach good and evil, from both sides of their forked tongues and speak of a god of love and forgiveness, who also happens to be vengeful and judgmental. It is enough to confuse the most sincere devotee. Meanwhile, this seems to be the greatest Ponzi scheme, ever launched into the hereafter. One that lures suckers in, through instantiating foolish beliefs in guilt and sin. The real message of extending unconditional love seems all but forgotten, while the esoteric teachings of the Gnostics, have been repressed and de-nounced as heretical.

The Islamic religion speaks for itself. It is an old world Goliath, in our midst. One more obsessed with covering the body, fasting and prostrating to the East at dawn, than seeking to promote genuine love and understanding. The blind dictates and codes of Sharia law, seem incomprehensible to any compassionate or progressive being. Maybe some of the original Sufi Mystics had grasped the original message, but their voice seems drowned out now. Replaced by that nebulous quicksand of ridiculous rit-uals and silly observances. Don't get me started on their fanat-ics! Then we have Judaism, which seems to be floundering in the soup, of its endless numerology schemes and sacred symbols. The imprint of the Sephirot, in the Kabbalah system, persuades me to contemplate less about divine essences and emanations, and to reflect more on crop circles."

This delivery triggered an old memory of a very symbolic dream. So I shared it, "One night I had a dream, in which four large blocks resembling ice were conveyed to me. These blocks glowed brilliantly, in the surrounding darkness and exuded a warm welcoming, yet ethereal light. I was hypnotized and magnetically attracted to each, like a moth to a flame. Approaching them, I felt my joy and peace increasing. I felt myself becoming more silent, restful and expansive as if I were reaching the peaceful center, in the turbulent cyclone of life. It was a supremely happy and restful place, from which I never wanted to depart. It was like Christmas time, and these were four gifts presented by the Divine. As I drew closer, I noticed a single word inscribed in each — the words **Truth**, **Peace**, **Love,** and **Bliss** respectively. All the blocks were identical, so, I could not grasp the meaning. Eventually, I realized, all aspects of truth, share the same essence and one can no more differentiate Truth from Love than Love from Peace and unconditional Joy. Once one arrives, at any face of Truth, one receives all four gifts. Now, I truly understand the message and the gift.

1. **Love IS!**

2. **Truth IS!**

3. **Peace IS!**

4. **Bliss IS!**

"Yes," the Lama responded, "Truth has always been Here. We do not need to create or manufacture it. It is causeless and timeless and beyond all our ingenuity and inventive capacities. We only need to discover it, because Truth created us. Our essential Being rests quietly within its soft embrace. Truth surrounds us in every way, within and without, as that all-loving, ever potent essence, that remains indestructible. Being perfect and self-contained, it lacks nothing. Instead, it is an eternal flame, whose light can never be extinguished. Within its welcoming manifold, all contradictions and dualities are quickly resolved, and all forms of sickness disappear."

AN ALCHEMIST COMES TO THE RESCUE

The Lama proceeded, "The great Grecian alchemist Hermes Trismegistus, knew all about essence. He had dedicated his life to finding and eliciting that potent elixir which could cure all ills. He excelled in many fields of practice, including astrology, cosmology, magic, healing and the occult and was as intimate with the Heavens, as he was with the nano-worlds of the subatomic. There were many esoteric secrets, buried in his mind and a cryptic, ineffable aura always surrounded him. Hence his name Trismegistus, which means '*Thrice-Great*.' Many felt he had discovered the root understanding and mystical principles which drive and propel the universe; the very fuel that powers the wheel of Kalachakra. After he passed, many ambitious, worldly folk started thinking his secrets must lie buried somewhere deep in his tomb. So one night, they dug it up. Sure enough, they found there a tiny scroll, on which was written two short phrases.

"As Within, so Without!

As Above, So Below!"

So this was the secret understanding and the fruition of his life's work. All appearances on the outside, were just a reflection, of what is going on inside. Our thoughts and beliefs, drive the entire world of our perception. Consciousness and perception exist then, as a duality pair. Perception being the passive reflector of all our conscious (and subconscious) mental activities. Changing our world was but a thought away.

At this point, I said, "This is very interesting because, in the current world system of Kali Yuga, we believe the opposite. We are convinced the external world shapes our thoughts and experiences and that the outer drives the inner. We foolishly conceive that if there were no outer appearance or phenomena, our inner world would cease to exist."

The Lama agreed, "Yes, this is what the world currently believes and how it behaves. Nonetheless, it is a classic example, of reversing true cause-and-effect and the key reason why worldly folk remain in bondage to ignorance. In truth, if one does not adjust their inner beliefs, the world of their perception will not change. All beliefs either bind us or set us free. They lead deeper into misery or else towards redemption. It is the veracity of their content alone that counts.

Our slavery then is self-induced. Each fashions a prison-house of their own unique design. Each is fully responsible for all toxic emotions, states of mental disillusionment and intense feelings of victimhood they continuously experience. As long as one's beliefs and attitudes are disharmonious with truth, one will continue to manufacture suffering, sickness, anxieties, and torments of every possible variety. Our individual and collective beliefs and attitudes are what have cause all the wars, tragedies, massacres, brutalities, pandemics and dark periods down the ages. These murky images derive from the inner content we cherish. All mischief, havoc, and tragedy arises in the darkened glass of our individual and collective mindsets.

Such was how the world of spacetime and bodies formed. None of this is true, and it need not appear at all. All is illusion propagating from ignorance. All covers Truth with the dark veil of Maya. In the relative world, our misbeliefs are as powerful as our true understandings. They feed the entire world of our perception and make the illusory world seem an impenetrable entity. Nonetheless, all, is nothing but a mirage, interposing itself before ever-present truth."

THE ILLUSION OF MULTIPLICITY

I was extremely puzzled by this content. So, I immediately aired my concern. "You refer to our individual and collective mindsets. Are these separate and autonomous and so is my liberation contingent on the beliefs others hold?"

The Lama welcomed my question and articulated the answer. He said, "No! There is only One Mind, and that Mind is a no '*thing*.' It cannot even be said to exist at all—at least not phenomenally. As you know, the sun's light can shine through ten thousand different windows at once, and yet this light arises from a single source. Thus, it is with the entire world of multiplicity. These separate windows are similar to your illusion of many minds. Nonetheless, all share in the same light and lifeforce. The pure essence of each aspect of mind always retains the same quality as its Source and is completely unified with it. A darkened, mud-smeared window represents the particular obscuring beliefs resident in one seemingly separate mind. Once that aspect removes all its obscuring beliefs, it is free of the relative existence. Then it shines with the same purity as its Source, and it becomes transparent to the light of Truth.

One's freedom is not contingent on the beliefs and actions of others but is ultimately reachable through one's own purification efforts. To the extent, that you remove hindering beliefs, you will shine all the more brightly. You can then pass on your knowledge and understanding to "other" aspects of Mind and accelerate their progress. Collective beliefs are powerful whether they be true or not. If true, they help liberate all aspects of Mind. If untrue, they spread quickly and rapidly paralyze and incapacitate all who are vulnerable to them. Their poison is the sickening contagion of wrong notions.

When one examines bodily tissue under the microscope, one sees many different cells separated by cell walls and competing for the same food source and nutrients. Each is looking out for its exclusive interests. However, when we examine the situation from a higher, more telescopic vantage point, we instantly recognize these cells are part of the same multicellular organism. They share the same life and body and are better off working in harmonious unison to support their joint interests. A good cell absorbs the right nutrients to survive and flourish. Then it goes through rapid rounds of cell division through either binary fission, mitosis or meiosis, which then preserve a healthy organism. Similarly, a bad cell absorbs various toxins, and so it spreads impaired chromosomes to its progeny. A single bad cell can over time bring an entire organism down, resulting in either sickness or death.

So it is with the microcosmic mind of man, in its relationship to the macrocosmic, One-Mind. The One-Mind is like the multicellular organism and the individual cells are like individual men. We know a single bad man who entertains wrong views can destroy or poison an entire nation with his corrupt ideology. Similarly, a Buddha or a Christ can uplift and inspire the entire world and the collective Mind for millennia, or even indefinitely. A Buddha or a Christ is immortal in more ways than one. She is immortal firstly because she has come to the deathless in herself. She is immortal secondly because her understandings, being pure and nondistorted cannot be destroyed or lessened by time. They go on being true forever and change the entire consciousness of humanity. Hence they liberate all beings into the peace and safety of the One-Mind. The mind is not pocketed into gazillions of islands, separated by walls of flesh and matter. It is impossible to fragment Mind; and nowhere is it discontinuous to itself! It remains always unified. It is how you are using it which makes the One appear as many. It remains the timeless-spaceless, form-transcending essence, from which all forms arise. The secret of a Buddha or a Christ is that they know the indivisible unity, potency, and autonomy of the entire organism of mind. Meanwhile, the ego would have you identify with just a single cell. The spacetime artifice first appeared, when pure Mind became defiled, and then it came to experience itself as consciousness. This impurity created all the seeming separations, partitions and distinctions that populate your world. It gave rise to the so-called world of multiplicity. All that is perceived remains just a projection of your thought and 'the perceived is powerless to perceive.' Understand this aphorism, and you comprehend all. Then you recognize the invisible dynamo which powers all worlds, both manifest or unmanifest. Purify your thoughts and beliefs and align them to Truth and you will perceive none of this. All will be vaporized in the light of your pure understanding.

If you are spiritually sensitive, you will feel the collective power and presence of the One-Mind at work. However, you need to look impartially and be tempted to put on the dark glasses of the ego. There are many examples of the collective unconscious, found in the realm of nature. It is there, as the supreme organizing principle in beehives, anthills and termite mounds. It is witnessed in flocks of birds and sensitive ecosystems. You may be surprised to hear that the collective memory of a beehive, is about six times the lifespan of an individual bee.

THE CONSPIRACY OF DARKNESS

We seem to find ourselves in an austere and isolating universe, that cares not for us and hopelessly immersed in a world of pain, loss, and separation. One impregnated with so many frightening aspects and twisted forms. Surrounded by armies of dark ones marching against us, looking to take the little that we have. A world of fear made real and given form. One where we cannot even unearth our real Self. Here all is so horrendously shallow, superficial and counterfeit in its motivating principle. It is but an opportunistic world that aims to enslave. It lacks any substance and authenticity and is replete with so many insidious presences ready to move in for the kill. Yes, our minds became very dark indeed, once we bite into the temptations of the unreal. Since then the inner lens of our thought only projects dark shadows onto the screen before us. Is it a wonder that we have lost all faith in truth?

In these shadowlands, we invest our self-made concepts, symbols, and forms with meanings; they are incapable of. None can approach Reality. This world of symbols merely represents our fall from wisdom and departure from the Kingdom. Perfect wisdom still exists, but it has become veiled by all the foolish ideas, skin-deep conceptions and dreams we cherish. Unless we dispossess all falseness, the immaculate gates of truth will remain closed. We cannot enter the portal to Eternity while clinging tenaciously to illusions, idols and wrong beliefs."

INTELLECT VERSUS WISDOM

ON THE TIBETAN PLATEAU

I interjected, "Removing hindering beliefs, seems very difficult to accomplish. How can I identify a hindering belief?"

The Lama smiled and said "Removing hindering beliefs can be considered the fine art of living since it leads to all real progress. It will expedite fundamental shifts in the quality of your life and awareness. It will ventilate your consciousness and rid you of all poisons. Thus you become spacious, capacious, free, potent and amenable to the radiant light of Spirit.

The whole game of life is not learning but unlearning. You must rip out all hindering beliefs which function as weeds of the mind. Such parasitic weeds can be very resilient. Often, they will not die, no matter how many times you spray them with pesticide. Hindering beliefs are difficult to identify because their true face is hidden and obscured by denial, and various psychic-defense mechanisms. Outwardly, they may appear beautiful in form, vibrant in color, and delicate to the touch. They may effuse a stupefying fragrance, that bewitches the senses and fools the mind entirely.

Secondly, hindering beliefs are attractive because they offer gifts. The mind wants to keep them for some treasured purpose. This empowers them to dig deep roots and to flourish. Mind seeks to protect itself through endorsing certain ideas and beliefs. It embraces those ideologies which offer it protection, security, gratification and potential prosperity on the worldly stage. A prejudicial man, for example, is unlikely go around his southern neighborhood chanting "**All is One!**" Such a statement runs antithetical to his prejudiced mind, and it will potentially turn his friends into enemies. Whether our opinions be right or wrong, we all have investment in our beliefs, and are unwilling to sacrifice them. Instead, we grasp to them unwaveringly, as if they were our lifeblood.

There is another serious problem. Beliefs do not simply hang out as lone wolves on the icepack. No! They like to congregate and head to the nearest bar. There, they slap each other on the back and are best buddies. They like to be in the company of friends and similar supporting beliefs. So when we tug on the roots of any particular belief, we are likely to be pulling on the roots of an entire universe. These roots are what hold a person's entire system of thought together. You will find that the relative mind likes to live in dichotomy and affirms polarized views and stances. This is its *Terra Firma,* and it strengthens the ego's hold over our thought and decision. All the time, it wants to retain strong opinions and make crisp judgments on everything and everyone. It soon establishes intractable views on good and evil, right or wrong, male and female, productive Vs. wasteful etc., all of which give it an illusion of power. It cannot tolerate any gray zone of compromise. It abhors the very thought that it lives entirely at the poles of a spectrum and so it never adventures out further from its front door. The conception that it is part of a spectrum that is constantly shifting and changing would crush it and destroy all its confidence.

The primary purpose of mind training is to provide the map and the tools. A map, by which you can better differentiate, the true from the false, the real from the apparent, the progressive from the blocking. Then you will no longer function, as a broken toy, which keeps tripping over itself. The secondary purpose of this mind training is to provide you with powerful Sutras, which can liberate you from the realm of appearances. These sutras can enable you to enter Nirvana unimpeded. Without the map, you will just be spinning your wheels. Many spend many lifetimes traveling in a futile landscape, unable to make any critical distinctions or fundamental progress. Unable to unravel the Gordian knot, of their existential selves.

Thus, they travel through a dream landscape and are tempted by all empty idols; the dream seems to offer. They are having *'The Nightmare of Adam'* and remain fast asleep in the garden of Eden without ever copping on. All their incorrect and conditioned beliefs keep them in chains. Meanwhile, the myriad temptations of the dream universe continuously bombard them; this dulls their senses and drugs them into submission if not outright mindlessness.

Meanwhile, the skeletons of past vengeance, regret, and failure, blindfold their eyes and molds them into highly judgmental beings. Bitterness, hate, and a litany of self-obsessions transform them into cruel, mindless beasts, who are incapable of impartiality. Then they wonder why they cannot experience, the naked, self-resplendent Reality, that exists all around. One that lies, just beyond the screen of their darkened perceptions.

I have taught the difference between the Relative and Absolute Mind. Now you must understand the difference between worldly knowledge and wisdom. The intellect is the home of all worldly knowledge. It represents the realm of the relative, conceptual, perceptual, differentiated and conditional. From here Mara's arrows shoot out, enclosing one in the darkness of denial and self-deception. Relative knowledge is always utilitarian in its nature, purpose, and scope. It strategically commandeers your ingenuity, inventiveness, ego vanity, and self-propaganda to ensnare you further in the Samsaric existence. It photocopies ideologies and exploits all forms of media bombardment to amplify its agenda. It is for this that the whole educational system seems geared. Intellectual knowledge deadens and dulls. It is the junk food of the mind, and it makes one mentally obese, inertial and severely paralyzed. Absorbing only this, into your system day-in-day-out, you fast become stupid, obtuse and complacent and ready to settle for a life of mediocrity, material comfort, and ease. Thus you no longer seek true understanding, and cannot discriminate the worthy from the worthless. Your mind becomes tarnished by all your chosen poisons and drugs of choice.

Nevertheless, despite your extremely superficial understanding, you go about with all the grandiosity, intellectual pride and superiority of the Pandit. You roam as a high-horsed primadonna who will bow to none. Your lack of humility and superiority places you on the wheel of ten thousand daggers. So you go endlessly spinning around until you are mindless with vertigo. On this wheel are the daggers of idolatry, specialness, self-preoccupation, worldly power, sensuality, pride, indulgence and fear, to name but a few. Yes, this wheel of the intellect just induces dizziness and confusion. It keeps you coming back time-after-time to this amusement park and the circus of life.

You never realize the degree by which the sterile intellectual realm covers the real world completely. Its knowledge cannot inspire because it was born, in the absence of light. Imbibing its content, one proceeds further down the hall of disenchantment and despair. Into the murky corridors of sweat, in which nothing can be known unambiguously. One has merely entered a hall of mirrors, in which the ego' thought alone shines and attracts. Yes, it gleams defiantly, as a beacon of false hope for all who would fumble and bumble for worthless trinkets in the dark. So they ignore the flimsy meretricious deception which leads men to their graves. Thus, do the fireflies of sensual pleasure, grandiosity, privilege, intellectual superiority and lust attract us to be consumed by their flame. The relative knowledge of the intellect, being transient and insubstantial leads only to more wars, genocides, atrocities and dark ages. It cannot quench one's thirst. One cannot be satiated by the foul water of a mirage but only by the pure vitalizing water of Truth.

Wisdom, on the other hand, belongs to the sphere of the supra-conceptual, undifferentiated and unconditioned. Its scribbles words in the ocean that can never be erased. Its Knowledge is imprinted into each living thing, and all are imbued with its timeless light and everliving presence. This presence comprises a loving field of infinite potentialities and unconditional bliss. Only a few overcome ignorance and reach to this Source—the pure realm of the Dharmakāya. Wisdom alone can ferry one gently into Nirvana.

For one who truly understands, nothing is higher or lower. Nothing is within and nothing without—there is no self and no other. Boundless freedom is synonymous with perfection. Holiness is being supremely aware of your essential and unalterable Wholeness. There is neither sickness, suffering, sacrifice, sin or salvation. No birth and no death. All such phantoms are myths emerging from the blind misinterpretations of ego orientated nonsense. Adopt such foolish notions, and you will cast a dark shadow over your Being, which then becomes projected as the relative existence. So you enter the hall of mirages and ignorance. Once you make that fatal blunder of thinking anything is outside you fall through the trapdoors into chronic victimhood and lose all access to the light."

IDOLS KEEPING US DREAMING

What the Lama said, had me hooked. No one had ever put it quite like that before. I was beginning to understand how all the contradictions and confusion in the relative world arose. We were once presented a picture of beauty and radiance but our sight has become myopic from our overzealous fixation on particulars. We were now obsessing over the pieces and missing out on the holistic majesty of the overall design. I finally glimpsed how it all came together. Realized, how our self-made web is spun, from nothing but temptations and deceptions. The hypnotizing snares of the relative world, cause us to miss out on the pure Buddhaverses. I suddenly remembered a phrase, H.P. Blavatsky, had written in her book '*The Voice of the Silence*.' Its meaning now became pellucid.

"The WISE ONES tarry not in pleasure-grounds of senses. The WISE ONES heed not the sweet-tongued voices of illusion."

[The Voice of the Silence]

Then Lama Dorje, sensing, I wanted to hear more continued. "It is only in the mind-generated artifice of spacetime, that conflicting thought patterns can wage out their wars. Our numerous attachments, mistaken beliefs, and insubstantial lusts serve as the cauldron for all our inner conflicts. Our idols keep us dreaming. They suck us into the vortex of time and away from the true present. They rob us of all our energies and leave us bankrupt. As we motor forward on this highway of the unreal, our eyes are blindfolded by our idol attraction. Undefiled Truth becomes hopelessly shrouded and sacrificed when we worship the unreal.

TRANSCENDING THE DUALISTIC MIND-FRAME

No one can awaken unless he transcends all dualities. Dualistic modes of understanding are essentially impure and a fundamental cause of our continued ignorance. Hence true Reality is shrouded and we continue to dream of a phenomenal universe. The relative existence depends intimately on dualistic thinking patterns to maintain itself. All dualities lead to distorted perception. Dualities always come in pairs, and neither side is whole on its own. Each half presents a partial picture and its polar opposite contrasts with it on every assertion it makes. Dualities represent splits, in that which is unitary, undifferentiated and forever unopposed to itself. Only when one comprehends the unique synergistic relationship of a duality pair, does one finally transcend. The relative existence only appears to exist because we focus all our attention exclusively, on one aspect of a duality and then take this to be the complete picture. Occasionally it happens that both sides of a duality are recognized, but their true relationship is misunderstood. For example, the relative existence recognizes both matter and mind but fails to diagnose their true relationship to one another. Instead, each is seen as whole and utterly independent of its twin.

Some dualities are obvious. The dualities of *Hot-Cold, High-Low,* and *Inside-Outside,* for example. Other dualities, seem obscure and go unnoticed by the deluded. The dualities of *Dream-Dreamer, Subject-Object, Pleasure-Pain, Male-Female, Consciousness-Perception, Mind-Matter, Space-Objects, Ignorance-The Relative Existence, Existence-Non-Existence,* are some examples of such. Ignorance alone fashions the relative existence and this includes all superstitions and false notions that have infiltrated our minds, to its deepest level. For example, one of the most pervasive, sacred and cherished beliefs is that the objective alone is real. This is the epiphenomenalist standpoint, and it reinforces the error that the subject is a mere product of matter. Thus the subject is interpreted as a chimerical apparition emerging from the chemical and electrical interactions of neurons, electrolytes, and polypeptides, etc. Those who uphold this view will never discern the fundamental emptiness of the "objective" existence and recognize it is a mirage. The relative worldview vehemently denies the intimate dualistic relationship existing between consciousness and perception. It does not deny our experience of consciousness, but displaces its cause to an external world of matter. This horrible and unfortunate reversal of true cause-and-effect guarantees our ignorance will remain. The phenomenal universe is seen to be self-existing, while the active power of the dreamer's mind in shaping and projecting it is passionately denied. Since the dreaming mind is beyond perception, quantification or empirical measurement, it becomes regarded as a myth. Thus the role of the subject is entirely deemphasized, and he becomes relegated into a mere object in his mind-dream. This false exchange and reordering of true cause-and-effect protects the erroneous premises of objectivism from ever being interrogated.

Each side of a duality pair depends intimately on its complementary aspect. Without the dream, there would be no dreamer since both exist in a symbiotic relationship. The dreaming mind projects the dream, and the dream, in turn, reinforces the notion of a dreamer. In the end, there is just mind, and that mind either dreams or it has awoken. Once you fully recognize, yourself as the dreamer; then you are ripe for awakening. Then you know all that is appearing "outside," is projected from within. Existence is void apart from your mind and thought. The dreamer is a pseudo-reality and fiction, generated entirely from the process of dreaming.

Similarly, the relative world behaves, as if our concepts of male and female can stand alone and independently. However, the concept of masculinity means nothing, however, apart from having a contrasting concept called femininity. This concept builds itself up through its displacement from what we consider the feminine principle and vice versa. Nonetheless, the true psychologies of all are strictly epicene and contain a blend of both. Each mind exists somewhere on that continuous spectrum going from female to male. Pure male and female specimens are hypothetical entities that do not exist. In fact, all concepts are hypothetical and are untraceable, once one seeks. They are apparitions of the conceiving mind. Concepts and conceiving are another duality pair."

Lama Dorje had cleared away many misconceptions in my mind. I could certainly see how ignorance and the relative existence were in a dualistic relationship. I now understood that once all ignorant beliefs, superstitions, and limiting concepts are eradicated, we freely enter the pure and potent realm of Nirvana. Until then the relative existence would remain to fog the mind. I could still not understand, two of the dualities the Lama had listed. So I asked, "Can you explain the following two dualities for me (i) *Space-Objects* (ii) *Existence – Non-Existence?*"

The Lama was delighted with the question. He immediately said "Try and visualize some inner object, such as a cup or a ball.

Now subtract all the space surrounding your chosen object and continue with your visualization. You will notice you can no longer visualize it. This is because all forms depend intimately on space to give them definition and shape. This also establishes their relationship to their surroundings. Space and objects are partners in the same phenomenal illusion, and continuously re-inforce one another. There can be no objects without the padding of space. Likewise, the illusion of dimensional space depends intimately, on the presence of objects and objective phenomena. Objects and phenomena help to establish distances in space and determine the number of its apparent dimensions. Dimensions become conceptually imputed based on the type of objects they can subtend. A space without any objects or phenomena would sit neutral, undefined and incommensurable.

Similarly, existence and non-existence are in a dualistic rela-tionship. The dreaming mind takes 'existence' to be that which is phenomenally present, or at least phenomenally possible. Something is declared existent when it possesses at least one phenomenal characteristic or attribute, that defines it. When all such qualities are absent, it cannot be sensed, perceived, con-ceived or measured in any way, and it is deemed non-existent.

A discerning mind recognizes that mere phenomenal absence is not sufficient proof of non-existence. It simply indicates that it cannot be perceived, conceived or understood by the relative mind. However, since its existence is transcendent over percep-tion, conception and relative knowledge, what else is one to ex-pect? So the relative mind is blind and remains powerless to grasp or fathom its greater reality. The supreme existence is far beyond all our concepts of existence and non-existence.

Take, for example a photo. It is only perceived because its negative is absent. So the relative mind, proudly declares it exists. Even so, all that is perceived only seems to exist because of the absence of its negative. However, we can easily place the same photo, adjacent to its negative and see both. Then, when we overlap them; neither seem to exist anymore since each annihilates the other. Our rational and reasoning mind knows both pictures are still present, but neither can now be perceived. Perceiving a complete blank, it foolishly declares both to be absent and non-existent. So it is with all images, perceptions, concepts, and understandings, in the relative world.

The great 2nd-century Indian Buddhist philosopher, Nāgārjuna taught:

(1) All Things Exist

(2) All Things Do Not Exist

(3) All Things both Exist and Do Not-Exist

(4) All Things neither Exist nor do Not-Exist

It all depends on one's vantage point or perspective. From the perspective of the relative mind, phenomena seem to be real. Taken from the perspective of the Absolute or Transcendental, they are known to be empty."

This oblique conundrum had my head spinning. I asked Lama Dorje to explain these aphorisms in more detail. So he continued:

"**(1) All Things Exist;** means the phenomenal world only seems real to the relative (or Samsaric) mind. In reality, all seems real in the same way as a distant mirage seems real.

(2) All Things Do Not Exist, means all phenomena and objects have no intrinsic Cause of their own. Being devoid of any inherent self-nature, they do not exist in truth. Their existence is merely a contingent one and dependent on other illusory phenomena and objects to gain their contrast and definition. Other illusions determine their unique shape and attributes. Otherwise, they would not appear to be at all. Ultimately, they have no real existence, and their seeming existence is a conditional one. Conditional existence, extends fully across the realm of the ephemeral and transitory.

(3) All things both Exist and Do Not Exist; means that from the perspective of Relative the Samsaric mind, the phenomenal world seems to exist. The Relative mind, however, is limited, partial and bound by ignorance. It deems existent to be all that can be conceived, perceived, sensed or otherwise known through the distortions of its relative thought. Enlightened mind, having dispelled all such ignorance, no longer witnesses this phenomenal world. It experiences only the pure realm of the undifferentiated which is a perfectly integrated unity beyond all attributes, forms or distinctions. The true Nirvanic State of existence; known only through the illuminating perspective of the Absolute. It relates to existence through supra-conceptual and supra-perceptual modes of mind and an advanced evolutionary consciousness.

(4) All Things neither Exist nor do Not-Exist; All seeming phenomenal existence is contingent on ignorance and the relative mind. While ignorance remains, phenomena appear, as mere hallucinatory byproducts and projections of this Relative Mind. This instantaneous condition is called *dependent co-arising,* and it is one in which our residual ignorance produces the illusion of form. Nonetheless, all objects and phenomena are distortionary products of false beliefs and unresolved dualities. When one stands with muddy wellingtons in a clear pool of water, ripples and murkiness naturally appear below. Even so, these ripples are absent, when one is no longer wearing dirty wellingtons. Likewise once one has reached the pure, undefiled understanding, one produces no further ripples and the limpid pool of the void is all that remains."

There was a lot here for my mind to digest. I asked about other barriers preventing our recognition of Truth.

"Another important impediment," he said, "Concerns all the hang-ups we have regarding good and evil and with moral systems and codes of conduct in general." Then he proceeded to provide more detail.

THE RELATIVE AND SUPREME GOOD

The **Relative Good** exists on the flip side of what we call evil. The Supreme Good, in contrast, stands completely unopposed by evil. The relative good is associated with whatever fulfills our attachments and desires. Relative evil is seen, as that which hinders our progress. For example, suppose you suddenly receive a large sum of money. This welcome boon solves all your financial problems, and you may declare it to be a blessing. Suppose, however that through your financial well-being; you start developing unhealthy addictions. Soon charities start pestering you a dozen times a day. You are becoming just a little frustrated. Then old friends/family start popping out of the woodwork, asking for money. You can no longer distinguish your genuine friends from your 'good time' friends. After a while, you may even start considering your financial boon as more of a curse than a blessing. You may begin to see it as somehow evil.

The relative good, is not always good in nature but only contingently good. It can just as easily be seen as an evil lurking in disguise. A big bad wolf dressed up as Little Red Riding Hood, bringing you a picnic basket. It all depends on your interpretation. On the flip side of all that is considered, '*the Relative Good,*' lies a dark one. This insidious presence is a mind-poison that can bind you even tighter to the world of foolish attachments and desires. The relative good clouds your mind and distort your perceptions, and it entraps you deeper in the hell of the relative existence.

The Supreme Good, on the other hand, always awakens you to Truth. It releases you from the Samsaric existence and the hall of ignorance. It bestows perfect understanding and brings self-liberation. It unchains your mind from all foolish attachments and wrong beliefs including your stubborn ego attachments to vengeance, possession, worldly power, sin and specialness. It gently transforms and heals. In consequence, you become more expansive, impartial and open to light. You detach from the false world of appearances and place your feet securely, on the path towards truth. Finally, the Supreme Good releases from the pernicious thought system of the ego. In its Vision, evil becomes unknown because evil was never anything more substantive than a misplaced dream.

THE RELATIVE AND SUPREME EVIL

We associate evil, with whatever denies us our desires, inflicts pain and loss or impedes our worldly progress. Such is **the Relative Evil**. Our casual labeling of it as 'evil' is solely the result of our interpretation. It is not implicit in the action or event itself. We are always taking a highly judgmental stance when we declare something evil. As William Shakespeare once wrote, '*There is nothing either good or bad, but thinking makes it so.*' He is referring to Relative Good and Evil, and he recognized their dualistic relationship. Were we to reinterpret our attachments and desires as keeping us in bondage, evil would be construed as a liberating force; and one that empowers. Most of us avoid pain and crave pleasure. Nonetheless, pain and pleasure exist as a duality pair. Whenever we experience pleasure, it means pain is soon on the way and vice versa. As for loss, it helps us to develop a greater appreciation for what we have. Gratitude is opposite to Grievance. If nothing ever became lost, we would take everything for granted and lose our sharpness. If all our problems were immediately solved and our needs met, there would be no creative evolution or growth in us. Problems move us out of our comfort zones and chronic state of complacency, and they convey us into the mysterious dimensions of life. That which seems to impede us most often enables us to flourish and become more ingenious.

Impediments can strengthen our conviction of our goal's worth and they energize and inspire our imaginations in accomplishing them. Alternatively, setbacks may lead us to reassess the worthiness and value of our goals. We may see the underlying futility of worldly goals and replace them with more meaningful spiritual ones. The relative evil keeps us very acute and vigilant of mind. It helps us to avoid all the pitfalls of complacency, indolence, vapidity, and over-indulgence. Under the right lens, it can be interpreted as keeping us on our toes, and more watchful of our mind and actions.

For example, suppose you invested, all your retirement money with a certain stock investment firm. The manager of the portfolio told you, this is an excellent opportunity and advertised excellent returns. He was such a charismatic business-man that you felt privileged to follow his advice. All the same, he was operating a Ponzi scheme and never invested any of your money. Instead, he lived the high life, from the proceeds of witless clients like you.

At some stage, you decide to withdraw all your funds and are shocked to find your entire retirement fund has been wiped out. You then curse yourself for your trust in others and fall into deep despair, feeling your virtue was turned against you. There is a silver lining in all this. This evil act has sharpened your wits and honed your powers of discrimination regarding human nature. You learned a valuable lesson. From now on, you will invest more wisely and cautiously before committing any time, money or effort. You will test the veracity of what others say, and take precautions to protect what is important. You are now more adept at separating the worthy from the worthless, and at distinguishing false prophets from Enlightened teachers. Vigilant also of all foolish ideologies percolating in the marketplace of the world.

So, the relative good and evil exist in a duality, within the manifold of the relative existence! Wherever one exists, the other is lurking nearby, just waiting for its opportunity to strike. Together they keep the fire of the relative existence going and they help you become more awake in your sleep.

The Supreme Evil is that which promotes ignorance. It, therefore, keeps you in bondage to the realm of appearances. It inhibits all spiritual progress and meaningful transformation. It often appears in the role of a temptress that bewitches us and baits us with foolish and worthless attractions. Attractions that ensnare us deeper, in the web of Maya. It promises us idols, glamour, fame, and specialness. Thus, we undertake timewasting misadventures and fail to invest in truly progressive paths of release. The Supreme evil, cannot last forever because all traces of ignorance will eventually be expelled from the One-Mind."

Lama Dorje's words had inspired me. They brought up some old memories. I was beginning to see some events in my life, from a more illuminating perspective. I decided to share, "I can understand how it all comes down to interpretation. The relative evil can often be seen as good if interpreted under a different light. For example, many years ago when I transitioned, I became increasingly isolated and cut off from the greater hub of humanity. I welcomed my transition as the joyous emergence of my more authentic self. Others, however, saw it more like a funeral and dropped out of my life. My eyes were opened, and I began to see how incredibly hollow and superficial this world is. Man is just like a tin whistle, without any holes. It makes no difference how much one huffs and puffs through this instrument; no soul soothing music is possible from him.

Since I had time on my hands, I decided to utilize it wisely. I decided to dive deep within and became stronger in applying my powers of introspection, meditation, and reason. I made my mind into my object of investigation and shone the inner light on itself. I became more competent at separating the worthy from the superficial and consequently I cleared away many sources of confusion and contradiction that had blinded me before. Since I eliminated all that held me ransom to darkness; I made an important spiritual breakthrough. After that day, I no longer felt alone. Instead, for the first time, I felt truly complete. I treasured being alone now more than ever. I was not unfriendly to anyone. I just did not depend on any 'outer' psychological supports anymore. I found no need to complete myself through others, as most do. I had successfully navigated past all fear clouds within and came to the Source of light. I had come to know my intrinsic wholeness very directly."

Then another example came to mind: "When the other yogis did not want to adventure here, I first interpreted this negatively. I conjectured that perhaps my adventure would be doomed. Now I can see, if I had not adventured here alone, I would never have been able to stay here in this Ashram because there is no room for anyone extra. I would have missed out on important spiritual teachings, and you would have found it difficult to get your generator up and running."

For me, this adventure and my transition, years ago were opportune events and not the result of some reckless attitude. There is a greater force behind the curtains definitely shaping these events. Both were critical to my spiritual progress and continued evolution. If I had not transitioned, I would have entered a degenerative spiral downwards. I would have probably become increasingly cynical and hateful of others. In the end, I would have hated myself most for caving in and not living fully.

Antagonistic forces were everywhere, pressuring me to bow down to the 'norms; of society. Yes, this army of Lilliputians was all-pervasive and acting as an invisible conspiracy. It did not matter that they came armed with mere toothpicks because collectively they could reduce a goddess to her knees. For years, I felt forced to pretend to be someone else and had to suck up the inner turmoil, in silence. The cost had been high! I drunk heavily, even to blackout and oblivion. In fact, my friends had christened me the Blackout King of Dublin. Sometimes, I would attempt to drive my motorbike drunk. One night I became intensely frustrated because the bike would not move, no matter how much I revved up the engine and pulled back on the throttle. It turned out that I had forgotten to take the lock off.

This situation all came to a head on a vacation to Turkey. I remember coming to, at a bar early morning and not knowing exactly how I got there. I had this faint recollection of working my way through a bottle of Jameson's on the plane the night before, along with a twelve pack of beer. Now, while others were joyously heading for the swimming pool or going for breakfast, I was trying frantically to figure out where my glasses, passport, and wallet were. Trying to resolve how I would pay for the drink in front of me. That next week was insane, and I will spare you the details. In summary, I became very sick and could not come out of my room for days. I was in a meltdown mode, and all tectonic plates supporting my world had shifted to an entirely different continent. During that time, a mirror was held up to my inner self, and I began to see who was buried alive, with all my games and charades, and dancing to the beat of another's drum.

Yes, I had become immensely disconnected from myself, in the game of playing "**Mr. nice guy,**" to all who wanted me to remain as I was—mere cheap photostats of themselves. After that, I began to instantiate serious changes in my life. I had always been a self-reliant and independent and always thought things out for myself. These were essential ingredients in the mix. Without them, who knows what would have happened? I may have ended up one of those tragic figures or suicides; we encounter only far too often in the field of life. In fact, I took positive pride in all who were independent and self-sustaining. I could never understand 'those lost souls,' who were content to follow society's blueprints their entire lives. Those drones who allowed the world of superficial appearances to determine all their values and time-allocations. Those pliant creatures who prostrated before tyrannical hyper-structures that dictated their entire lives. Dictatorships that told them when it was OK to take a vacation, and when they could go pee. Such tyrannical entities pruned and groomed them into well-manicured birds until they were devoid of all spirit, character and independent will. Reduced to human androids, staring blankly at life. Going through the motions of a program written by a faceless corporate beast, whose only goal was to thrive, by any and all means possible. One that cut mercilessly cut the legs out from under all who humbly supported it. Yes, it did not seem to matter how many rivers of human blood poured into the cocktail of this stark ideology. I even treasured all vestiges of self-reliance I witnessed nature and the wild. I had a strong preference for the lone-wolf over the pack-wolf. When I was young, I had a farm cat called Tiger, who was tremendously self-reliant. She was jet black and a lean, mean killing machine. I had seen her on occasion stealthily prancing through the grass, only to then rapidly dart twenty or so yards or more and pull a bird straight from a tree. She would often go down burrows, only to emerge some time later, with a rabbit firmly locked in her jaws. She even attacked the neighborhood dogs, and when she played with a live mouse, it was so fun to watch. She would lie casually in the grass, as if on a siesta or play a game of "Walk-the-dog" with a Yo-Yo. Every time the mouse thought it was finally getting away, she would calmly stick out her claw and yank it back.

Yes, Tiger was no house-cat. She did not care to sit idly indoors all day, luxuriating on a comfortable sofa and wait for others to take care of her like some Cleopatra pandered to by slaves from the colonies. No every fiber of her being was armed with a purpose and exploited to precision. She was a living dynamo of the animal realm and one of unspeakable perfection. I didn't even like cats, yet this cat had taught me a thing or two. Finally, I had to go live in a remote part of Ireland for a few months to learn the Gaelic tongue. During this time, Tiger was left on her own. She was foraging one day some distance from where we lived when she was struck by a car. I was very sad to hear the news, yet grateful that it happened suddenly. She was not a cat to be gradually wound-down by life. No! She lived like a bolt of lightning and died that way.

ADVENTURING INTO THE SUPRA-CONCEPTUAL

The Lama remained in silence, as I went through my inner thought regressions. Finally, he responded, "You certainly provided excellent examples of Shakespeare's famous words in motion. It is our interpretations which transform the relative good into evil and vice versa."

I asked where he had learned to speak English so well. He said "I am a Tertön and a Translator and I search for lost sacred texts and manuscripts. There are hundreds, if not thousands of lost texts up there in the mountains. Lost by those who perished while carrying them back from India, Nepal, Sikkim, and Bhutan. In many cases, they were complete originals, and they embodied great esoteric secrets. Secrets which had the power to transform the entire consciousness of humanity. Eventually, I realized that many of our sacred Tibetan texts were unknown to most and therefore of limited power to effect world change. Consequently, I began translating them into English and other languages and disseminating them worldwide, to all who would listen. For such purposes, I also produced an updated English-Tibetan dictionary. Now I will continue with the teaching!

The world appears on the screen of our self-limiting concepts. We never see things directly, but only through the convoluted mesh of all our biases, preferences, desires, hatreds and false understandings. As a result, the Supreme Reality remains unknown. What we perceive only reinforces our wrong beliefs and circumventing thought patterns, and it seems to justify all our elaborate psychic-defense mechanisms. In ignorance, the world appears, and once right understanding is attained, this phantasm melts back into the void. Nevertheless, the undifferentiated remains the pure underlying essence of all and the essential backdrop of existence. This mysterious unseen essence is known as the *Dharmadhatu*. Even though it is extremely potent; it is not any '*thing.*' It is equivalent to Nirvana and the void and can only be apprehended through a pure non-judgmental state of mind. A single instant, without judgment, offers us Eternity.

On this journey to truth, one is not to look for meaning in symbols, words, concepts or forms. Symbols are merely pointers, and they can direct as much in the wrong direction as in the right one. Symbols are powerless to contain truth. No one has ever reached the Ultimate by clutching to symbols. You can only ever reach truth, by venturing fearlessly beyond all symbols. *No symbol can represent Totality,* and not one can aspire to replace the reality of unconditional love or bliss. Remember, *form is never content*, and it is content alone that you are after. All that is meaningful and transformative originates from direct experience of content. This map of mind-training is merely a navigation device. It can lead you to transcendence but is not a replacement for any experience of the ultimate.

There is a light within that remains timeless and pure, and unfading in its radiant power. This light is only revealed when you eliminate all shadows that hover over your mind. Your misplaced understandings are your only barrier to Truth. Worldly learning, has filled your mind with so much junk. The thick accumulation, of which has caused you to lose all clarity. So you picture a brutal, chaotic world permeated with madness, hopelessness, and despair. A barren world in which you feel

abandoned by the divine. A world in which illusions continuously hound you. A homeless depot for vagabonds in which you feel
continuously drugged, dumbed down, confused and unsure of
yourself. Be confident that you will attain to luminous perception once you purge all false ideas from your mind. The dark
mantle of wrong beliefs is all that prevents this light from shining outward. Once this veil is removed, the duality of perception
and consciousness disappear, and you become immersed in
Truth in full visceral awareness. Then you experience naked reality in its full dimensionless splendor. Then crutches are needed no longer. Instead, you remain as a timeless knowledge and
can experience no loss or diminishment of joy ever.

Truth has always been waiting silently in the endless present.
This instant is our only Gateway to the Eternal. The dark clouds
of ignorance and conditioning force an apparent continuity to
the world of time. Thus, illusions perpetuate ad infinitum! Truth
remains ours unconditionally, and it is so close that we cannot
even perceive, think or breathe without it. Truth is Life, and yet
this Life is in our mind. There is no Life apart from the Mind. We
live and operate out of mind always, whether awake or dreaming. Everywhere we go, our mind is generating the hologram of
the world. Truth cannot be lost, only forgotten. Our enchant-
ment with worthless things seems to keep it at bay. Many lifetimes we have traveled in dreams, unaware that truth even exists at all. Far beyond and above the clouds, we have formed,
Truth still shines. It will be witnessed immediately once we un-
do all falseness that pervades our mind-system."

With this, Lama Dorje ended this discourse. He asked me to
meditate deeply on what he had said and indicated; he would
start the next discourse in about two weeks. That would give me

time to digest and mature in these ideas and gain more meditative expertise. He had given me a lot to reflect on. I was already
contemplating the world of multiplicity and trying to separate
essence from form. I also began brooding on the critical
differences between intellect knowledge and wisdom. Then
there were the thorny briars of Relative Good and Evil, and all
the dualistic thinking modes in which we had become hopelessly entangled.

I found I meditated the best after some rigorous exercise. So I
decided to hike the next day to Tholing Monastery which had
been constructed the year before Atisha arrived in Tibet. He had
spent three years here at the red monastery teaching disseminating the purest and most potent esoteric teachings of the
Buddha. Old buildings, houses, monasteries, and caves, etc. always gave me the willies since so many memories and impressions were stored in these locations. I felt that the emotional
and psychological energies of those who visited or lived in such
places for long periods clung to the very atmosphere. Many
times, it happened in the past, that I would go to rent an
apartment or stay in a hotel only to immediately start running
for the door. Nothing was visibly wrong or askew on the surface,
but something deep within me had become extremely agitated
and alarmed, just being there.

Often I detected an unseen anger or sadness in the building or
apartment, that was coming in loud and clear. At other times, I
would enter a very humble looking apartment and feel tremendous joy emanating from the walls. The message would be silently playing in my head, *"You need to lock-in and get this place
now. Only good things will happen to you here. It is positively
brimming with new life potentialities, friends and exciting oppor-*

tunities ahead." I fully believed that each building, relic, utensil or complex functioned like a time-capsule. Some carried important messages, written thousands of years before. Many messages were still out awaiting delivery and would only be released when the right person came along.

Hence, I was eager to find out if any such message was waiting in my inbox when I arrived at the Tholing monastery. After all, I hadn't checked this particular P.O. box in over a millennium. As I approached, I could see, in its immensely dilapidated condition it was barely hanging on. It resembled now a worn out Methuselah or Gandalf the Great. It had obviously known better days and seen happier times. Nonetheless, it had stood here steadfastly and defiantly for over a thousand years, while nearly fifty generations had come and gone. All came with various ambitions or noble intentions. Each fell into the grave, exhausted, burned-out and corroded of spirit. Yes, mildew and rot had set-in, on all. This monastery had once been very young and vibrant, and it had welcomed many admirers and guests. There were times of great celebration in which beautiful paintings, mandalas, prayer-wheels, and monuments had been created or revealed. Times when those who sought the pure life and the enduring comforts of spirit had roamed the earth. Generations when monks would spend months or years, carefully composing just four lines of poetry to perfection—like some Japanese *Haiku.* They would consider this time well spent. This world, was so different from the one we have today that is incredibly impatient and drowning swiftly in an ocean of useless knowledge.

As I looked around within, it evidenced the brutal destruction of many of its monuments and paintings. I surveyed it all with tremendous horror and sadness in my heart because of all the neglect. The far greater crime was that the world didn't care anymore. It had become too obsessed with various political ideologies, Hollywood movies, tech-toys and social media self-propagation sites. These had become our modern gods, and we didn't give a rat's ass about anything else. It was not a question of paper or plastic, for we had become both. Yes, we were paper-mâché figures now inhabiting a plastic universe of things. Barren, lifeless and artificial to the bone. No spiritual seed would ever grow in us, ever again because we had exorcised all that was noble and good. We were empty, empty, empty of all life-giving nutrients. Defunct beings that would never flower. Time to be taken out the back now and shot or chopped up for used parts.

Despite its old, haggard and worn down look, there was something tremendously alive in this monastery. It was young in spirit, and it excelled in wisdom. Its spirit was deathless, and its sagacity could never be taken away. All its stripes and scars had been earned in the battlefield of life and in the quest for perfection. Even so, it remained unscathed, despite the destruction of the ages. Unmitigated in its capacity for engaging endless joy and true life. It remained as a young child forever curious and adventurous. Even though many world-systems had passed; its essential spirit remained unconquered and undiminished. A mystical fragrance continued to emanate from all its pores for it had crystallized all that was potent, and of value across the ages. They had become part of its inner flesh and bones. Sure its outer "phenomenal" face had picked up some wrinkles and blotches over the years, but its inner one remained radiant and serene. Ready, as always to bravely go now, where no monastery had ever gone to before—through the gates leading to the eternal.

SUTRA 1: CONSIDER ALL PHENOMENA AS DREAMS

FIRST MORNING LIGHT ON THE HIMALAYAS

Lama Dorje started the morning saying. "This powerful Sutra of Atisha is the only one you need ever know. It is the healing touchstone, that can instantly vaporize all your illusions. It will evaporate the dense fog of ignorance that beclouds your mind. Perhaps you have heard of the philosopher's stone, which medieval Alchemists sought to transform the base metal into gold. Likewise, this Sutra can transform your mundane worldly mind into a perfect harmonious alliance with the formless and undifferentiated realm. Once you come into absolute union with the all-powerful One-Mind, you will reign supreme. Yes, it has the proven power to bring Enlightenment to all who fully penetrate the esoteric meaning of its message. It has the capacity to dispel all phenomena in your inner and outer worlds, and to illuminate you with the very face of reality itself."

At this point, I interjected with, "Can you begin by telling me exactly what a Sutra is?" He continued, "Exoterically a Sutra is a short phrase or aphorism, usually given by an Enlightened Master. It can rapidly accelerate your spiritual progress and lead to meaningful transformation.

Esoterically a Sutra is an extremely potent key to Self-Liberation. This key only works if you are in a ready state of mind. Once your mind becomes truly receptive, open and unbiased, then the Sutra's underlying meaning become self-evident. Then you are instantly transported into the greater reality; towards which it is pointing and it reveals its secrets to you. Otherwise, it is entirely useless, just as words on a page are useless, if improperly understood. Symbols can represent different things to different states of mind. What seems like nonsensical gibberish to some, can represent potent realities to others. All depends on your degree of conscious evolution and the quality of your awareness.

Some, for example, completely miss the meaning of metaphors. Metaphors are wasted on them because their minds are incapable of reaching the higher realms of abstraction. They mistakenly think that the perceived universe exists, while the unperceived does not. With Sutras, the goal is to grasp the essential higher meaning and to expeditiously induct what they are directing you towards. Only then do you receive the gift, they impart. It is impossible to become nourished, on a diet of symbols and words. Only by distilling their true underlying content, at the level of your being can you ever be nourished. Your true

Being is not deceived like your superficial ego mind is. It demands the real, and it demands essence. It knows true nourishment demands fully imbibing veracious messages to your core.

Many have heard this Sutra, and yet it triggered no effect because they are deeply asleep and words are just words to them. They live in a perpetual state of confusion and know not themselves, nor the world they appear to inhabit. They are incapable of metaphysical abstraction and cannot decode the higher meta-realities, which are all about. That superfluid existence that the senses are powerless to depict. To them, the world is just a fuzzy lukewarm place at best—about the same temperature as their minds. Brimmed with the confidence of the arrogant, they never distinguish any signposts in the dream. Then there are others, whom we call 'the simultaneously born.' They hear this Sutra just once, and the next moment they are Enlightened. They possess the pure capacious power of mind which can instantaneously reach liberation. Thus they are easily freed from the entire world of appearances.

The simultaneously born are completely *sui-generis* and are gifted with a naturally heightened state of awareness. They are capable of viewing the world of perception, through many different layers of abstracted understanding simultaneously. They see what others miss and decrypt powerful diamonds of unrealized potential in our very midst. They are quick to pick up on key insights and impute relational models to the world, that others cannot even fathom or grasp. They are fearless pioneers of the inner world and rigorously honest in what they know. They are not like the herd but work things out from first principles and therefore will never accept secondhand opinion in place of first-hand knowledge. Thus they remain untainted by all the dream's petty attractions and supremely aware of all its pitfalls. This enables them to rise above it in an instant.

You are now listening to this Sutra and retain the free will to either treasure or discard it. You have the power and discretion to discern its immense value or else to see no value at all in it. You can harness its power and underlying meaning, to trigger a quantum leap in your consciousness and thus become rapidly liberated from the dream of transience and death. Or you can use these words as just another ego souvenir. Something to wear around your neck and show off to your friends at parties. Doing so, you will remain just a troglodyte in your cave and never reach the advanced Turiya state of consciousness.

THE COMMITMENT PROBLEM

Many are afraid to make firm commitments and prefer to remain on the fence. After millions of years of conditioning, we possess a host of unnatural and exotic tastes and desires. Yes, we want to accumulate an abundance of shiny trinkets before we go up in smoke. Likewise, we are eager to engage in myriad meaningless misadventures. Our bucket list is mostly composed of gaining more possessions, pleasures, experiences, and merits—but nothing that is genuinely worthwhile and lasting. It is rare to find a person, who can fully commit to some pure ideal or understanding known to be true in his heart or one fearless in their approach to life and ready to leave no rock unturned. Those who are impartial and honest in everything they know and do are scarce to find. Truth does not reveal itself, to those who are happy to play games of self-deception. Neither does it reveal its gifts to profligates who continuously vacillate and procrastinate their way through life. It bypasses all who shamelessly indulge their fantasies or spend their days looking in the mirror. For those cosmetic souls who are supremely uninterested in ever peaking below the surface, the wrapping is the gift and they cannot escape the prison-house of the Relative World."

I said, "Yes, I know a number like that. It is a very fake and superficial world we live in. I see such worldly people crawling about everywhere, rising out of the gutters of our planet. Judge Judy personality types, shoveling out unsympathetic caustic rhetoric through venomous tongues. They make me feel nauseous and raised my BP. They are so 1-dimensional, clinical and unrounded in their thinking. Their vertical worlds are all about procuring bread and butter, possessing the latest model car or else a fine yacht in their backyards. These earthly and materialistic street-cats are always seeking to dazzle all their friends with their latest collection of junk. Or else they pound them into placid submission, with incredibly tiresome conversations and tall-tales, that go on for hours. It feels like a cerebral cocktail of blunt-force trauma, and I just want to run, whenever I am forced to attend one of their barbecues. They belch out their strong, overbearing opinions on everything from politics to healthcare, to immigration. Never listening to themselves it seems, but perfectly happy to spout out their verbal diarrhea in every direction at once. It seems they make a concerted effort, to fill their lives with so many meaningless distractions so that they can avoid facing themselves. Dare open your mouth, to speak about anything more stimulating and intriguing, and they just look at you blank. For a moment they remain stumped. Then you hear the rattling within, as they start dismantling and coming apart. Their inner temperature is rising, and now their rage starts spontaneously emanating in bursts. They have morphed into petty, ratty beings, who are likely to say anything that will hurt. Suddenly you are made to feel diminished to the size of a worm and supremely unwelcome to enter their petty nexus of privilege. Or else seen as some alien lifeform, hailing from the far side of the cosmos. A spaced-out viridian green monster that is so out of touch."

The Lama continued, "Yes, those who are easily satisfied with all sorts of worthless attractions, cannot reach truth. One must fall into the sulfurous soul-crushing pits of absolute disenchantment before the real magic can begin. Entering the palace of despair, you fully comprehend how all your wild and wacky plans, dreams and schemes brought you nowhere. Only now are you ready to receive the gifts of truth. There are those who preach that '*The Temple of Wisdom, is reached through the pathway of excess.*' Even so, most to whom, this aphorism appeals are self-indulgent voluptuaries, sybarites, and epicureans, trying to justify their wicked, wicked ways. They blindly follow the pathways of the senses and course the river of Lethe to states of abject mindlessness. There is nonetheless a nugget or two of truth to this aphorism. Complete indulgence does ferry one expeditiously to absolute disenchantment. Thus it prepares one for wisdom. Only one who fully engages in life comes to see that all idols are made of dust. Then they are ready for something more substantial. Then they are ready to trade or sell everything to procure that priceless pearl of wisdom."

A DISCIPLE LEARNS AN IMPORTANT LESSON

Then I asked, "**What is the best attitude or tone of mind to take to make progress with this Sutra?**"

Lama Dorje went on, "I will tell you a true story that may help. A disciple came to his Zen master. He was ready to leave the Ashram, where he had spent many years. He was severely disappointed, with all his Master had taught him. He said, "I have read all the scriptures, esoteric texts, and Sutras, you have given, and I have meditated upon them deeply. I have endured so many pains, sacrifices, and deprivations. Long periods of silence and ascetic discipline. Undertaken so many intense yogic practices, asanas and sadhanas, and yet I have accomplished nothing. There has been no fundamental shift in my awareness, no quantum leap in my consciousness. In fact, nothing at all has occurred. I am essentially the same man, who came to this Ashram many years ago. Except now, I am so much older and worn-out from life. I could have lived a life of utter indulgence, and probably been far better off."

The Master immediately agreed with the disciple. He said, "*Yes, your eyes are so lackluster; so full of worldly appetites and lusts. You are still consumed by the outer.*" So, he asked the disciple to go for a small walk with him. The disciple expected it would be a very refreshing walk intermixed with some light bantering talk and climaxing with the Master finally conceding his failure. As they were climbing along a promontory of a nearby lake, the Master suddenly pushed the disciple off into the lake below.

Since the disciple was a weak swimmer, he instantly started flailing about in the icy water. The Master then descended to the lake and placed his foot on the disciple's head. The disciple was at this point positively beside himself, struggling and gasping to get the essential oxygen; he needed to survive. Just as he was about to drown, the Master took his foot off the disciple's head and yanked him out of the lake. Then he said, "*Once you seek for truth, with the same intensity and fire, as you have just now struggled for oxygen, it will come easily to you and on its own.*"

Yes, only when we develop the intense willingness needed, to penetrate the meaning of this Sutra *in-and-out*, will it not disappoint. Then you the dreamer will instantly awaken from the dream and recognize that your whole life up to this moment, has been nothing but a dress rehearsal. An endless series of dreams, seeking to light your awareness on fire from within. Despair is the great liberator because it purges your mind of all ephemeral fantasies and future desires. Doing so, it transports you wholly to the Eternal Gateway of the present moment and places you in an impartial and unbiased state of mind. Unless your adventure here, bring you to yourself, it brings you nowhere. Only then will you see through all appearances and realize nothing has ever been outside the dreamer's mind. Then you will see that all phenomenal existence, and all your life experiences up to now have just been an oneiric outflow, sourced from within. You know now with certainty that the mind of the dreamer alone is real.

A deep heavy slumber is the pervasive state of the world. That is why endless wars, brutalities, and cruelties bubble up from time-to-time. Every generation seems to have at least one major war. Because every time the collective mind becomes thoroughly sick, it fantasizes again, a dream of power. Then self-serving megalomaniacs find it easy to seize control. We only enter a state of war because the collective mind cannot contain its madness and rage any longer. So the world becomes thoroughly drenched in rivers of blood and vengeance, once more."

THE HIERARCHY OF ILLUSIONS

The Lama continued, "The dreaming mind sees a hierarchy of illusions. A hierarchy uniquely established by its judgments and evaluations. What it values or desires most, rises high on its hierarchy and becomes amplified into its perceptions. All else is quickly excluded. Out of the deceiving web of its partiality arises a world of various contrasts, orders, and levels. Judgment is a dichotomizing force, that places one in a highly differentiated existence. One in which competing concepts reinforce the pseudo-reality of one another. Yes, illusions depend intimately on a vast network of other illusions to lend themselves, any semblance of credibility. Even so, all illusions are equally untrue and have no place in truth. All the same, the mind that accords value and reality to illusions, cannot stop from dreaming. It becomes hypnotized by all its arbitrary wishes and wants and by all its special hates. Deeply enmeshed in the screen of its mental fabrications and confabulations, it becomes drugged by a very powerful hypnosis, which keeps it fast asleep. Thoroughly identified with the surreal content of its dreams, it is unable to awaken! For it has accorded reality to a host of splendiferous illusions, that momentarily tantalize it into submission. So each dreamer lives in a world of self-generated hallucinations. Trapped within the nebulous haze of belief phantasms powered from his mind is where he spends his entire life.

He fails to see that each dream is just his autogenous projection onto the screen of the void. A projection that perfectly depicts the hidden content of his inner thought. It images to him all his hopes, aspirations, judgments and fears. The dreamer does not readily catch-on because these images, impressions, and beliefs have become unconsciously infused over many lives. It is indeed a motley spectacle, ranging from the mythical to the mundane. All kept buried deep below through denial and self-deception. All this content, still very directly affects all his experiences and perceptions. He does not realize that his perceptions have no reality and that he is the sole dreamer of the world he experiences."

WHY THE DREAM IS NOT RECOGNIZED

Now the Lama and I engaged, in a brief colloquy. He had brought along some food to eat and some herbal tea. I asked him, "Do you miss any aspects of the dream? Is there anything in the greater world outside, you would like to experience again? How about sex, drugs, fame, booze, fast cars or plenty of exciting experiences? I can visualize you now heading down the Vegas strip with a beautiful woman hanging off each arm and jewels on every finger. Wearing designer clothes spun from silk and illuminating all with inspirational speeches. Assuredly, neophytes would pander to you and lap up every word you speak and apotheosize you as a living God."

Lama Dorje continued "You were just telling me a short while ago how nauseating you found it to attend a barbecue populated by obnoxious, opinionated assholes and morons. As Shakespeare, once said '*A fool's paradise is a wise man's hell.*' That is how I feel about all such novelties, esteemed in your world. They are but the foolish desires of an immature mind. Of one steeped in ignorance—not knowing where to turn to next. All foolish wants arise out inner emptiness. All that is transient is a poison, and it will exact an equal amount of pain in time. Just watch and see! In this Ashram, I have everything I need. A beautiful view and a life of utter simplicity. One low in stress and full of mindfulness. I spend each day completely absorbed and intoxicated in the divine. Because there are no real distractions, I can easily transport myself to any inner realm or mental state, I wish. I can travel at will from states of absolute restfulness and mental quiescence or else to pure Buddha Kingdoms, suffused with a very high quality of thought. I even enjoy my work here fixing things or growing plants and vegetables. I see my entire life as a meditation. I have all the food I need, and it is very healthy and nutritious. There may not be a Starbuck's nearby, but as you have already noticed, I can make a nice cup of Chai and Herbal tea. Why would I ever care to leave this place, to venture out into that mad jungle? That arena of crazy psychotic animals and serial killers where identity theft, fraud, spam and all sorts of other superficial nonsense bombards you 24x7?"

Then I inquired. "**Why do we not recognize the dream?**"

Excellent question! He said! "The dream-states can be very powerful indeed. In the dream, you see many jazzy, zooty and snooty characters, magically coming and going, Numerous relatives and acquaintances being born, growing old and then dying. It seems everyone needs to have their spots and stripes in this jungle. Their special scars, war wounds, and weird idiosyncrasies. It is quite the kaleidoscope of freaks, geeks, and misfits. An avalanche of aberrant and grotesque behaviors, and embittered souls looking to suck you dry. Yes, it is a world rampant with psychic-vampires and bloodsuckers of every possible variety. Thus you see friends appearing and disappearing, some gaining in notoriety and fame. All hypnotized by various vulgar and meretricious attractions. All extremely motivated for a brief period while they ferociously accumulate certain toys or accomplish certain ideals. Each mesmerized by his special dreams. They all bite down hard and fast, on the carcass of the world and call this life. Then slowly you see them becoming more disenchanted, sick, mutilated, desiccated, frozen, circumvented and transmogrified back into lifeless and lusterless corpses.

The dream is quite a hologram of technological wizardry, innovation, colored lines moving fast across our screens, birds singing in the sky, junkies getting high on LSD and wanting just to fly, New-Age hipsters seeking to heal, and magic swirling rockets powering to Mars on zero-point fields. Many thinking they just slid on a P-brane or have fallen into the supergravity field of a parallel universe. Only to find themselves quantumly entangled into a mundane world of tramps, fags and vagabonds, where they can no longer afford the gas bill and have to live off food stamps. Yes, this is your dream, so do not be afraid to come out with your hands up and take responsibility for your wondrous creation. Aren't you so proud of it? Isn't it such a darling? Here is a bucket, if you want to throw up! Ultimately there is just One-Mind. This is the artifice where we place all our cardboard boxes and come to file away all our special grievances, petty prejudices, jealousies, hatreds, volitions, capricious wants and foolish notions of self-power. Our wish is its command and how we use our mind-power determines what we perceive.

Consciousness is just an illusionary modality of experiencing ourselves through the split-mind of our personal ignorance. The capacity to conceive is inherently formless because one cannot conceive of conceiving. It is only the objects of conception that ever take form. What appears 'out there' is but the projection of all your conditioned beliefs, wish fulfillment desires, fears, idols, and fantasies. Reality remains spaceless and devoid of things. It is of the nature of ideas. What you see, is but your own wicked or altruistic thoughts and scripts playing themselves out on the screen of your perceptions. Just look at how many illusions, have arisen out of your firm belief, that you are a body! Without this bodily belief, you would find no need for tables, chairs, food, clothes, shaving creams, insurance bills, TV screens, jobs, health prescriptions, opioids, yoga classes, security devices. . . And so forth. All these needs are built-up very carefully and meticulously in your mind to support that tiresome and nauseating world, your bodily beliefs warrant.

The body is your root illusion, yet one you have become deeply identify with. Through it, you strengthen the epiphenomenalist belief system of the ego. So you welcome in a world of magic, consumerism, materialism, genetics and medical science. All are mind-made worlds that further cement your bondage. Your essential mind is free of all form, obstacles, and hindrances. In its raw and pure, unimpeded and independent of the five skandhas. Even so, this impure mind experiences itself as consciousness and so witnesses the relative existence. Such is the fall of Adam and his dark dream. **Consciousness has never been in the body; the body is but an apparition in consciousness.** The relative world is nothing but a quantumly collapsed product of your consciousness. One composited from all your arbitrary thoughts, volitions and fears. It is not without, but within. Adjust your eyeglasses up and down or press your finger against the side your eyeballs and see how the world moves in correspondence. All this should be incontestably indicating from where it is sourced!

THE MONKEY'S PERSPECTIVE

THE MONKEY GOD ON THE BRIDGE IN RISHIKESH

D oes a monkey share your world? Or is its world a product of its peculiar limitations? Would you be willing to highlight for the monkey, what is false in its world understanding because the monkey believes it perceptions to be 100% true. It cannot understand that the many fleeting forms, movements and smells it witnesses are merely a product of itself. The end product of its unique level of conscious evolution. All the distortions, amplifications and unique colorations that constitute its particular experience are shaped and filtered by the capabilities and filtering templates resident in its monkey mind.

Using the power of induction you must surely suspect that there are numerous similar highly faulty images, concepts, and false formulations, showing up in the sky of your mind. These manifest into your unique world experience. Many are karmic imprints and the residual arising from your past life experiences. Such are the Vasanas. Powerful inner forces, resident within the psychic matrix of your subconscious. They automatically direct your decisions and behaviors and establish filters on your awareness. They function as distortionary elements that twist and turn, mold and shape. Defiling truth, and reimaging it into a world of mere appearances.

Once you realize the world of perception is just a reflection and not out-there, you are beginning to understand this Sutra. Then you are beginning to understand the chimerical nature of the dream. A dream you appear to inhabit as some animated object or corpse. You begin to glimpse how the dark cover of your misunderstanding and former impressions, covers over the real. That what you perceive, is being driven by your pervasive state of ignorance. Then you know that all forms and phenomena appearing in it are your mind-driven hallucination. Meanwhile, truth silently awaits for you, to awaken from your dreams.

RELINQUISHING THE FALSE IS THE PATH TO WISDOM

Truth is always self-consistent and it leaves no room for any duplicitous content or contradictions of any kind. In the relative world, truth can seem like the many-headed monster of trickery and deceit. One that charms and beguiles with games of artful legerdemain. One possessing many faces. The faces of materialism, pleasure, power, worldly justice, vengeance, complexity, chaos, isolation, and mercilessness, to name but a few. Sadly the faces of unconditional love, mindfulness, peace, bliss, abundance, and limitlessness seem nowhere to be found. They have been eroded from the mountain by the corrosive force of our worldly natures. All we are left with is the Mount Rushmore of our ego. Yes, all becomes interpreted and valued differently by the relative mind. Nevertheless, the face of Truth endures and can never be eroded, except in the landscape of illusion. It remains completely unified. Yet, it can only be known where there is no duplicity and self-deception. Purification of thought is needed to reach it. Then your mind becomes truly radiant and no longer entertains any source of darkness. Then the light of truth within streams out into your perceptions. Then all false appearances and fleeting forms generated out of your misbeliefs disappear.

It may surprise you to know that the real world is not like this. It has no bodies mindlessly perambulating about, infused with all sorts of wicked ailments, deficiencies, wants and perverted desires. There are no vehicles, buildings, hospitals, food shelters or weapons of mass destruction. There is no pollution or ecological devastation—no melting of the icecaps. No sociopaths, psycho-paths, cyber-thieves, or neurotic individuals surfacing from their ghettoes and technological tombs, looking for their next victim.

In the real world, there is never any diminishment. Nothing ever tires, grows old or weary. All exist in light, and every idea is imbued with potency beyond your wildest imagination. Shining and shining forever as a transcendental masterpiece of beauty, that is forever giving of itself. All these worthless appearances that surround you only arose from the conditioned residuals implanted by all your faulty understandings. They can be con-sidered part of your antediluvian or classical mind-frame. Your post-separation, Samsaric lower mind. Once you use the sword of discriminating wisdom, to uproot all false beliefs, the chick-en's head will have been severed forever. Yes, it may appear to wiggle and waggle about for a while, but it will soon drop life-less to the ground. It was carrying all the momentum of your conditioned beliefs. Perception was always just a mirror, in which you saw your thoughts play out. It merely represented the quality of your conscious evolution. In this dark and grimy mirror appeared the world. Many images are born and forged from your conceptual misunderstandings and beliefs, as from all your unnatural desires and fears. Each of us is the projectionist and we have covered the walls of our caves, with so many shad-ows, phantasms, and chiaroscuro. Grandiose pinups of the tacky and the vain. Foolish images written in crayon, scribbled by a ghetto artist, which nevertheless we use to complete ourselves. Our wanton, impure, and unwholesome thought alone is in need of healing. We must dam the well of our desires, quench the illu-sory fires of our anxieties and fears. Relinquish all our confusion about ourselves. Clarity is the holy grail, we desperately seek.

Our confusion has produced a crepuscular world of make-belief—a weather-beaten shack that should be rapidly bulldozed to the ground. It is a desolate desert of the spiritual, rather than a refreshing oasis and presents a bleak landscape in which we identify as bodies. This has led to all sorts of anxieties and ills. Yes, we have all fallen into the well of ignorance and believe we are a body. It is only by nuking all our faulty understandings that we will see it disappear."

ALL LIFE IS AT THE LEVEL OF THOUGHT

What the Lama had said, about the world being nothing but a projection of images, fueled by ignorance, really had an impact. He had succinctly explained how all phenomena were simply mirages of mind, and of the nature of dream. This images only appeared, where first there was impurity. My mind was bubbling like a cauldron of inspiration, and my entire old worldview was severely shaken. So I was not a body, after all, navigating mindlessly about on a chaotic planet. This was the reason; I never could understand the world I lived in. Because I did not live in it, it lived in me and who could ever understand a dream? Its many symbols and metaphorical imagery were just projections of what the mind itself wanted to hear and see.

However, I immediately thought of another important question to ask: "If all phenomena are empty, insubstantial and of the nature of dream, does life even exist at all. Or is everything just an illusion?"

Lama Dorje was delighted once again, by my line of questioning. He knew it meant I was attaining to real insight. So he expounded in detail on this topic.

"The universe is infused with life. Only this universe is not outside your mind. All life is of the nature of mind. When you view the universe, it seems that consciousness exists across a vast spectrum. In our explorations here, we come across many lifeforms, which are so hypersensitive to their immediate environment. They can tune in and respond, to such a vast range of frequencies and movements, even to remote astrological phenomena. Many lifeforms even extend their antennae to detect vibratory phenomena, that seem miraculous by our standards. No other lifeform possesses the peculiar quality of life we call self-consciousness.

You should reflect deeply on this thought: *Consciousness does not go anywhere. It cannot go out, nor is it a part of the world you perceive. Rather the world is a moving shadow in it. There has never been any lifeform outside your mind.*

Whenever consciousness becomes parceled, containerized or restricted to a particular range of frequencies or abilities, then it appears as a particular lifeform. This lifeform remains just an appearance in your mind. So it also, with the entire world of objects and phenomena. There is nothing dead or inanimate because all shares in your mind and thought—and your thought is life. It is the only life any lifeform ever really has. The particular body you perceive and identify with is not alive, the way you think it is because anything perceived has no power to think or perceive. The appearance itself can never be alive, any more than a shadow could be called alive. Instead, each is just a reflection of your thought. That is its entire life!

You may have heard of the pre-Socratic philosophers, known as Hylozoists. They developed great intuition, to the world around them. They knew the secret and were thoroughly cognizant that even matter that seemed static and dead was very much alive. They knew it was alive, not as a thing, but as a thought. Obviously, they saw fire, water, air systems, as well as planetary and cosmological bodies as possessing life, in the same manner. They did not stop there. They understood that rocks, buildings, mountains, cooking utensils, chairs, etc. were also throbbing with the same life energy of thought. To them, nothing was separate, and all was in a powerful, seamless interaction with everything else. There was just one life-force present everywhere and anywhere. All individual lifeforms were part of this supreme unseen entelechy. One that remained unseen because it was intimately joined to our minds as well. In fact, in essence, it was just Mind. A One-Mind which was pure and indestructible. One that could not be ravaged or dissected. All forms and phenomena represented projected manifestations of its thought. This was our real Mind and real Self. Many druids, mystics, alchemists, yogis across the ages, also knew this esoteric information. So they were able to connect and communicate, with much greater intimacy with the world around them. They were able to understand things from the inside. They did not view the world as a catalog of separate objects and surfaces. Their intimacy made it possible for them, to extract potent elixirs, cures and healing remedies that helped catapult us meteorically forward into a New Age. Their wisdom and methods have long been forgotten and are no longer taught. Once science came to the forefront, we were duped into accepting certain hedonistic theories that examined the world only at its presented surface. The world became shallow and interpreted as one of separate objects, linked by phenomena. Examining and understanding things from the outside, we had barred ourselves from mystical union. It was not long before our intuition became dead. Hence, we now take pictures of a Tsunami, instead of running for the hills. All these great mystics, alchemists and philosophers have always agreed that "**Life alone IS**." Having probed deep in their investigations of the true origins and nature of Life, they had answered important questions, such as:-

What does it Mean to Live?

Where exactly is the Source of Life located?

When Does Life Begin?

Does Life come to an End?

Why do we see such a Diversity of Lifeforms?

Is Static and Inert Matter Authentically Dead?

In the end, they had found that nothing is separate or external and that all is of the nature of mind. A simple understanding and the real TOE. The impact of this realization was tremendous and paradigm shifting. They proceeded to teach, that to truly live, one had to free oneself quickly from all fears, defensive strategies, and petty interests. Instead one was to give oneself unconditionally to all. Life was of the nature of boundless communication of high-quality information and thought. To live selflessly and to disseminate the pure perfume of one's being in every direction at once, without any sense of regret, was the only true way to live. Their metaphysical intuitions, spiritual insights, and visions had brought them to the temple of wisdom. Unfortunately, they were powerless to transfer this wisdom and understanding to others. This is because it is a tacit and wordless understanding, that must be experientially felt and known within oneself. It must be palpably understood at the visceral level of one's whole being.

This profound esoteric wisdom became lost when the druids and mystics went out of vogue. Facts and dry intellectual knowledge came onto the horizon instead. This is because facts can easily be conveyed, communicated, illustrated or e-beamed to others. Hence, the superficial worlds of Science, Biology, Finance, Medicine, Technology, Genetics and Warfare soon proliferated. These phenomenally-based belief systems came in the guise of our saviors and protectors and our understanding of the world diminished to the level of surfaces. This "New" knowledge was easily digested by our mental bodies, but toxic to our spiritual one. This is the real reason for our present state of confusion, conflict, and anxiety and why we no longer feel truly alive. Consequently, we have become ravaged with so many strange mental sicknesses, psychoses, and neuroses. When the spiritual is absent, the world of prescription drugs, painkillers, opioids and various addictive tendencies must rise to fill in the void. Our world is now one of never-ending consumerism, shameless tabloids, and endless invasive marketing campaigns. A world of terror, information wars, propaganda and serial killers. Of Ted Kaczynskis' carrying a lethal payload to the Sunday market. A homeless depot where all fragmented and isolated souls, are trying to up their game and going in for last fourth of July that blows the competition away.

The vitalizing life-force needed to restore and heal us can only ever be found at our centers and never at our peripheries. Sadly, we exist now only at the periphery and surface and never penetrate to the level of essence. Our learning is too superficial and it does nothing to imbue us with increased life and expansivity of mind. It fails to make us more compassionate, forgiving and concerned about the needs of others. Instead, it is utilitarian and there to support the machinery of lifelessness, corporations and special interests. It is good to remind ourselves at times what Oscar Wilde once said: *Nothing worth knowing can be taught."*

Lama Dorje had provided a powerful perspective both on the past and the present. It seemed that in many ancient systems we were far closer to tracing the mystical essence, which held the key to our liberation. Yes, the ancient alchemists and mystics had demystified the world of appearances and avoided making artificial separations between the world of the organic and inorganic. To them, the world of static matter and organisms were all powered, by a single unifying life-field. It seemed all our rigorous classifications had only thrown us further into darkness. Steeped us in the grandiosity, pride, and conceit of superficial knowledge. We remained blind and arrogant horsemen, gallantly riding over the edge of the cliff. Plunging deeper into the abyss of our self-generated ignorance. I was interested in learning more about the powerful deception of Scientific knowledge. How it had attracted us so mindlessly like fireflies into its false light. How it hypnotized us so compellingly, that we became voraciously consumed by it. I asked Lama Dorje, if we could provide some more history. So he continued with his insightful delivery.

THE SCIENTIFIC REVOLUTION PROPELS US DEEPER INTO THE ABYSS OF IGNORANCE

"Slowly, the world began to see that these druids, alchemists, and mystics were onto something of tremendous import. The realization dawned that there were hidden powers, in this world of matter and phenomena, that remained untapped. Powers which could become, our holy grail to lives of longevity, ease, and bliss. These powers we now wanted to extract and master. So a divide-and-conquer approach was taken to the world around us. Everything was exhaustively investigated, analyzed, quantified, labeled, gauged, calibrated, tagged and bagged and then placed on the shelf before us. Once labeled, we became conceited with our new conceptual understandings and figured, we now knew all its secrets. Just a few unimportant bits of information needed to be added later to complete the picture. Simply by enumerating an object's attributes, capabilities, and phenomenal interactions, we thought we understood it its entirety. Nonetheless, we remained as ignorant as ever and deeply submerged in the subaqueous realms of false knowledge. We had never really fathomed, a single thing to its essence. Never arrived at the authentic seat of its being. All our knowledge was delusory, superficial and self-deceptive.

That seed, which was the essential innermost component to life, remained an elusive mystery because it could never be revealed through any phenomenal or conceptual means. The phenomenal and conceptual could only take us so far because their scope was limited to the surface reality of appearances. Bombarded by the perpetual mind-flux of artificial labels, classifications, and designations, we became addicted to our superficial games. And drawn to those wicket pursuits of sophistry, dialectics, false-reasoning, number-crunching and endless data-massaging to support the evidence we wanted to hear. We came to believe in circulatory cause-and-effect and made numerous unfortunate cause-and-effect reversals. Even so, all we were ever doing, is scrying into the crystal ball, of our self-made conceptualizations. We still did not understand a single thing from the inside-out, as the druids and mystics had before us.

A great cost of applying the Scientific method was it unfairly relegated the world of the unmanifest and undifferentiated into the waste paper bucket. It was considered a black netherworld unamenable to scientific scrutiny and so actively dismissed. Anything which could not be readily quantified, labeled or symbolized was deemed taboo or else irrelevant and inconsequential. Only those findings which could be studied objectively became emphasized in the greater picture. The world of the formless and unseen was considered far too subtle, elusive and nebulous to support any meaningful investigation. So, the greater sciences of mind, consciousness, and spirit became archived away and placed on a dusty ledge where they remained for centuries. Any open-minded researcher, who delved into these murky worlds was swiftly deemed a quack, who was idly chasing ghosts. Any quantum shift in the new world order was deemed far too heretical. So our evolutionary trust and research became profoundly circumvented. More like that of straight-jacketed knights peering through tiny visors in their metal headgear who would be ready to strike anyone down who even hinted at saying anything rebellious or seditious to King and Country. This New Order focused on the exterior and the surface world of appearances. Even the shadowy meta-realms of sorcery and witchcraft received greater emphasis and respect in this old world scheme.

Likewise, the more fluid inner cosmos of our dreams became trivialized. Dreams were perceived as endless streams of mostly fallacious images, and nonpertinent to worldly affairs. All the mysterious symbols, motifs and hidden metaphorical content, pervading them were considered mostly a private affair. Because our dreams could not be readily grasped or decoded, their healing symbolism went completely unharnessed. Likewise, the powerful connections our dreams shared with the vast reservoirs of our unconscious knowledge remained lost and undeciphered. Nevertheless, newly accessorized with our vast accumulation of facts, empirical knowledge, and exotic sounding words, we felt we were making excellent progress. What we were entering, however, was a truly dark age in which the skin-deep macrocosm of materialism, consumerism, self-absorption and outward obsessions took over. Soon other themes became articulated also including pollution, ecological devastation, drug dependency and privacy erosion. For the first time, we saw a proliferation of new insidious weapons, that seemed capable of threatening us with complete extinction. None of this mattered a whit because we were not happy anymore. We had lost our hearts and all meaningful connection to our true Identity. We had entered a barren cul-de-sac where our online personas took over and became even more real to us, than our physical bodies. We had transformed overnight into a mob of androids and human robots, who blindly accumulated worthless knowledge. Immeasurably addicted to all those sterile inorganic facts, we could exploit to mass-produce the toys we wanted. Stubbornly indifferent to anything that could meaningfully transform us.

The world became polluted, and our minds became nothing but pestilential garbage dumps. Havens of pure filth and trash, full of obsolete and stillborn knowledge. Worse than a whore's underwear after a night at the harbor. Our thought processes became so torn and shredded by numerous contradictions and obfuscations that a new industry of mind-numbing drugs had to be unleashed to sedate us with its poisons. The pharmaceutical industry exfoliated overnight, dazzling us with its endless array of powerful concoctions. Ones that could send our neurons dancing the Tango across our hemispheres, then shuttling back through all synaptic connections, like they were on the slide in Waterworld. Meanwhile, we would peer out from our vapid lifeless sockets, looking like pure clowns. Clowns, that had lost all their perspicacious capabilities for reason, intelligent insight, intuition and visionary experience. Yes, the planet of the Apes was back up and running. Only those tongue flapping demagogues who could pander loquaciously to swarms of mindless beings, while taking cash injections up the ass, could be elected as president.

All had metamorphosized into was a hub of commonplace Philistines, buzzing about in noxious landfills. We had become cold, calculating machines, who knew the price of everything and the value of nothing. Capable now only of manipulation and exploitation. We didn't have a clue how to be truly empathic and altruistic. Instead, we had become predators on these landfills, who cared not a toss about the needs of those around us. We deemed our existence as that of biochemical engines packaged into meat-suits, and were willing and eager to be twisted into profit.

Nature seemed to have lost the upper hand along with all its magical, inspirational properties. Yes, it had fallen fast from its former splendor, radiance, and glory into the gutter below. Now standing there, raw and naked and completely demystified before us—it seemed more like a plain Jane. The hidden powers of the cosmos were worshipped, no longer because we had humbled, tamed and subdued this beast. Yes, we had become its Master and were now the ones carrying the whips. So we cut it up and gored it and placed it into our tiny little boxes. Boxes we painted over with the artificial veneer of our superficial knowledge.

A dark overlay fell upon our world, that hung like clusters of dark billowy clouds over our souls. Since spirit and mind had been relegated into the trash, we found ourselves drowning violently in the pretentious soup of senseless and hollow sounding terminology. Uncontrollably flailing about in a veritable quicksand of words, symbols, concepts, and equations that we nevertheless now idolized. We came to inhabit a stark object-orientated universe. One in which we saw our existence as that of mere objects. Day-in, day-out we were mentally invaded by a never-ending plethora of mind-blowing information. New research on phenomenal interactions, technological innovations, and medical advances. We found ourselves immersed in the cruel sea of endless paperwork, logistics, new regulations, statutes, edicts, treaties, provisions, lawsuits, codes of conduct, patents and copyright infringements. All of which became interweaved like weevils, lice, glowworms, and animalcules into the fissures of our everyday existence. Our souls cringed in their boots because we had fabricated for ourselves a world of escapism, delusion, desolation, and isolation. An exhausting world of so many meaningless things. One steeped in disillusionment and despair. One that would soon become the blueprint for our entire destruction."

PRACTICAL APPLICATION OF THIS SUTRA

All this had been an eye-opening revelation for me. Lama Dorje certainly portrayed in-depth how the dreamworld had evolved into such a fearful, overly complex, and meaningless place. "So now you are wondering how you can use this powerful Sutra?", he asked.

"Yes," I said, "It seems so abstracted and high level, that it completely eludes my mind, how I am ever going to unlock its power. If my liberation is contingent on examining all phenomena exhaustively as a dream, then I will just become hopelessly depressed and concede failure. That approach seems even more futile that counting the grains of sand along the Ganges. It may motivate me to take the addiction highway instead to reach the celestial realms of the Buddhas. So morphing into a hobo, like Kerouac and hopping aboard the trains of alcohol, drugs and various hallucinogenic agents to enter a very psychedelic and multicolored landscape."

Lama Dorje continued, "Fortunately, you do not need to penetrate all phenomena as dream, to become Enlightened. That is just the overall intention. Once you recognize even a single object or phenomenon as a dream, you will promptly see the entire dream nature of all. You must understand that nothing is ever separate from anything else. All that is perceived is fused intimately in the higher reality. It all exists in a hyper-manifold and transcendent order from which even mind cannot be excluded. All separation is an illusion. Once you penetrate a single phenomenon or image to its core, you will quickly be released because the light you recognize in it, is the same heavenly light that suffuses all.

Perhaps you have heard of the demiurge, the artificer of all world systems. One whose eyes and ears are everywhere. One who smells through every nose, tastes through every tongue and lives through every order of being. Every orgy of man, woman or beast becomes intimately threaded into its greater bliss and never-ending circus of indulgence. Yes, its tentacles are everywhere, and there is no action or motion apart from it. In its vast scope, the duality of motion and stillness completely disappears. It remains unseen because it represents that greater entelechy of Being. Yet, it is the one responsible for all the artful conjuring tricks that deceive you. Our lives are mere VR simulations playing out in its great cosmic brain. It remains the code master, deceiver, and spinner of countless universes and it basks forever in pure light and formlessness. It is the Bill Gates of the spiritual realm, and none can come to see its true face, without truly deserving it.

You must move out of the ego comforting pastures, which pertain to the world of specifics. Rise beyond the contagion of all worldly thought and apply this Sutra diligently and indiscriminately—to all phenomena seen in both the seemingly exterior world and those of the inner realms. All perceived with your mind's eye is of the ephemeral nature of dream.

The quickest way to have success with this Sutra is to pick a single object and stick with it. Something that seems static, on which you can place all your focus, without any distraction. Such an object will work better to prevent your mind from wandering. Pick something that you love, because you are undertaking a voyage into the sacred. On this journey you will be bypassing, all ego barriers generated from your worldly thoughts and ambitions. You are attempting to reach the greater field of loving light which embraces all. The goal is to merge the loving light already within with this "outer" object. This immaculate, potent and radiant light powers all motion and life. It is indestructible and boundless, and likewise immanent in this object, you have chosen. The light which seems locked within this frame, is held ransom there only due to your ignorance. Once you successfully connect to its real essence you will have reached to the very hub of Life itself.

To accomplish this, you will need to rid yourself of all trashy knowledge the world has ever given. All that which is false and superficial. Such unreal fictions establish illusory boundaries and partitions to your Real Self. All function as a darkening distortive mental overlay and they impede the inner light from radiating out into perception.

In the final analysis, you will be doing absolutely nothing, but doing so in full awareness. This is the most potent and productive activity; one can ever undertake. **Because once you stop, the world comes into true focus and you perceive all in a holy light.** Move, and you will know nothing, see nothing and understand nothing. Instead, all becomes darkened and distorted by your mental fluctuations and lost under the dark veil of all your Self-obscuring activities. Your doing has caused all your problems up to now. Mental motion and wasteful action have left you crippled and blind. It has enabled numerous phantasmal images which do not genuinely exist to infiltrate your inner landscape.

ATTAINING TO NAKED PERCEPTION

A dam once perceived with Vision in the Garden of Eden. Regrettably, the moment he thought he could usurp his Creator, he fell into darkness and succumbed to the hypnotizing drug of sleep. He remains asleep in that Eternal Garden, and he is you! His dark thought poisoned the well of our entire Mind, with impure and false ideational content. Nonetheless, we can reattain naked perception, if we know how to go about it. To accomplish this feat, we must eliminate all alien ideas and distortions that have infiltrated our mind system. Purge all that which camouflages Truth, which prevents it from being recognized Reality in its naked essence. We have become blinded by numerous erroneous thought-forms, imprinted over eons from the tarnishing influences of civilization, culture, dogma, worldly goals and various morality systems. Blinded also by that superficial knowledge, accumulated through the intellect. Mentally shaped and molded further by environmental and astrological influences and relative perspectives.

Then there is that confounding thought prism of all our predilections, partialities, biases, fears, jealousies, attachments and incorrect understandings. Many are blinded further by their dreams of vengeance and retribution for all past brutalities and injustices they have suffered. All of this functions as a powerful web of deception that ensnares us, in the three hells of the relative world. It forms a dark cover on the mind and it keeps us endlessly chasing the phantoms of past regrets and also our future dreams and aspirations. All this junk percolating through our value system makes it impossible for us to distinguish the worthy from the worthless, the eternally true from the simply fleeting and transient. So like Don Quixotes, we keep tilting aimlessly at the many windmills of life, and embrace a fatalism that fully guarantees our rebirth.

If we are to regain our original purity of mind, which alone perceives truly, we have some serious spring-cleaning to do. All those skeletons, mannequins and teddy bears of our pet beliefs must be expelled from our closet. We must become fearless and swiftly divest ourselves of all unworthy guides, and futile defenses we tenaciously grasp to protect ourselves in this dark world. True understanding alone is to be our guide. Our faith in ultimate veracities and timeless wisdom will quickly vaporize all mists of ignorance and it will transport us rapidly into the light. Then we will behold the Uncreated One everywhere. At that moment, the world of multiplicity and phenomenal existence will be completely consumed in the bonfire of Self-knowledge and luminous understanding will return.

THE DETAILED APPLICATION

This dreamworld is plagued with so many unnecessary barriers and partitions. Illusory walls surround all objects you perceive. Thus mind, seems to have crystallized and congealed into endless arrays of statically frozen and seemingly lifeless forms. It is a bleak picture imaged by our worldly minds, and one vigorously shaped by the conditioning power of our beliefs. Now after millions of years, it all seems to have become, a powerful, impenetrable fortress that completely clouds our essential Being. Nonetheless, this seal can easily be penetrated with the right attitude, intensity, and key. This Sutra is the key. So developing the right attitude and intensity is all you need to accomplish. You must come with an expansive, impartial and diffusive awareness—that innocent and unknowing mind of a newborn. Retaining an inquisitive, playful and open attitude to life is critical to your success. Then give your chosen object all your presence and attention. Allow yourself to become completely absorbed in it, and simultaneously exclude all else from the manifold of your mind. Do not allow yourself to become mentally-clouded by your biases, false beliefs, expectations, partialities, memories, feelings of limitation and conditioned understandings. Retain your intense focus while also remaining supremely aware. Be resolute in your determination not to let this object out of your focus, until it has revealed its true nature to you. The light within it wants to join with the immortal in you because you both share in the same Life. Regrettably, myriad illusions have interposed themselves as a screen which seems to keep you separate. Realize from the getgo that all sense of separation is illusory. It is just an artificial mesh induced by ignorance and the immense conditioning power of the dream.

Now you are ready to transcend all appearances. The web of complexity is powerless to hold you back unless you allow yourself to become partial and mentally contracted. Do not be deceived or attracted by the gifts of littleness. The priceless pearl has always been here in full sight. Available were you not blinded by false knowledge and the hypnotizing power of expectation. It is these alone that place themselves, between you and truth. All phenomenal existence will come tumbling downward like a house of cards, once its worthless offerings no longer tempt you. Then you will see the many as One and the One in many. The formless and Faceless One that is yet the Face of all. Then you realize you too never had a face. Your dream-face was just an ego mask, generated out of your lower mind.

To reach the supreme goal, your perceiving must become a mode of apperceiving. You must maintain full conscious remembrance of yourself as a non-defiled awareness while looking outward. Do not become bogged down and overly-focused on the world of specifics because you are searching for the common presence that pervades all. All objects and phenomena are mirages arising out of your momentary mental colorings. They reflect nothing but your conditioned beliefs and adapt, as your beliefs change and your awareness increases in its capacities for subtlety. It is you that have cookie-cut your world, through so many pernicious and narrow–banded mental ideologies. These alone create all the walled partitions in your object-orientated universe. Such partitions were never there but were mind-made from the nexus of your erroneous thought and limitations.

When you consider all phenomena as a dream, you are acknowledging at long last, the direct relationship, all shares with your mind and belief. All are mental creations and images forged and shaped, in the firmament of your indigenous thought and desire. Cease thinking about one, and it becomes diminished in your perceptions. Then it disappears from view and regresses back into seeming non-existence. Change any of your thoughts concerning it, and it is instantly forced to adjust to correspond.

Maintaining an intense, impartial, and conscious awareness ferries you into the bosom of the formless One. Your non-attachment and non-judgmental attitude transports you into the unitary powerhouse, in which all is joined forever. The Immaculate One is a faceless, spaceless nonentity possessing no inside or outside. A benevolent immutable being, devoid of all attributes and differentiation. A Being that seems absent when the phenomenal universe is present, and present when the phenomenal universe seems absent. Once all your conceiving stops and all conceptualizations drop, all phenomenal appearances begin to merge and disappear back into the Great One's womb. It takes but one timeless instant, for your entire world to explode into light. Penetrate to the light in one appearance, and you see the same light in all. Then you gain passage to the seat of infinite aliveness, that powers all Being. Then you cease to be a phenomenal being because you have realized your Immortal Self and regained the vision of your original face. Now you know, where you have always been–NO-WHERE! There has never been any "WHERE" to go to. You have always been that *no-thing,* that yet gives rise to all. Now you have reached the silent realm of pure potentiality, from which all worlds are formed. The Source of all and the invisible potency that lights all universes manifest and unmanifest.

Do not be afraid to break all dark seals of conditioned thought and to adventure far beyond the petty kingdoms of the ego's world. Make the welcome sacrifice of all false ideas that becloud your mind that block your vision. Then you will enter the vaporous state of consciousness and find yourself resting in the quiescent and immaculate state of mind. This is the door to all Buddha-lands, in which the natural light of spirit shines freely, effortlessly and forever."

OTHER PATHS TO TRANSCENDENCE

Then I said, "This Sutra seems to offer a great return on investment. Is this the only way of transcending or are there other paths and keys?"

The Lama responded, "There are many paths up the mountain to transcendence, just as there are many ways to skin a cat. Many are slow and arduous and take forever. In such complex, convoluted routes, the thorns of worldly attraction and vengeance continuously stick in to make one bleed. I offer you the most direct path up the mountain. One on which the influences of karma will have no effect. Such influences are powerless to hold you back because they can only ever extend to the world of time—not to Truth. The realm of pure understanding, known through naked perception is non-karmic and timeless. Reaching this Holy Abode is only for the bravest and quickest of mind. It is for those ready to die this instant and be reborn and those naturally superior in the quality of their awareness and thought.

Many prefer to take the slower paths of, the lower yogic practices instead. They use pranayama to still their mind and thought, thus entering the vaporous world of the unconditioned. By huffing and puffing, they course the life-force of prana up and down through their Ida and Pingala Nāḍīs. Thus they stimulate the psychic nerve of the Sushumna Nāḍī, which runs up the center of the spine. This threadlike nerve once awakened carries the serpent power of kundalini rapidly to all the other chakras, like a laser beam. As a result, all illusory notions of separation disappear. But first, the "external" existence becomes more diffusive and begins to melt away. Then one enters the state of Nir-vikalpa Samadhi.

However, this is a slower path since it is conditional. One only retains the bliss of Samadhi, through ongoing pranayama. It is best to recognize that the yogic paths of **Hatha Yoga** (postures), **Pranayama** (Breathing Exercises) and **Dharana** (Concentration) were never intended to be the end-goals in themselves. They are intermediate junctures, which aim to condition the body and bring a halt to all mental processes. By stabilizing the mind, one reaches its natural and quiescent state. Then the true nature of the phenomenal world can be seen directly. Then you know the true relationship between mind and matter and perceive with naked perception. Others use **Gibberish** to reach the same state of mental quiescence. By constantly chanting gibberish, they inhibit the conditioning power of their thought. Speaking nonsensically for long periods, they freeze all analytical and linear processes of thought, cranked out ceaselessly by the mind's engines. By inhibiting all activities of the lower mind, they weaken all identification with the dream. Thus they open their world up to ever fresh perspectives. Their mind is restored to an unwritten slate, upon which Truth can once again shine."

Then I asked the Lama if he could provide me some example of what is gibberish. So he quickly spouted out the following phrase:-

"I caught this morning a boson squirting its pee into the sea of quantum-gravity. It didn't see me, who was happy, sappy, dapper in my nappy, crapping, laughing, while cowering and showering behind a battering ram, subsumed by thoughts of drowning, frowning and thinking of Wham and the last pixie-mas of the

snowboarders and doomsday hoarders at the borders of the Trump towering infernos. Where shrimp gumbo, fried beans, sombreros and peyote smoking banditos were blowing Yaks, Yeti and smoke up my ass with a snow-blower powered of coke, meth and vintage sweatshop sweat."

The important thing with gibberish is that it be nonsensical and spontaneous. Once the mind attempts to master it or attach meaning, it is no longer gibberish but the ego creeping in, rejoicing in its ability to formulate non-conditioned mental scripts. And that is the whole crux of the problem. Man thinks all meaning is within his tiny scope, rather than transcendent of his limited domain. He thinks he can possess and master truth and does not recognize, Truth embraces his being in its entirety. For it is from Truth he was Created. To become Enlightened, man must first be transcended. This fiction, we call man, is just a temporary depot and stopover, a gas station in the relative existence where he needs to become wise. Man can never be the goal because such a goal is meaningless—he remains just a mirage in his self-made dream. There can be no substance ever in the relative. All rats squeal, abandon and cave the same, once they get the whiff of bacon, coming from another. To reach truth, we must get out of our way. Eliminate all smugness, conceit, arrogance, pomposity and other foolish airs; we idly attach to ourselves. All that nonsense which makes us feel more superior in the dream. It just generates an image built on sandcastles.

Understanding and unlocking the power of this Sutra can be considered **the Yoga of the Great Symbol**. It is the yoga of knowing the mind in its naked essence. The Great Symbol is that which transcends all symbols and forms. Since it represents Totality, it can never be symbolized. As you make progress, you will understand that the visible universe is constituted of nothing but ideas and that the mind and the world are inseparable. Then you are ferried from the realm of the phenomenal to the noumenal, the manifest to the unmanifest, the mind-made and projected universe of things, to the uncreated, formless, ever-potent and undifferentiated!

Enlightenment occurs spontaneously once one intuits, and fully understands through introspection and reason, that nothing intrinsically IS. All phenomena and images are the outcome of your mental colorations and the residual of past impressions. Each must come face-to-face with his raw nature and pure essence as Mind. He must pullback all curtains that cloud his vision and be fearless in uprooting all ego weeds that have grown from eons past."

BREAKTHROUGH

MOUNT KAILASH

E verything happens for a reason. Existence is the consummate magician, and it works in very oblique, crafty and miraculous ways. She loves to paint myriad designs in chiaroscuro, which bewitch the senses and tantalize the mind. Her vast intelligence and vision are often only comprehended many years later when events and experiences become reevaluated, in the rearview mirror. Then all becomes crystal clear and is seen as part of a masterful design. Every moment she is holding out a golden treasure, silently waiting for us to unwrap it. She always brings us exactly what we need, which may not always be a carbon copy of what we desire. But once interpreted correctly, the light is there! Nothing happens accidentally, that is for sure. Each experience in the dream can be used to promote self-growth and healing transformation. The present moment is the gateway between the illusory and the real. In this time transcending portal, all stands still—and exists in infinite glory. This eternal portal is the fountain of inspiration, and it triggers mystical experiences. Here, the abode of Enlightenment! Many squander this moment and every moment of their lives by allowing their minds, to recklessly wander. Fortune, nonetheless, favors the brave and if you stay on the roller coaster long enough, without judgment and fear, you are in for a hell of a ride.

Lama Dorje's teachings had truly hit the nail on its head. He had taught me just how the relative world arose and was maintained. He had helped me understand the nature of dualities, and how they distort our perceptions keeping us ransom to darkness. He illuminated for me, the critical relationship between consciousness and perception. My mind was simply bubbling like a cauldron full of new insights and life. I was beginning to cognize how time was non-objective but psychologically driven instead—that its apparent passing was very intimate with our state of awareness. This illusion would come to an end when all our ignorance was dispelled. Now I could understand most acutely that male and female energies were never isolated and split-off from one another. These existed along a continuum and were dualistically interdependent. Yes, the animus and anima were present in each of us. If we looked closely enough, we would recognize that we were continuously switching between the two. These inner entities simply wanted to hold hands and join in holy union. Sadly, repression in our society was pulling them asunder. The less dominant party always felt forced to live out a life of silence, sentenced deep into the bogs of the human psyche. Impelled to live along a tenuous fault-line, that it felt powerless to escape. Many meta-selves lived and roamed deep within us, each seeking desperately to gain full control. Each, only able to take command at the switchboard for a few minutes, before being forced to move on. Before long another would pop-up to oust it. These meta-selves were often vengeful and spiteful with one another, and it seemed highly unlikely that we would ever patch a peace agreement, between these warring parties. No wonder there was all this confusion, turmoil, and restlessness in the world. It was all perpetrated by the schizophrenic story playing out inside our heads. Each of us had our San Andreas, Mount Kilauea or Yellowstone going on in inside that could erupt at any moment. Every so often, it would release powerful waves of destruction and torrential downpours of hot lava and ash.

I understood markedly that mindfulness, self-remembrance, and introspection, were key tools to a life worth living. These practices were the panacea for finding sanity and joy. After all, hadn't Socrates stated so succinctly, long ago, that '*The unexamined life is not worth living.*' Without the critical remedy of mindfulness, one simply lives as a machine, and soon falls prey to the many insanities and evils of the world. Yes, we should not swallow, all that we are forced to imbibe in the relative world. In fact, none of it because this knowledge is superficial and unnourishing. It is but a complex edifice built on a foundation of untruth. All worldly paths lacked meaning because they were paths deeper into the snares of Maya. The modern fields of Science, Engineering, Technology, Medicine, Genetics, Pharmacology, Space exploration and so forth, were all cul-de-sacs. Our stunning complicity to these modern gods arose from our deeper insecurities. We imagined ourselves as living in a minefield of a Mad Max world, and these had morphed into our patchwork solutions. Their aim was simply to make our life in the ghetto as comfortable and tolerable as possible. We did not suspect that there was anything worthwhile below all the debris, pipe bombs, noxious fumes and mangled bodies; we saw littering this minefield. Because at rock bottom, we did not genuinely know ourselves. We operated as superficial and circumscribed beings, who were *'faking it 'till we could make it.'* We grasped tenaciously at all outer gods, who then functioned as surrogates for our lost knowledge. Now, the extreme difference between wisdom, intelligence and knowledge were also becoming apparent to me. Intelligence was just the tool, but not the fruit. This tool could be deployed for destructive purposes, just as easily as for constructive pursuits. Worldly knowledge was a great burden on our backs. We had the illusion that it enhanced us in some way. Instead, it maintained our blindness and pseudo-bondage to the realm of appearances. It served as just more chains and manacles around our minds. Chains that guaranteed we would eventually grow weary, sick and old. Yes, all who eat of this fruit would certainly die. Wisdom alone was the fruit that could enliven because it alone was harmonious with Truth. Wisdom was spacious and the exact opposite of worldly knowledge. It would be reached, when we unburdened ourselves of all that junk and trash, worming into our minds. Then alone we would travel light and unhindered, untouched by the world of appearances and discern the true nature of reality and living presence in all! I went back to my hut and began reflecting on this Sutra. I fully realized that unless I unlocked its existential power, it would remain just barren words. Yes, it would sit there on a flea-bitten alcove in my mind, as just another trinket for the ego to gloat over. Reflecting on this Sutra's meaning, I fell into a deep sleep and had a marvelous dream, which soon became a nightmare. It began with me meeting my brother and his wife for dinner in their high story apartment. While appreciating one of their paintings by Hieronymus Bosch, I noticed water at my feet. It was rising rapidly. In just a few moments, it had us completely submerged. Then all the walls came crashing down. I felt myself suffocating. Within a short while, I had detached from my body. So I was dead then! Even so, I remained hyper-vigilant and well aware of my surroundings. Then, as I started navigating my way out, I came across a friend who was wearing green jeans and a purple shirt. I immediately had the flash thought, *"There is no way in hell, he would ever be caught dead wearing clothes like these."* That was my trigger to enter a lucid dream.

In this lucid dream, I visited three Kingdoms. The first Kingdom was the world, of all my heart's hidden desires. Anything I craved, coveted, desired or desiderated would instantly become manifest before me. I could manifest many worlds at once. They would appear like holographic images on so many flat screen TVs, and covered my entire perception. They presented a higher multi-dimensional reality, that I could freely enter at will. In each world, superhuman lifeforms would appear, and provide me with their full loving attention. These celestial presences were inspirational, kindhearted and serene, and seemed to know all my heart's instantaneous needs. Words were unneeded here and entirely obviated as a communication medium. Yes, the primitive nature of all forms of verbal and symbolic communication was all too evident here. And seen as equivalent, as trying to run the stock exchange using an abacus of chestnuts. Instead, all was transferred in blasts of unspoken images.

These benevolent presences were extremely intelligent and capable of communicating through highly abstract thought-forms. Complex ideas, they would instantly relay through images, which made their content simple, lucid and self-explanatory. Through alien tongues, they delivered the intended meaning and made it immediately transparent. It was all very dizzying. I began to realize that I could now intimately understand, what before would have been pure and complete gibberish. I could decipher in a moment, what before would have taken many years. I was flying through these psychedelic worlds, feeling completely relaxed and light of spirit. Here there was no sickness, loss or pain. No diminishment ever of one's strength, vigor, and vitality. No decline or attenuation was possible in one's acuity or clarity of mind. In fact, my depth of understanding seemed limitless. It was all well beyond my power of imagination, visualization, and cogitation skills, to even remotely grasp the endless vistas of thought and world potentialities, latent here. I wanted to remain here forever and never to go back to that boring, mundane lifeless world of pettiness and small-minded ideologies, that I had left. That bleak world of '*Joe Six-packs*' and tiny, fleeting morsels of pleasure. Of pain, bills, disenchantment and despair, where everything constantly broke down or wore out. That wasteland where one felt more disempowered, disenchanted and despairing with each passing hour. Where sickness and death aggressively snatched away all that one cherished for a while. The world of a single channel of perception and such a monotonous script. A swamp of the mind, one felt hopelessly stuck in, until it .played itself out. It represented such a vapid world that needed to be quickly bulldozed to the ground and shredded into a gazillion pieces. Then the epiphanous realization dawned, that our world was in that shape already. For a few moments more, I looked back with awe and wondered about this world of my heart's delight. I was feeling like a boxer in *animal farm*, peering at all the pigs feasting at the table. Thinking to myself, *all pigs are equal, but some pigs were evidently more special than others*—something that a Snowball or Napoleon might have said.

Then I was ready to move on. I realized this world had no back-drop to it. There was something tremendously empty in this perfect paradise. All was given too easily, so there was never any feeling of accomplishment. Since no one suffered, there was no one ever to console or heal. Since all were so hyper-intelligent, there was no one to teach or inspire. Yes, I had felt no sense of purpose or value there. More like a hoover sucking up never-ending streams of information, with no end ever in sight. Yes, it felt like a modern day brain-farm, and I would just be one of the Cyborgs. A mere cog in the centralized Borg chip of the One-Mind.

Then I visited the Kingdom of my hates. Here I immediately ex-perienced the most extreme panic, anxiety, and revulsion. My fingers and head began to tremble and shake uncontrollably as if I had a nervous tic disorder. There were all these revolting, ugly mischievous creatures running about, doing all sorts of re-volting things to one another. This was the world of the living dead, where toxic, angry, soulless people circled about like vul-tures. The special hell reserved for all those, who cared only about themselves. Here there was no forgiveness, gratitude or appreciation—only condemnation and spite. It was infused with psychic-vampires, leaches and gaunt figures of every possible variety. These means spirits hovered about, awaiting their per-fect opportunity to strike. Some were morbidly obese, weighing well over a thousand pounds. Others looked so frail and bony as if they were wearing their skeletons on the outside. Many ran around naked. One came by and dowsed my drink with some incredibly repugnant and gooey substance which made it taste like ear-wax.

Then there were those who took pleasure in torture and victimization of the weak. These relished impaling their victims and stretching them out on racks. Then they proceeded to lacerate and tear away any remaining flesh, before pounding and smashing their bones to dust with large hammers. They took great delight in using the power of their imaginations, to inflict the most ingenious forms of suffering and torture. It was all tremendously sickening and hard to deal with. I found it very difficult to hold onto any remaining threads of my integrity and sanity while experiencing this dark place. A fierce energy welled up inside of me, urging me to deny and condemn this world outright. It took enormous effort to restrain myself from making any judgment.

The final world was very blasé indeed. In it, no one cared about anything at all. Nothing carried any life, significance or meaning. It was a dry, barren, listless world where there was no passion, enthusiasm or mental fire. A placid, vapid world, of flatfish personas with no developed notions of good or bad, right no wrong. Everyone went about completely de-energized. They moped and dragged themselves about from one soul-crushing orifice to another. It was impossible to shock, awe or inspire anyone. Yes, life here was an entirely gray, goalless, apathetic and cheerless existence. A world of supreme routine, neutrality, and indifference. It elicited from me no emotions whatsoever. It seemed all had flat-lined so long ago. None were showing even the merest blip of life on my biometric Geiger counter. After a while, I could not tolerate the heedless indifference, a moment longer. It seemed the worst hell of all to be trapped in its manifold for endless time. I wanted to escape as fast as my boots would carry me. However, I remembered once again not to judge or condemn it.

At that moment, I directed my conscious mind back to my life in the Tibetan hut. It suddenly felt welcoming and more like home. The morning had come, and I somehow found myself still alive, conscious and grateful. On the surface, everything seemed the same, as before. All the same, something powerful had happened. Everything looked and felt so different in an indescribable way. All seemed presently infused with a single energy and life-force. Even the most mundane object, seemed to be sparkling as if it was carrying all the significance and meaning of the universe. All the strict partitions and delineations that nominally surround everyday objects had faded away. Instead, all was effortlessly blending and diffusing into one another. Even the space itself felt tremendously alive.

Suddenly remembering the Sutra, I began to fathom its true and hidden meaning. This world of my everyday existence was also another dreamworld. No more or less extraordinary or solid, than any other. No more substantial than my lucid dream, from the night before. Now I understood, everything was simply an extension of the dreaming capacity of my mind; I had actually died the night before. Nonetheless this death was an illusion since consciousness itself is deathless. All was appearing now as I expected it to be but this was because my mind was recreating the universe. I began to realize that perhaps, I had never awoken from my dream. My apparent awakening was pseudo, and just another part of the fabric of a dream. I began to panic, thinking that someone would find my body in a few days and take it out and bury it.

The question remained, "**How could I be sure one way or another, whether I had ever woken up or not?**" I could no longer trust the deceptive information propagated by my senses.

Because my conscious experiences from my lucid dream were just as real, vivid and valid, as the world I was now experiencing. I had entered worlds, which I would never consciously enter in endless lifetimes. I became extremely anxious to prove to myself, that I was genuinely awake. All the same, how does one do that? We always just assume we are awake! I no longer had any leveraging point, by which to differentiate the landscape of dream from my regular day reality! By what special criteria I asked, could I make this critical distinction? The seeming "waking" and "sleeping" dreams were recognized now, as no different from each other. Each was the product of the powerful hypnosis of conditioning, expectancy, and false beliefs.

At that moment, I had the comprehension that I had never experienced the true present. I had been everywhere but to the naked present. All I ever had perceived, was that which my intellect and unconscious beliefs directed me to see. That is, I was always seeing and interpreting life, through the complex maze of my memories, ideas, expectations, desires, needs, concepts, ideologies, beliefs, theories, opinions, defenses, instinctual reactions and so forth. These were all the traitors that had suffocated my life and blunted my capacity for authentic living. They had imprisoned my mind in the heavy shackles of spacetime, ignorance, and conditioning. All of which hung, as a dark obfuscating mantle over my mind. They forced the real present to disappear completely.

Yes, I had never been truly living. I had been living, instead, through all those mind-molded algorithms and filters that were inherited from my past and projected into my future. The present that I knew was just a dream projection seen through the lens of my anticipation and memories. My "seeing" and "experiencing" of life was from the artificial and unreal vantage points of the future and the past. I had simply spent my whole life living in a dream, and taken it to be reality. The enormity of this self-deception was stunning. The depth of my delusion was beyond comprehension and world-shattering. At that precise instant, I decided to nourish no more dreams. I wanted reality straight up for once. I understood now that thought was the enemy all the time. One could never think their way to Enlightenment and emerge out of the sewer of the mind and the world. Rather thinking created the entire maze. That great murky ocean of memories, concepts, and conditioned beliefs was the only barrier to Truth. And now the stopper needed to be yanked so that all the filth in the cesspools of my thought could flow down the drains of my mind. Disappear into the nothingness from which it came. Then, I remembered what Lama Dorje had said. Once you see the light in one object, you will rapidly see the same light in all. I took my doll out of my bag. This doll, I had always brought with me everywhere. She held power to pacify my mind instantaneously, whenever I felt anxious, uncertain or worried. Her serene eyes soothed me immensely. She always exuded the same unconditional loving energy. It did not matter how much I changed, or the world did. In those moments, when it tottered about and seemed to be falling apart, the constancy of her presence was reassuring. I looked at her with that intense penetrative awareness about which the Lama had spoken. I inwardly said, "If all is dream, she too must be nothing but a dream. She is not really there, just an appearance in my mind. An appearance that was continuously being recreated, on a moment-to-moment basis. Recreated, through the extensive conditioning power of my mind and thought.

Now under my intense and powerful gaze, I began to see her dress changing color. It went from a cerulean blue to a light purple, then back again. So the colorations on her dress were tracking my mind's thoughts. Then I saw her eyes becoming more liquid in appearance and moving slightly about. Then her facial features were beginning to melt and flow. As I continued with my intense gaze, undistracted, her body began to sway over and back. Yes, it was obvious now, that she was ceaselessly being created and dissolved out of the power of my conditioned awareness.

At that moment I was for the first time able to go beyond the veil of all conditionings and obstructions. I was moving in a different dimension now. The dimension of the true present. A silent dimensionless dimension. One that was always here, but squarely missed. One that had always been frozen over and dismissed through ignorance. Lost in the haze of my mind's perpetual grasping after futile dreams. At that moment my doll exploded into light, as did everything else in the room. All became blended and immersed as One. There was but a single light everywhere. I realized that this light was coming from inside me. In fact, it was the radiance of my real Self, and there was no longer any sense of separation anywhere. There was no "*where* " anywhere because my inner and outer worlds had merged. My thought world and that of my direct perception were now inextricably fused. All was emerging from within and spontaneously powered by the quality of my ideations and awareness. There had never been any objective existence—that was the supreme joke! A joke, I had nevertheless spent lifetimes to demystify and uncloak.

This unmoving, potent and tremendously alive stillness was the fundamental backdrop all the time. This majesty had always been covered by our dreams of vengeance, change, and desire. As I looked downwards, I began to see that my arms, legs, and entire body had also disappeared into the light of my newfound vision. They also were nothing but conditioned aspects of a dream. I had spent many eons entertaining a series of long, bad or mediocre dreams and never comprehended, that all was being generated by my thought. I had forgotten true cause-and-effect and lost access to this inner light somewhere along the way. Now all dream fiction was over because I had awakened. All my lives had finally come to fruition. The only purpose of all dreams had been to make me so miserable, wretched and despairing, that I would finally awaken. Once I committed to bargaining with none, the Supreme One came. These dreams had nonetheless served a holy purpose. They had increased my resilience and lit my awareness on fire, thus leading me beyond their petty scope forever. Yes, I had finally come to the boiling point and evaporated into a vaporous light-filled consciousness, that yet contained all. There was no *"where"* now for dream fiction to continue to write itself. The slate of my mind was radiant and wiped of all. No idol would ever again gain the strength, traction, and conviction to delude and hypnotize my mind so pervasively. I understood the meaning now of *"I am the Alpha and the Omega"* and *"Before Abraham was, I Am."* Because in one single instant, the illusions of spacetime and the world, had come to an abrupt ending. Nothing had ever happened, and nothing would ever happen again because nothing had ever been. This was the supreme Truth! The reality of the unconditioned, timeless and undifferentiated existence alone was real and everpresent.

SUTRA 2: PROBE DEEPLY INTO THE NATURE OF UNBORN AWARENESS

MANASAROVAR LAKE

For many days afterward, I was in a state of shock, at what had occurred. Since I was undergoing turbulent inner changes, I did not go out much. In any case, there was no "*where*" to go to anymore, since all was known now as a pure projection of mind. Life inside the hut was a full experience—nothing further could be added! I realized those who travel idly about doing a host of meaningless things, do so because they have never come to themselves. Yes, life inside the hut was as colorful vibrant, potent and alive now as anywhere else. Even the simple mud floor with its straw had transformed into something entirely magical, and it exhibited a psychedelic and multidimensional splendor. I found myself immersed in this vaporous flux of energy and light that was boundless in every direction. All was perfectly representative of my newfound purity of mind and I felt lovingly immersed in the uncontainable and dimensionless. Nonetheless, there was no center to this vortex of whirling forms effortlessly blending into one another. The radiant brilliance of which shone far brighter than ten thousand suns. It was a warm, soothing light, and I felt ecstatic and blissful, encapsulated inside its womb. This resplendent luminosity shared no connection with the weak artificial worldly light but was instead a scintillating and inextinguishable blaze of eternal grandeur. One as intelligent and nurturing, as it was illuminating. It seemed that every cell and atom of my body was now singing harmoniously as one and all floodgates of my senses had finally opened. All were chanting out the great OM of Being in perfect synchronized unison. And yet I knew no cell or body had ever really existed. Nevertheless, I found that I could see, hear, smell and taste like never before. All unnatural layers had been stripped away. I recognized incontestably now that I had always been traveling inside myself.

My mind was struggling to fathom and integrate what had happened. Words I found, to be redundant, powerless and alien entities, belonging to the false and foreign world, I had known before. Barren impotent squiggles in the sand and ones forever incapable of grasping the real. Yes, they were mere symbols of symbols and hence twice divorced from reality. From the transcendental perspective, nothing at all had happened. Truth had always been Here! Now, it had simply been revealed. From a relative and phenomenal perspective, everything had changed. Because all happenings had ceased and all worlds had disappeared. All happenings were recognized presently as illusory. With some trepidation, I realized with dismay that nothing had ever happened. My existence had always been nothing but a personal hallucination. That posed a major problem! When all happenings cease, the relative mind can no longer survive.

Yes, my dream had been fatally smashed and obliterated beyond repair. I was immensely grateful, yet also awed because when you stand at the gate of the timeless, you simultaneously collide with the infinite. Intellectually, I knew of course what had occurred, yet the implications were staggering. Mind-boggling beyond words or worlds. I felt eternally suspended and left hanging over a limitless abyss. Dispossessed of all past and future and all else on which I could hinge my existence. I could not see any value in meeting with Lama Dorje again to continue with the discourses. After all, what could he teach me now? All teaching had become superfluous. He was, after all, merely a dream image, projected from my mind. **Who speaks to an hallucination, except a madman?** Yes, the bodily figure I had conversed with before, was gone for good. It had always been just a luminous image and part of my greater Self. He would simply mirror all the changes that had materialized within me. On another level, we were more intimate now than ever before, because we recognized our unity in the selfsame Mind. As I reflected about it more, I realized, he might be able to help me resolve or better interpret some of the inner volcanoes that were transpiring. When we finally met again, he knew right away that there was no more need for any further clarification on the first Sutra. He had been wondering what had kept me hung up in the hut for days and had even been mildly concerned. He figured I must be indulging in an extended period of solitary meditation.

After a long silence, he spoke. "So now you are Enlightened! You have seen the dream for what it is. You find yourself, completely immersed now, in the Turiya state of consciousness. You can see the living dream directly and have recognized all other states of consciousness were false. The waking and sleeping states, the states of hypnotized awareness, of subliminal and supraliminal cognition and those of the death, after-death and rebirth states, all pertained to illusory mind-generated worlds. Worlds created out of the dust of ignorance, inherited karma, and conditioned belief. Now you have reached that immaculate state, in which consciousness has dissolved back into itself. One in which, the looms of Mara have stopped spinning their webs of powerful deception. You have reached to the pure unborn and natural awareness."

"Yes," I responded "I am comprehending, at last, the absolute absurdity of my whole life up to this point. Laughing hard for having taken it all so seriously. It is evident that none of it ever happened! My entire life story, existence and the apparent con- tinuity of my dreamworld became molded with perfect consistency to all my mental scripts. However, I am no longer running or licensing these malware scripts, which wreaked such havoc in my mind. I am no longer chasing after the dream's idols because I see all are fabricated from dust. It is only now that I am fully grasping, what each one cost. Yes, the joke had always been on me. It is so glaringly clear-cut to me now, that thought was always the enemy. Decidedly toxic to one's progress and lethal in high doses. It had led directly to all acute states of inner turmoil, mental unrest, dream identification and pandering after wasteful passions. Sickness, suicide, death, and rebirth were just some of its nasty byproducts. I understand that the entire web of Maya is spun from our frivolous ideations. The thought world constructs all hells we will ever see or experience.

I had made my breakthrough after recognizing thought needed to be bypassed entirely and that something new was needed—the *no-mind* state of Buddha consciousness. A pure quiescent state of mind in which we are serenely present and no longer producing any poisonous fluctuations of thought. Only then could we pass through the eye of the needle into the true present. So had I entered the quiet eye in the hurricane of life! The restful center of the storm that remains unaffected by dreams. I came to see, that the joke had always been on me and that time was always just an illusory apparition arising from my scripts. A ghost, emerging from the movements of my thought. The '*Deus ex Machina*,' of my thought. I had articulated so many wonderful stories about my life, past adventures and where I would go to next. Crafted numerous spellbinding fictions about my birth, progress, good deeds and entrepreneurial spirit. Yes, I had become quite the magnanimous dream figure, in my mind. A beacon, I hoped others would look up to in awe, or at least in admiration.

However, I have been swiftly yanked off my high-horse and came to understand all was empty mind-dreams. Enlightenment robbed me in many ways because it left me bare and exposed! It deprived me of all my delusions, foolish fantasies, and illusions and the entire world I had known before. It simultaneously granted the gift of everything and nothing. Who would have thought, that it could be one of the most humbling of experiences? Yet even that is not true! For it is not any particular experience, but arrival at the very basis of experiencing itself and entering the gates of true, naked and unadulterated Being."

He continued, "Now you can just relax! Settle into your new-found knowledge and wisdom. You have always remained, this indestructible awareness of infinite potential. An awareness that cannot be zapped or annihilated because it has no form. Of course, all your illusions had to disappear together—how else could it be? Because all propagate to support one another and all arise out of ignorance. Death and birth were always just the same illusion because the same erroneous belief powers both. That epiphenomenalist belief that consciousness is embedded somehow in the body and matter. Now you have seen through both and realize there was never any birth, simply because, there was no one ever to be born. There will never be a death, for the same reason. Awareness is not born because its essence is spaceless, timeless and formless.

There has never been any way to disappear out of the unity of Whole-Mind. **Who is there to disappear? And where could you ever disappear to?** You spent your whole life pandering to so many false and foolish appearances and reacting to a world you believed to be outside. In doing so, you replaced firsthand knowledge, with secondhand opinion. Now you realize, nothing ever was exterior nor holds any power over you. You have always held the keys to the Kingdom. You chose your bondage, just as now you find yourself released and free.

In the dream, you thought you were special. You constructed a life history, you ego esteemed and saw as worthy. You believed all your life-experiences, degrees, qualifications, skills, exotic adventures, etc. augmented you in some gratifying way. They did nothing, but engrave a complex dream image into your mind. This dream you mistakenly took to be yourself. Your dream image became further strengthened by all your foolish opinions, stances, ideals and values. Now you know this dream image was entirely false and insubstantial and built on nothing. No such person ever existed. Your self-made conceptions and experiences were all like empty words written in the ocean of the void. All were powerless before truth and incapable of changing you in any real way. The Self alone IS, and there is no 'other.' The Creator is never separate from His Creation.

Specialness, vanity, and superiority were just idle games you played with yourself. Games played out, in the greater field of your perception. You have always been unified with Truth and empowered out of its Totality. Only the defilement of ignorance shielded this from your awareness. Now the dream has ended, simply because you the dreamer have awoken. It was your strong identification with the dream that kept you asleep, just as non-identification and non-attachment led to your awakening. You had always taken the Self to be merely an extension of the ego self. Now you realize it was a *no-self* and that the self you invented, was the only barrier. Likewise, you recognize there has never been any phenomenal world. All such craven images merely represented fluctuations, in the sea of your awareness. Fluctuations, driven by the winds of impurity and the obscuration of ignorance. Presently, you find all such impurities have been eradicated from your belief, and so the sea of your Mind has returned to its tranquil, clear and quiescent state. That state in which all becomes authentically known because all is understood unambiguously and without any hint of distortion. All inner and outer boundaries have dissolved, and the senses have been internalized.

So you have come to the calm place of rest in the center of the cyclone. The quiet eye of the storm and the zero point of consciousness. One that the phenomenal world is powerless to reach, so it cannot displace or torture you anymore. For this is the sacred kingdom of luminous clarity, in which all yogic Siddhis and miraculous powers are born. Arriving at this holy juncture, you have come to the end of time and reached the other shore. You have merged with the sea of the *Dharmadhatu*. That fathomless Source, containing infinite potentialities, which is yet the seed of all. It is a sea beyond the reach of the five Aggregates (or Skandhas) of Form, Sensation, Perception, Conception, and Consciousness. Its unadulterated essence is even beyond the reach of all Rishis, Asuras, Avatars, Demons, and Gods.

Similarly, all celestial kingdoms and pristine Buddha-lands cannot compare to it because all cerebrated kingdoms contain mental forms and therfore embody some distortion. Thus they still hint at some degree of impurity in the mind. In you present state the Kingdom of wisdom and thought gleams in its most potent, abstract and purest essence. Nothing can be apart from this sea and be real. In its seamless Oneness, all is intricately and inextricably fused. Yes, the Whole was always immanent in every part, and thus the immense value of every part is beyond all reckoning. To lose any part, would destroy all meaning implicit in the Whole. Reality remains indivisible and infinitely potent wherever it is found — and Reality is everywhere. The microcosmic mind of man is just as powerful as the Mind of the Absolute, once it has awoken to it-Self."

THE SPECTRUM OF HUMANITY

Lama Dorje had illuminated for me our real nature as a deathless awareness and transmitted the wisdom that all was part of an undifferentiated Oneness. From this Oneness, all springs forth and comes into apparent being. Nothing exists apart from it. The true meaning of the first Sutra seemed all too self-evident now that I had unlocked it. Its sacred knowledge was an open secret. I asked the Lama, why more don't grasp the existential meaning of the Sutras? He was happy with my question and said "The Spectrum of Humanity can be said to be composed of five distinct genotypes of people:

1) Drones

2) Scam Artists

3) Ego Inflated

4) Disillusioned

5) Truth Seekers

The **Drones** are all those minions, mummies and walking dead you see everywhere around you. They live out their lives in chains, serving the interests of all the large corporations. Functioning as servile peons, to all oligarchies, aristocracies, and plutocracies of this world. Over time, they morph into hyper-institutionalized and semi-lobotomized beings. Ones, self-sentenced to lives of drudgery. They love to be in harness with the bit showing between their teeth. They are in steep denial of the whip, that is always at their backs and are content to have their lives parceled back to them, in tiny morsels of freedom, per ton of sweat hours. In their imaginations, they like to think of themselves as cutting edge pioneers, world-changers and as movers and shakers. So they eagerly embrace all corporate value systems, mission statements, and codes of conduct. They thrive around anyone or anything that tells them how to live and what to value. Thus they lock themselves into very conditioned, limiting and restrictive patterns of thought. Value to them is always found somewhere on the outside. So they are found smothering in all the regalia, pomp and accolades of some outfit or else engaging some crusade seen as far greater than themselves.

In the end, they are all just sad workhorses, serving the profiteering engines of utilitarian enterprises. Swamp creatures who drag themselves daily through all the mud of the working world, without ever capturing a single glint of light. Over time, they become rigorously closed-minded, tunnel vision and positively bourgeoisie in their prevailing attitudes and no longer amenable to radical changes and transformations. Functioning instead, more like stiff-lipped, stolid folk, whose features seem chiseled in a lackluster cuneiform. Primitive insignificant creatures, who remain as mere silhouettes of all they could have become. Their spiritual potential never blossoms. As they age further, they become unable to decouple themselves and their lives from the gods of the corporation. Their greatest fear is giving up their chains and finding freedom. It is only a matter of time before they become worn down and desiccated and ready for the recycling bin.

Then he said, there are the **Scam Artists**. This group represents all those slick willies, con-artists, opportunists, and deceptive manipulators who have infiltrated every orifice of humanity, like cockroaches. Those who merchandise only in half-truths and bold-faced lies. White lies or black lies, it is all the same to them. They love to live the good life and off the back of another's sweat. The less they have to do or think, the more they pride themselves. They are cunning and vile, yet skilled in the dark arts of guile, deceit, duplicity, and legerdemain. They like to come across as bons-vivants and connoisseurs at times. All the same, their stark and enduring reality is that they are nothing but relentless attention grabbers, schemers, voluptuaries and pleasure seekers, whose gods are money, worldly power, and privilege. Two-faced beings with impure motives, who will only ever present to you, those defunct pieces of information, that serve their better interests, personal agenda and end goals.

Thus they create palindromes of deception and glowingly declare, that the projected end always justifies the nasty means employed and that a brutal and decimating means is often necessary. Yes, their cruel, heartless idealism can always justify the number of heads hanging from a string over their mantlepiece. Their whole psychology has become so warped, twisted and convoluted by all their evil ways, that it resembles more a rat's nest or a Gordian knot in a hyper-dimensional space. Nor can they be honest, about anything. Transparency is the last thing you can expect even though they toss that word around profusely. Some can be open-minded, but unfortunately are too myopic to see through the perpetual haze of their self-crafted distortions. Like the drones, they see all value on the outside, and it is in this artifice they play all their Machiavellian games of manipulation. The external world is that special, exclusive human arena of crazed animals where they feel superior and vindicated and alive.

The **ego inflated** are all too pervasive, in every cesspit of humanity. They run around like a tribe of hungry ghosts, flailing at witless victims while spewing all their credentials and experiences from the sides of their mouth. Yes, they will extort every opportunity to draw more energy and attention towards themselves. Taking great pains to cultivate their personality myths while propagating endless hype, propaganda, and confabulations. This is what floats their balloons after all, but it is one always ready to burst. One innocuous comment idly passed can be enough to set off an explosion or a locking of horns. Let the buyer beware, because they cannot even pass a compliment without expecting some ROI. Their lives are a game of constant one-upmanship, and they retain a persistent and insatiable need for ever more feathers in their caps, notches on their belts or exotic plumage in which to prance around in. Their adventures and conquests will always be better than yours. So they proudly go about with their display cases, taking their dog & pony show from one place to another, hoping to suck in a few more witless victims. Some half-baked fish who will peer at all the trophies and idols on exhibit there. Malleable patsies, who will flatter them with all sorts of social niceties and commendations. Anything at all that can send their self-images skyrocketing into the stratosphere. But do not be fooled! They place all the jewels and spoils they have carved from humanity on a special altar in their private ego bubbles. This becomes their place of daily worship, and the only gods they will ever entertain.

Then there are the chronically **Disillusioned**. These are the army of sluggish, disenchanted and inertial beings, who have seen through the deceptions of society and the man-god of their egos. Having penetrated past all worldly value systems, worthless accolades, they know the futility of all forms of self-glorification. They often find it very difficult to fit in, or to gain the required momentum to follow any pursuit. On the surface, they look lusterless and tamasic, but inwardly they can be fathomless. Most become cynical, sardonic and contemptuous and always ready to puncture any dream. Being naturally apathetic and unproductive in the conventional sense they roam friendless on psychoplanet as veritable anthropophagi of the human spirit. They are disillusioned because they have seen through the myriad illusions of Maya and know the essential emptiness that pervades the relative world. Unfortunately, they have not found any positive value, ideal or understanding that can substitute or compensate for their profound state of disillusionment. Some settle for a life of routine, while others drop off the radar completely. Unlike the previous genotypes who are all worldly in their disposition, this group is neither worldly nor otherworldly. In fact, they are immensely directionless beings, and flicker like a compass needle under the Aurora Borealis. After a time, they lose all social calibration and inbuilt GPS, and function more like Doomsday Preppers. So they build a cement fortress around their minds, to shield themselves off, from the greater world. They see value nowhere! Neither in the world without nor the one within.

The last group is the **Truth Seekers**. These relentlessly pursue the goal of liberation with an intensity and fire that is breathtaking and inspiring. They will leave no rock unturned and are ready to topple every statue, idol or belief that stands in their way. Yes, these are the spiritual anarchists that have come to destroy all worldly value systems. They are immune to the vices and seductions of pleasure and pain and seek neither. They will pander to no gods of the relative world. All they desire is to peek under the sheets and go far beyond the veil of Maya. To rise above all the chiaroscuro and deceptions of the worldly dream and reach that Truth which is fathomless, formless and infinitely potent. Their intuition tells them that the phenomenal world is a deception, a façade, and a mind-generated hallucination. Something placed here by a higher power to keep the children busy, until they get fed up and spiritually mature. They feel if they can just peel away the layers of subterfuge, arti-fice and conceptual abstraction, they will finally reach to the core and enter the transcendent reality that is just beyond appearances. Their one aim is to move away from the kiddies table once and for all."

"Geez," I said, "You sure know how to shovel it out! But it seems to me, that there are only two distinct classes of people — **(1) The Quick** and **(2) The Dead,** The dead being all those in the first four groups, you have just enumerated. Yes, these are all the worldly folk, who cherish the worthless. Those content, to live their lives in darkness, restricted to the pernicious and pes-tilential thought processes of the ego world. They do not know themselves, and so they flounder around broken-winged, searching out those wide-eyed, gullible beings, who will listen to all their cockeyed tales and idle chitchat. They all work in collu-sion to blunt the sword of one's will and spirit. Yes, they are all shameless slugs, and thugs hovering on the face of the relative existence, sucking up pleasure and attention, while doing their utmost to bring others down. It is of these that Jesus spoke, when he said, "*Let the dead bury their own dead.*" [Matthew 8:22]

They have eyes, but they cannot see, ears but they cannot hear, minds but they cannot think. Only their tongues work and these they use for fellatio and cunnilingus or else to spit out the vilest and most wicked rhetoric and nonsense. Their world is veiled by the dense obscuring layers of their desires, attachments, fears, and self-obsessions. The lids of their eyes are hooded like serpents. Enmeshed in the fat obfuscating fleshy mushroom cloud of all their self-deceptions and distortions, they peregrinate myopically about, claiming to know all and to be Masters of the Universe.

Then there are the **Quick**, who were thrown in mercilessly to the same pond but they have risen through the murky waters and found the light. Since they are blissfully immersed in the light of Reason and pure motive, evil is unknown to them, and this is their wisdom. The world of appearances does not deceive them, nor are they sold on any petty offerings in the market-place. These are the truth-seekers, who have removed all inner distortions. So they look out now in the radiant light of innocence and spirit. Their power arises from being knowers of the Real. Since their inner eyes have opened, all tenebrous veils of the conditioned existence have long fallen away. Their second sight has made them invulnerable, to all the frivolous and small-minded attractions of the worldly paradise. Traveling lightly, they move with ease and grace through all worlds and ferry the raft of their mind effortlessly, into the tranquil quiescent lake of Nirvana.

The Lama's inspired words on the genotypes quickly crystallized in my mind. I began to see all these deluded beings as programmed goons and robotic zombies, caught in a mesmerized trance of their personal making. All somnambulists walking one-by-one, and two-by-two, into their allotted slots in the ark of the genotypes. This judgment day cortège seemed to extend backward endlessly. It was populated by all those beings, that I had ever known—either briefly or else for my entire life. Even so, one slot was not filling up. The one reserved for the Truth-Seekers. The Lama explained, "Yes, to find an authentic Truth-Seeker, is very rare indeed, less than one in a million. That is why these Sutras go on misinterpreted and locked for most."

SUTRA 3: LET EVEN THE HEALING REMEDY GO FREE ON ITS OWN

THE GANGES NEAR ITS SOURCE

What the Lama Dorje had said was both fatidic, inspirational and perspicacious. He obviously possessed a rigorous mantic and divinatory understanding of what constituted 'unborn awareness.' He knew this resplendent awareness was the underlying plenum in which the true state of existence became perfectly reflected. It underscored a reality blocked to most. This world has always been a headache, without a head. Gladly now, this head had been cut forever. Cut by the sword of discriminating wisdom. Yes, I had slashed the Hydra-headed beast of Maya and mercilessly decapitated it. By applying the powerful healing remedy, I had seen through the dream and awoken to the light of my Self-nature. Now I was going about like a Banty rooster, immersed in my newfound state of peace and bliss. I had become one of the immortals, invulnerable to all illusions. All my worries and cares melted away and fear had gone into hiding.

DREAM HYPNOSIS AND OVER-ATTACHMENT TO THE REMEDY

When I next met the Lama, I was positively euphoric. He asked about my thoughts and feelings. I said, "I feel free, light and expansive for the first time in my life. I have escaped from a tremendous jail or fortress and one that seemed to offer no hope ever of release. Some penal institution, akin to Black Dolphin in Russia. I always thought of unconditional peace, only in negative terms. Treated it, as if it were simply an alleviation of pain, unrest, turmoil, and fear. Now I see it entirely differently and in positive terms because it has given me such clarity, bliss, freedom, and receptiveness of mind. Darkness and confusion are no more. In contrast, everything is imbued with tremendous meaning and recognized to be of the nature of perfection itself. I feel I was ensnared in the clutches of a very powerful dream, without realizing it. The dream of fear and unending misery. One that held me completely consumed and hypnotized. One that had gone uninterrupted, for possibly hundreds of thousands of years, if not longer. I had spent lifetimes, experiencing myriad mindless misadventures and futilely grasping at straws. All those headaches and hangovers that come from drinking from the cup of the world. Even so, I had gone on begging for more and never realized that no dream could ever offer anything of lasting value. Yes! There was no trophy ever to be found on the outside. Just those fool's gifts, that glitter and shine so endearingly in the dark, but all are worthless at their core. More like something, one might pull out of a 5c 'lucky bag'. They offered psychedelic arrays of sensual attractions and all sorts of flatteries to beguile the mind. Gifts that would persuade it to keep up its mortgage payment on the body. Meretricious temptations that would entice it to continue to decorate and adorn the body's lawns and prune its rose-gardens. Now, I see that all dreams were powerless to bestow any real gifts because each was born in the darkness of my ignorance and confusion. Each was just an outward representation of my internal sense of inadequacy. It was the dream that had obfuscated my true worth. It was the true nature of the seeker that alone needed to be found. However, this remained unknowable, so long as I remained fast asleep."

Naturally, there was a feeling of great indebtedness to the potent remedy; Lama Dorje had given me. For it had finally released me from my self-made hell. I wanted to cling to it forever, as a small child does to his teddy bear.

THE DANGER OF ATTACHMENT TO THE REMEDY

L ama Dorje listened attentively and then responded, "The only purpose of the first Sutra, was to awaken you. In this goal, it functioned admirably. Like an ancient Rosetta stone, it enabled you to decode your true Identity as the dreamer. As a Holy Grail, it brought the cup of life back to your lips. Nonetheless, if you insist on clinging to this remedy, now, it will transform into yet another attachment, that will finally poison you. Spiritual attachments can be most insidious of all attachments. They can be the most tenaciously grasped and the hardest to get rid of. If you repeatedly apply this remedy over-and-over, everywhere you go, you will just be inducing a form of self-hypnosis. You cannot synthesize, nor manufacture your ongoing safety from the dream, by auto-repetition of words. That would mean your source of safety was causal and artificial. Your natural awareness is now awakened, and repeating mantras now will just put you back to sleep. You have to trust in Truth for it alone can guarantee the protection needed against all demons that seek to infiltrate your awareness, and it will do so unconditionally and always.

SUGGESTED PRACTICE

The most important consideration at this moment is that you do not allow yourself to become forgetful. Abide constantly in your newfound awareness. Let the fruits of your newfound understanding sink deeply into your unconscious mind. Once they take root, all remaining false perceptions cropping up on occasion will soon depart from you forever. Yes, at times, there may be lapses in your awareness. Certain dream fragments may reappear on the screen of your mind. You may feel threatened by this. Fearful that you will once again become dream identified. All such ego imprints, psychic-residuals, and sense impressions were built-up over eons, through the power of conditioning. These cannot endure when no longer powered by your mind. Your relative mind is like the Chicken's head that has been cut. It may still walk about for a while more and take a few more steps. Don't be overly concerned, because soon it will collapse lifeless to the ground forever.

The light of Spirit imprisoned within has been released, and this is presently illuminating all your perceptions with a timeless fragrance and radiance that you never thought even possible. It is bringing to you, continual remembrance of your true Reality. You feel cradled in the arms of unconditional love because you have found the fountain of Life. You have reached the clear light, that is eternal. This light can never depart from you because it has always been here. There is nothing apart from it. All former poisons, attachments and worldly desires have lost all power over you. In the vaporous state of consciousness that you now abide in, it is only a matter of time, before the entire phenomenal existence disappears for good. It will evaporate through your newfound vision, as mists do before the morning Sun—never to reappear. It was always lifeless and insubstantial and held no power.

All you need do is remain hyper-vigilant in your Self-remembrance. Vigilance will automatically prevent any future dreams, idols or temptations from rushing in and clinging to you. Remember, "others" may still think of you as an image in the world, possessing a body. You, however, know that you are no longer in or of the world. Their misplaced dream projections have nothing to do with you. Their perceptual errors simply reflect their own state of ignorance. You are well beyond being tarnished by worldliness. All worldly illusions are powerless to reach, where you Are Now. Powerless to diminish your perfect state of rest. For you are blissfully immersed in your Eternal Home."

SUTRA 4: SETTLE INTO YOUR ESSENCE NATURE; AS UNLIMITED AND INDESTRUCTIBLE AWARENESS

THE AUTHOR MEETS WITH A LOCAL ATTRACTION

I had always wondered what my original face resembled. At first, I imagined it was some physical face, like that of some primitive beast or savage. Then I thought it might be something highly serene and noble and impregnated with numerous virtues and ideals. One beaming effulgently, as a beacon of strength and light for all humanity. I visualized it as a hybridized fusion of a very select group of noble, virtuous, charismatic and strong-willed beings from the past. Illustrious figures such as Marcus Aurelius, Plotinus, Eva Peron, Osho, Meher Baba, Milarepa, Richard Feynman, Zeno, Parmenides, Socrates, Joan of Arc, the Buddha, Lao Tzu, Ramakrishna, Shankaracharya, Sri Ramana Maharshi, Florence Nightingale and so many others appeared as part of its fabric. All because this powerful mosaic of beings had inspired me to some extent along the way. As I advanced in my Scientific understanding, my original face started to take on a more psychedelic, multidimensional and holistic appearance. It became a curved spaced spread across the Akashic Field that enfolded limitless universes and infinite potentialities. In addition, it contained all my memories, experiences, virtuous acts, aspirations, innate capabilities, latent strengths and so much more.

Now that I had finally found my original face, I was completely stumped. It had nothing at all to do with this vast panorama of beings and fields of multidimensional spaces that I had envisaged before. Nor was it tainted by my illusions of grandeur. These were all dreams of my relative mind and mostly projections of the ego. My original face, was not some complex picture, set in some highly elaborate, ornate and disproportionate frame. Or an expensive masterpiece, on which I could place all my jewels of deified beings, past glories and conquests, along with all my dreams of illusory love and sacrifice. Instead, it was a pure, simple and light-filled picture that possessed no frame at all. One immensely fluid, dazzling and sublime. One timeless, spaceless, formless, faceless and deathless. It was representative of an ever-potent Identity that could never be eroded or erased. An indestructible, pristine and immaculate awareness, in which all things happen, and from which all phenomenal universes are born. One fully radiant, vibrant, ecstatic and alive. One that encapsulated even Eternity and the wisdom of the One-Mind. This is why it had evaded me for so long.

The Lama advised that I settle deeply into my essence nature and to fully embrace and explore my original face. To take in, all the profound implications, it portended. He said, "The quality of an essence determines its power and scope. The spiritual realm is one of quality, not of quantity. For example, you know that even a single seed can yet produce a great forest. Even in the world of Science, we can draw parallels. We see that a single thread of DNA can contain the entire blueprint for a new species. Therefore it may contain the recipe for entire new ecosystems and advanced ways of living. Alternatively, it can be used to clone organs, such as the heart and liver which enable us to live far longer and experience a more enhanced quality of life.

In the cyber-universe of technology, we likewise find many illuminating examples. The single concept of "Windows," for example, has completely shaped the way we communicate and interact. It harnesses and streamlines our most excellent creative instincts for reinventing, refashioning and reframing the world around us. Other emerging fields such as nanotechnology, robotics, control systems, heuristics, biotechnology, etc. all exfoliated from just a few key ideas or concepts. The most powerful essence of all is mind. Mind, as a pure awareness outshines all since it gives rise to all. Nothing is apart from it. In its warm manifold, we live, experience and grow. We can use its knowledge to gain liberation, everlasting love, and bliss or else to unleash vengeful weapons of mass destruction.

With your newfound vision, the source of all that is miraculous has been revealed. Now that you possess a pellucid understanding, you know with certainty that Absolute Reality in its raw, and pure essence contains no appearances. It does not humor the false worlds of the phenomenal and conceptual nor entertain distortions and fabrications arising from erroneous beliefs. You see that all apparent motions and appearances were unfortunate byproducts of the relative mind. Trapped beneath the suffocating veil of ignorance, you had cherished certain wrong beliefs. These alone kept the machinery for dreaming alive and operational. They accounted for all dark, nasty projections that showed up in your perceptions. So your mind morphed into an event-driven engine, whose entire momentum was fueled by all your foolish desires, idols, fears and unnatural appetites.

Having taken yourself to be just an image in a dream, you had always felt incomplete. Thus, your undertook a vain search for idols, hoping one day to fill the void in your soul. You then attempted the most futile of all tasks—patching up holes that were never there. Hence your frustration and ultimate failure! For you were attempting to fill in and patch all those fissures, and cracks arising from your self-deception, denial and ever-tenacious clinging to the illusory. The myriad dark caverns that arose in your mind were simply sandcastles that depicted your fall from grace. So you came to inhabit a world of littleness, in which you walked around as a scarecrow, ragged and weary and lost to yourself. Awaiting the vultures and hyenas of the dreamworld, to come and pluck out your eyes. It was such a futile and fatalistic endeavor to attempt to find value and completion, in anything "outside" your mind. The treasure-house was always on the inside and so close, yet where you never dreamed of looking. You did not know, how to look, nor how to treasure. You had forgotten the true criteria of worth. That which is everlasting, ever-potent and limitless is alone of worth. Once you devalued "others," you had also devalued yourself and so disfigured the true face of the eternal in all. Shrouded by your personal ignorance and self-deception, the face of the Creator became hidden from view.

You had come to an extreme in which you thought it the height of absurdity, even to question the origins and nature of your dream machine. The dream seemed so ominous, manifold and fearful in its consequences. It held your very life, so precariously in its paws. It ruled your world entirely and whipped you about there like a ragdoll in it. You never questioned the dreamer's true essence, apart from the dream. Never realized that the multiplicity of developments and refinements in the dream's evolution had simply mirrored the ongoing evolutionary changes happening within you. They reflected the ever-increasing subtlety of your consciousness. So your consciousness had become just like tinder, desperately waiting to be set on fire from within. Nothing was ever outside! Nothing was ever happening! All happenings, were reflections of your misplaced thoughts, projected onto the screen of the void.

Now you fully realize, the dreamer's mind alone was real. All it needed was healing and awakening and true understanding was the only cure. Yes, your dreaming mind was always the priceless pearl, you had so desperately sought. Regrettably, dazzled by the world, you never looked at mind in awe. Instead, you had used and abused it and wastefully squandered all its power. You made mind into a slave, pandering after all the body's manifold needs and lusts. You downgraded it into an errand boy, a femme de ménage that idly chasing solutions for the body to keep it from falling apart. So it became subjugated to your passions and false protections. *This is what you did to essence.* You sold in the marketplace and traded in for a dream of servitude.

For a while longer then, some scattered fragments of the dream will continue to appear on the screen of your mind. These scattered dream fragments keep arising from the junkyard of your unconscious. They represent many long dead skeletons and useless artifacts of thought. Ones buried deep from a time, seeming beyond all conscious memory. For the descent into dreaming has been long, hard and torturous and it has been going on since ancient times. The relative world could never have appeared were it not for all those illusions you cherish that are born from ignorance. Nothing can usurp the power of Truth, and nothing can destroy essence. Now that you have found the true Identity of the dreamer, these foul-smelling vaults and ancient caverns have become exposed to light at last. This light is unborn awareness and it will heal your entire perception of all its distortions. As each past skeleton is reintroduced to conscious awareness, it dissipates in the light of your newfound awareness. Thus your world glows all the more and springs of nascent vitality, gush forth to charge and replenish you with new life and resolve. You will never realize how truly thirsty you were until your cup has become completely filled. As you continue to abide more in your indestructible essence, you will cease to react to all dreams. Phantoms and false appearances, will soon lose all residual traction in your mind. Unpowered by toxic ego trains of thought, they will arise no more. As all remaining dark clouds disappear your eternal inheritance of Nirvana alone will shine in a cloudless sky. The Great One will then take you into her Bosom, and you will be seen no more."

SUTRA 5: BETWEEN MEDITATION SESSIONS, CONSIDER ALL PHENOMENA AS ILLUSORY

A HIMALAYAN MOUNTAIN PASS

The next time, that I met Lama Dorje, he asked, "*How are your progressing with settling into your essence nature?*" "It is hard to explain," I said. "Initially, as my awareness and sense of presence intensifies, I begin to see the whole room flowing about, including the walls. Everything fast becomes fluid and malleable. All objects soon lose all their sharp edges, definition and artificial boundaries and begin effortlessly diffusing and blending into one another. It seems space is gobbling them up and in turn being gobbled up by itself. Soon all merge into this great throbbing Oneness, and disappear. Then the entire dream of phenomenality is no more, and there is nothing left to be perceived. Then for long periods, I feel all existence as a vaporous flux of benevolent light, cradling me with love, and unconditional bliss. I am high above the world, abiding in a non-dualistic awareness, in which all is formless and undifferentiated. This seems to be a very pure awareness since it is free of all forms, worldly dreams and all notions of bodily consciousness. All in the lower world is powerless to inflict or spread its contagion here. For Here dreamer and the dream have fused and doing so both disappear into a far greater unity. No longer is either reinforcing the pseudo-reality of the other. At times, I need to shake myself out of it. Only then do forms begin to reappear.

THE GREATER ENTELECHY OF BEING

Then, I walk over to the small mirror, and I notice it too has lost all its solidity and seems surrounded by a rim of light. The light flickers on and off a few times. I recognize, this as the sign, that time itself is dilating, and coming to an absolute standstill. I am entering the eternal present. Everything is hopelessly enbosomed is this whirling vortex of energy, whose Source is invisible. I see many different faces spontaneously arising and falling in the mirror before me. It is quite a motley procession and hard to place each according to the unique age, culture or civilization they belonged to. Some extend far back into the distant past and can be quite scary and intimidating to look at. Sometimes they are missing teeth or eyes, or else they may have large scars, ghastly disfigurements or missing limbs. Some resemble a Cro-Magnon species of men and women. Others look at me blank and emotionless as if resigned to the special destiny life had in store for them. A life now long erased even almost from the Akashic Record, it seems. Then others appear, who are far more refined in appearance and demeanor. These delicate and esthete ones exude a calm, dignified, and regal air. Such figures are epicene by nature since they posses characteristics or both sexes. I feel there is something I have in common with them all but for the life of me, I cannot place it. Each appears just for a few moments and then disappears to make way for another."

The Lama listened silently, then responded "Yes, these are all the figures from your past lives. They only reappear after your Enlightenment. They have always been present and available to you. However, you were too blinded by your spacetime dreams. In consequence, your awareness got funneled to just the immediate past and present, and you could not perceive them. Time was never spread out linearly or serially as you had mistakenly thought. Nor is it objective in nature. It is nothing but your mind and its strong conditioning that enforces the apparent continuity of time. All these figures remain part of your overall memory and were stored deep into your unconscious. However, these memories could never rise back to your conscious awareness, because you closed the gates. The narrow filter of your conditioned belief patterns had blocked them out.

All of them had an important evolutionary role to play in bringing you to where you are now—which is *no 'where.'* They/you had to live and learn important life lessons so that you could eventually transcend the dream. All helped your consciousness to evolve. All were part of the wood and tinder needed to light your awareness on fire. You should be grateful to them all. All made you what you are today, which is a *no 'thing'*—a perfect and pure awareness. More accurately, they brought back into your awareness the fact that you were always a *no 'thing.* All of them are you, but only at the level of essence. They can be considered, you in metamorphosis spread out over the canvas of phenomenality and time. You had always identified with just one limb on your body. The limb of your present life. But now the centipede is rising back from below the surface. The light has come, and you are now seeing the greater entelechy of your Being.

SOME SIDDHIS ARISING FROM ENLIGHTENMENT

Having awoken, you will notice, that soon you will have gained mastery over certain aspects of the dreamworld, whenever it reappears. Certain miraculous powers will come naturally to you. They arise from your heightened state of awareness, and from your knowledge of the true nature of existence. It is just like in a lucid dream, when you gain certain powers and control, once you realize you are dreaming. Only now you have awoken from the dream of the relative existence and the so-called phenomenal world. You always considered yourself Awake, but you never really were. You were just dreaming with your eyes open. For example, you may have gained already the psychokinetic ability to move objects at "distances." Attained various shape-shifting abilities and thus now able to transform your seeming physical form, through thought and concentration. The Siddhis of **Anima**, **Mahima**, **Laghima**, and **Prapti**, we have spoken of before. The ability to directly manipulate and shape the macrocosmic world and the natural course of nature itself is also possible. Using the **Ishita Siddhi**, for example, you can change the weather, the course of the tides or the natural cycle of ecological events, Hence, you can bring, much needed rain in times of drought or even fruit to blossom when it out of season. This Siddhic power is extremely potent and it can even be utilized to move the planets and comets out of their normal orbits.

Then there are some basic Siddhis, which most Enlightened minds pick-up on almost immediately. The ability to hear and see things remotely becomes very easy because you will just be surfing through the cosmic mind-matrix of the Akashic field. You will find yourself becoming immune to the extremes of weather, poison, fatigue and have no need to sleep. Sleep is only required for those worn down by destructive thought patterns. They become easily exhausted from all those pernicious and internecine battles waged daily by their inner demons. You may also have already begun to prognosticate certain events from the seeming future. Abilities for precognition and retrocognition are not rare to the Enlightened because the entire spacetime landscape played itself out in illusion so long ago. In fact, it played out at the instant of Adam's fell asleep in the Garden of Eden. Now that you have the more sublime view, you can see simultaneously all that has ever happened and all that yet seems in the future.

Most who are Enlightened find they can communicate clearly into "other" minds very crisply and unambiguously even at vast distances. Such communication power arises because they have recognized all Mind is One, and know that it is continuous and spaceless. They, therefore, find no real barriers or obstacles within it anymore. Nothing can hold them back from penetrating through to all its aspects. They use this understanding to influence "others" and to change the natural course of events. This particular ability or Siddhi is known as the **Vashita Siddhi**. You may also find that you can go days or weeks without needing any food or drink or sustenance of any sort. All because you have recognized the body as empty and illusory. This particular power is known as **Haadi Vidya**. It was mobilized by many Enlightened Masters, including Bodhidharma, Milarepa, Jesus, Therese Neumann. In fact, many accomplished yogis today use it today whenever they want to be left alone for extended periods of Sadhana. They prefer the rewards offered by deep states of meditative absorption to any petty hard-earned gifts of the world. They also make use of the **Kaadi Vidya**, which makes them immune to changing weather patterns. Thus they can stay out in the hot sun for days on end without getting burnt or de-hydrated. Likewise, they can roam naked on the glaciers without ever freezing to death.

THE SOLID AND VAPOROUS STATES OF CONSCIOUSNESS

In this pure non-dual state of consciousness, you undoubtedly experience heavenly moments of unconditional joy and one-ness. Extended periods of complete intimacy with Truth are the norm. Once you transcended the dreams of duality and form, your consciousness moved from the solid state into the vapor-ous one. The solid state is synonymous with the dualistic mind-frame of the world. In this state, one perceives a multiplicity of objects and phenomena and considers them real. It presents a bleak and static world picture and arises from the restrictive, controlling and strictly partitioning consciousness of the tyran-nical ego self. Here everything and everyone is seen from a utili-tarian and exploitive perspective. Each seems to occupy a pri-vate bubble, around which they rapidly establish a vast network of defenses. Knowledge that is specific, and relative is valued and worshipped over that which is far more potent, generalized and abstract.

Those who operate in this world, seem to have a gazillion needs and are never satisfied. They want to be pampered and spoiled, and yet they cannot take any responsibility for their thoughts and emotions. They are like babies peeing down their legs, then crying out for help. It is an unstable and insane race of voracious, insatiable beings who have much in common with the realm of hungry ghosts. So they occupy their days, chasing after endless new inventions, innovations, and toys. Dedicated to meaningless pursuits whose end-purpose is to gratify all their bodily wants and lusts. Ones that embroil them deeper in the pseudo-comforts of materialism. It is a world of shameless marketing, intelligence wars, propaganda, money manipulation and operating strategic Coups and takeovers to expropriate the resources of all.

Now that you have entered the vaporous state and transcended the realm of appearances, all has melted away. The dream of the phenomenal world dissolved into non-existence, once you resolved all dualities. You reached the zero point of consciousness. The consciousness of consciousness, in which the self-reflective mind has taken itself, as its autogenous object of investigation. So it stops projecting form. Now you see yourself flickering in and out of existence, like an apparition in a dream. There comes the feeling that "**I Am**" followed immediately by "**I Am Not**." This oscillation can go for hours or indefinitely because you have arrived at the very root of Being and the source of all projection. The feeling of "**I Am**" arises whenever you are projecting. Then the world and the body stream back into your awareness and once more appear on the screen of the void. The feeling "**I Am Not**" arises, as your awareness intensifies and increases in purity. You are entering the projecting booth and experiencing yourself as the projectionist of the dream.

Recognizing that there is no one in the house. Since you are "seeing" through the greater vision of Spirit, you can see no form.

This pure realm you are bathing in during moments of "**I Am Not**," is the essential backdrop of all existence. The unmanifest and noumenal Source, which is also a nothingness. Yes, nothing can exist apart from it. From this great plenum of ever-existing fullness, all form and phenomenal universes become extruded into seeming existence. Ignorance is the fuel and fear and passion are the gasoline. During the oscillation, the world of perception, and the perceiver are collapsing into one another. You come to recognize your true essence as Mind. And intimately understand that the realm of perception, the perceiver and the act of perceiving are seamlessly interfused. None have had anything to do with you and your essential and immutable Reality. They were not your business, but merely mirages arising in your sleep. Mirages you became deeply identified with and took to be your true Self. Nonetheless, the Absolute has no room for any such foolishness. It does not pay homage to appearances, born in the dust of your ignorance. It does not heed any splits or separations, seen by the dualistic mind-frame. In the powerful light of your Self-nature, Reality becomes revealed. Yes, this vaporous state is the realm of the immortals. Beyond mice and men. Here, all illusions are powerless to enter, and nothing can distract or tempt. You find yourself gently rocking back and forth, in the great quiescent sea of formlessness. Endlessly intoxicated in states of deep bliss and relaxation, safety and invulnerability while feeling your absolute potency and dominion over all. Functioning more from the elevated stature of a Supreme Master who reigns over all universes and all states of being."

ENLIGHTENMENT AS THE NEW BEGINNING

Then I stated abruptly, "**This is all very well, but Enlightenment does not pay the bills.** Those who aren't Enlightened, cannot recognize it in another. They continue to wander about in their deep state of sleep, projecting their very limiting thought patterns and beliefs on those around them. Also, it is difficult to maintain the necessary heightened state of awareness, indefinitely. Whenever I don't, the old dream-world comes rushing back at me again and seeks to make continuous assaults on my peace of mind. Whenever I feel compelled to take care of some trivial tasks, I see the body arising out of the mists once more. Before I know it, the whole quality of my awareness is no longer the same. That extremely tranquil state of mind, I was resting so nicely in, has been replaced by a hive of nonsense activities. The phenomenal universe is back up and running and going at full steam. I begin to hear all the screeching sounds of the world and feel invaded by all the pandemonium and petty annoyances. My former serenity now seems more like a long-lost dream. Yes, I am back in the mud of the world and feel humiliated by my rapid descent."

Lama Dorje laughed wholeheartedly, then spoke once more, "Yes, Enlightenment is a bit like owning the Cullinan diamond, before it ever got cut and polished. You know the immense value of what you are holding, but to others, it still seems just like an ordinary dirty rock. You cannot cash it in, because there are only a rare few gem experts circulating about, that can genuinely appraise its worth. To all others, it is like you are trying to pawn off Kerry diamonds to the witless and docile. They smell a door-to-door salesperson and so miss out on the excellent opportunity to be spiritually healed. So, yes I fully understood your difficulties and dilemma.

People mistakenly think of Enlightenment as the end of the road, when in fact it is just the beginning. True, you have broken the hypnotic spell, binding you to the Samsaric existence. You have lost all continuity with the past and to all that you "knew" before. You have no reference points left and no bearings. Now, that you have finally tasted the bliss of True Being and entered the exalted realm, it is hard for you to launch any excitement or enthusiasm for the world of shadows. When all you believed in were shadows, you were at least somewhat content in your discontent and happier to settle for the world's sad offerings. Now that you have transcended all dualities, you would like to abide uninterrupted in the unconditioned reality. You would like no more phantasms or worldly distractions to arise and interfere.

You must realize that you have just destroyed the seeds of dreaming. The tree and the fruit still remain. This tree of the phenomenal existence did not appear overnight, but grew and evolved over countless millennia. Now it is only maintained because of the power of your conditioned beliefs. So for a while dream fragments will continue to reappear, even though their cause is long gone."

Unwinding the Phantom Universe

My logical and reasoning mind was having some difficulties with this explanation. I said:

"Surely when a cause is gone, then with it also go all its effects. Once one has seen through the spacetime existence and penetrated beyond the veil of ignorance, then how can the conditioned existence still retain any power?"

Lama Dorje, fathoming my line of thought said "The conditioned existence never held any power since it is illusory. However, it does possess great traction in mind. In the Absolute, Cause neither appears nor disappears. It simply always IS, and it exists as a beacon of radiant purity that is forever unchanging, omnipotent and indestructible. In the world of time, no Real Cause has ever been. What is hailed as '**cause**' in the relative world, is just a pet term idly tossed about! Just like a child can wave a magic wand and then believe that this invests his toys with powers they do not have. So dreamers exploit the term 'cause,' to account for certain belief dynamics and magical principles, wrongly accumulated in their minds. For example, they believe miraculous terraqueous forces like gravity, electromagnetism, radiation, inertia, vibration, etc. power the entire world of appearances. Nonetheless, all their mistaken notions of cause are rooted in their ignorance.

With Enlightenment, you undertook that quantum leap in consciousness, and this exposed the dream for what it was. Your original face, long hidden and defiled by illusions came back into view. In moments of complete awareness, you feel one with the

Presence of the Absolute. In those times, you can see incontestably that no 'thing' ever existed. The phenomenal world only re-
emerges when you lose your natural awareness. Then it becomes contaminated with the unreal due to your identification.
Then you begin to nourish foolish fantasies related to ego idols.
So whenever you lose vigilance of mind even temporarily, it
reappears from the mosaic of your conditioned thought patterns
and beliefs. Thoughts patterns that yet remain deeply unconscious to you.

Self-awareness and phenomenal existence cannot exist simultaneously. The appearance of one leads to the disappearance of
the other. Non-identified awareness is phenomenal absence, just
as identified awareness is phenomenal presence. Once one falls
again into the trap of becoming dream identified, one forgets
themselves as the dreamer. Then the dream assumes command
and seems very solid and substantial, and it retains the potential
to become very dark and seedy indeed."

I was beginning to see the underlying sense, contained in the
Lama's explanation. After all, a shooting star can still appear to
be present, even when its cause is long gone. Similarly, a picture
or image can temporarily appear on a blank wall, if the image
was focused on long enough, beforehand and then you glanced
at the blank wall. Beliefs and experiences are no different. Past
events and experiences, particularly traumatic ones can continue to haunt the apparent present because such experiences have
left strong indelible imprints in our minds. Thus they can continue to exert a strong conditioning influence on present perceptions. Extrapolating this idea to all our beliefs, memories,
experiences, biases and predispositions, we recognize the
ultimate veracity is that all dreamers are just continuously reliv-

ing their past in the apparent present. All that is appearing in our world is arising out of that vast unconscious reservoir of our beliefs and former impressions. It is only at the instant of En-lightenment, that one sees the true and naked present, for the first time. Then one breaks through the seal of all their condi-tioned thought patterns.

I said, "it seems as if the phenomenal existence is just like a vast magic show. This magic show can only maintain the mirage of its existence, through our entrenched beliefs. Once we no longer cling to such foolishness, all phenomena arising from them falls away. The videotape of our conditioned unconscious projections just needs to play itself out. Presently, I am just rewinding the videotape, and getting ready to bring it back to the store and tell the clerk what a shit movie, it was."

Lama Dorje seemed pleased with my grasp of this Sutra and said "Yes, it seems that you have caught on to the essential gist of the matter. We had spoken before about the chicken, that had its head cut off. It will continue to prance about for a few moments more. Since it still carries the momentum of all past energies and events, set in motion, before its beheading. So it is with the mind. Our pain, anxieties, and fears often remain, even after their cause is long gone. Consciously we know, there is nothing to worry about, but we cannot relax. The realm of the unconscious is vast and an entirely different beast to deal with than our conscious one.

THE LANDFILL OF THE UNCONSCIOUS

One way to look at the unconscious is to see it as a gigantic landfill. A dump that accepts all thoughts and beliefs of the conscious mind, without asking any questions or making any judgments. So like a perfectly servile slave, it accepts all requests from its master, no matter how ridiculous, puerile or quixotic they may be and its master is the conscious mind. It does not allow itself to become partial to any particular task; it is given. Instead, it functions as flawlessly and efficiently as it can, to bring into fruition all requests and desires of the conscious mind. It uses all information available in its vast store in accomplishing this. It does not make moral judgments on what is right or wrong, good or evil, or it would never get all its work done. It simply embraces all that is useful and ignores and discards all else as useless or redundant.

The conscious mind, on the other hand, is very selective, close-minded and judgmental. It possesses very narrow filters and recoils from anything, not to its preference, taste or desire. Anything unfamiliar, alien to its filters, or transcendent of its thought gets blocked out and put off indefinitely.

The dream fragments that you now see reappearing, from time-to-time, got stored away over numerous past eons, in the vast storage locker of your unconscious. They became denied and so forgotten. Nevertheless, their pseudo-existence can still exert a very powerful, commanding and hypnotizing influence over your world. The *'out-of-mind'* became *'out-of-sight.'* Unfortunately, the corollary of this is untrue because the *'out-of-*

sight,' is not necessarily *'out-of-mind.'* These dream fragments were once in your conscious awareness. They became consciously digested and assimilated before being stored away. The landscape of your perception predominantly displays the content of your unconscious mind. It pictures to you all that which was vacuum sucked into it long ago.

Now it is slowly and gradually releasing its contents through the narrow filters, that your conscious mind will allow. Except, now your filters have all been disabled, and the motor has been placed in reverse. You are taking a journey back to your beginning, Coming to the Absolute zero, from which no more phenomenal worlds, will ever be able to regenerate. Now is the time of spring cleaning for your unconscious mind. The opportune time for raising it out of the garbage can and ridding it of all impurities, accumulated over eons past. All appearances will soon be fried for perpetuity in the great bonfire of your newfound light. Soon the unreal world will be gone forever.

The important activity for you presently is to remain vigilant and not slip back into the coma of dream identification. There may be times when you feel the dream hypnosis, to be too overpowering and mind-consuming. In such moments you can actively apply the method given in the first Sutra, to dispel all appearances. Thus you will avoid falling back into any identification with the dream."

SUTRA 6: THREE OBJECTS; THREE POISONS; THREE ROOTS OF VIRTUE

A LOCAL WATERFALLS THAT I FOUND REFRESHING

It was two weeks before I met Lama Dorje again. I wanted to know what special attraction their isolated and rudimentary lifestyle held for them. I said, "I noticed that you and the other monks spend most of the day either at work or in meditation. On occasion, you are absorbed joyfully on a mandala, which you then quickly destroy. Is this all the excitement and entertainment you need? I mean, it seems even more primitive than the lifestyle of the Amish."

"What would you have us do?", He responded; "Play bingo on a Saturday night, or mercilessly beat a golf ball around a course and traipse after it for many miles, in the lashing rain? We could all head to a rock concert to get our ears blown off; then get caught in a swarm of sweaty grabbling bodies and drugged to oblivion. So feeling like sardines trapped in a can, while ferociously seesawing back-and-forth amidst the mangled heaps. Or maybe we could drop some Quaaludes, only to start wildly thrashing about the place like cows with mad cow disease? Hell while we're at it, why don't we all head to Lhasa on a party bus and get mindlessly trashed, as you western folk do! Then start climbing up all the fountains and peeing on all below. Serenading the moon with our wolf cries while gentle releasing tears from our urinary tracts. Then listen to the drips make their soothing splashing sounds like frogs launching into water.

Unlikely to happen! Childish entertainments are only for those deluded souls, who feel unfulfilled in themselves. So they go about searching the world for all sorts of substitutes and compensations for their loss of identity. There is no lasting satisfaction to be found in idle entertainment. Lasting happiness and contentment can never be derived from the physical but only within a mind that has reached perfect understanding. One thoroughly absorbed in pure and potent contemplation reaches easily to bliss. We do not aim at any doing, but our complete undoing. Supreme inaction and motionlessness of mind and thought transport one into the quiescent state of Buddha consciousness and this is the most potent and satisfying form of action.

As for mandalas—they help strengthen our creativity and visualization powers and enable us to spread healing influences across the One-Mind. They also enhance the capacities of our mind for abstractive thought. We destroy them to signify the impermanence of all things in the relative world. Now, I am going to teach you about the three poisons, which alone keep one fettered to the relative existence. They perpetuate all dreaming and worldly misery and are directly responsible for keeping Nirvanic bliss at bay. These three root poisons that instantiate the hell of the Samsaric existence are:

1. **Fear**

2. **Attachment**

3. **Ignorance**

Fortunately, each of these poisons has a very powerful antidote, which can restore the original purity of mind. So providing lasting freedom, from all Samsaric existence."

FEAR

I then asked, "**Can you explain these mind poisons, in more detail?**"

He proceeded, "Fear is the number one poison, responsible for all your misery and ills. The presence of fear, in its many variegated forms, always signifies a lack of Love. Whenever you fail to be loving, you will always be fearful. You will then feel compelled to adopt a false identity to protect yourself and your little fiefdom in the sand. Thus, you morph into a lone separated being, in a seemingly cold and hostile universe. A fearful identity emerges that seals you in airtight and it functions as an ego defense against Love. In this loveless world, you feel isolated. Through fear, the voice of the ego strengthens, and you lose sight of your original Identity, as all-encompassing Being. This world of fear is fabricated entirely out of your thoughts. **It is done unto you as you believe.** The presence of fear in any form arises from all your mistaken and fearful interpretations and nothing else. There can be no fear, where there is no distortion, and there can be no distortion, where there are no wrong beliefs.

Fear keeps you hostage in a dreamworld and throws away the keys. This dreamworld then becomes magnified and gains complete power over you. You rapidly dwindle into a minuscule speck of dust. An avatar made of clay and mud, begging for pennies and loose change and dumpster diving for morsels of stale pizza in all the ghettoes of the world. All your thought processes become obsessed with stealing more power, and you engage in pitiless attempts to gain some mastery over your dreamworld. You seek to carve up some life-space for yourself, by brutally cutting another down. Is it a wonder, that a world of vengeance and retribution arises swiftly before you? Then you scamper back to cower in your little homunculus of clay. Your next move is forging alliances with special friends to protect yourself. You begin surrounding yourself with a dizzying array of self-made defenses. Nonetheless, it was you alone who licensed and welcomed fear into your mind and all the power, it seems to possess is actuated by your poor choices.

Some ego fears are understandable considering its intractable and rigid bodily identification. Hence, you fear disease, suffering, loss, poverty, starvation, and death. Other fears of the ego require a little more scrutiny to arrive at their real metaphysical roots. Examples include your fears of **Freedom** (*Eleutherophobia*), **Nothingness**, **Infinity** (*Apeirophobia*), **Eternity and Heaven** (*Uranophobia*). These all seem to have a psycho-spiritual basis, and all relate to the ego's immense desire for control and underlying fear of inconsequentiality. The ego fully believes it can become more substantial by controlling all events, people, and circumstances. Even so, it can only maintain this illusion of control through limiting the horizons. Only thus can it retain any sense of magnitude in your mind. It feels itself suffocating in Eternal conceptions such as boundlessness, freedom, and infinity. It opines such abstract notions as rubbish and steers you quickly back to the world of specifics. Then cautions that such ideas pertain to a non-existent world of ideals and therefore cannot be important.

Likewise, it is quick to equate any teaching on nothingness, as one of embracing nihilism. This is a cheap tactic designed to scare you off. It sees nothingness as a doctrine of deconstructionism leading to self-annihilation. Inside it shivers, intuiting nothingness as a power that can topple all its carefully erected sandcastles. Ones it has spent many decades meticulously constructing and decorating into something, it deems treasurable. Nothingness is simply the realization that the relative world is illusory since all that is relative only has a contingent and conditional reality. Each perception is, therefore, of the same order as an hallucination. Nonetheless, the ego desires you ignore all this and implores you to make this hallucination into your home. Its goal is that you see the world rather than your mind as the unshakeable bedrock on which to pin all your hopes, faith and investments for Salvation.

You may well ask, how can a false identity ever find itself in this dizzying web of its distorted perceptions? Unless it becomes loving again, it can't and won't. It will just continue to react viscerally to the many dark images, it perceives on the screen before it, and these images serve to reinforce its fears. So, like the dog found dead, in the amusement park, the only solution is to stop barking at the myriad ugly reflections, seen in this hall of mirrors! Only then will you realize, there is nothing to worry about. Fear has no real Cause. All dark and twisted images, showing up in your perception arise from your aggressiveness and the malicious thoughts generated from within your mind. All negative thoughts, moods, and emotions are working in collusion to co-produce this bleak world you see. Hence you feel continuously tormented, victimized and even crucified.

THE ANTIDOTE TO FEAR

The dream of fear, being of your making, has no power over you. It is merely an outward projection of your state of mind. Only by administering the cure, at the level of your mind and thoughts, can the cure be efficacious. The first step then is for you to take back full ownership of the world you see. The next step is for you to practice unconditional love as the antidote. This will erase all inner thoughts of fear. From a worldly perspective, this means you must become forgiving, compassionate, altruistic and understanding of the sad plight of all around you. It is futile attempting to be loving to others if you do not love yourself. One cannot give what one does not have or is unwilling to accept for oneself. Unfortunately, most of us are completely loveless, even to ourselves. We allow our minds and bodies to be mercilessly flogged, annihilated or bent into submission. We continuously endure tasks we abhor and are eager to sign on the dotted line, and so place our lives into sweatshops. Soon we end-up as prostitutes of the psychological and physical realms, and hear the sound of the whip cracking every moment of the day declaring its authority over us. Some cut up and flagellate their bodies in an attempt to eviscerate their inner pain and guilt. Others are on such serious trajectories of self-destruction that they make the kamikaze dive bombers look more like a flight of Dodo birds. Then there is that carnival of vicious and insidious animals in the arena who just love to hate, brutalize and deceive. They will claw desperately at your coat-tails trying to pull you into the gutter. Yes, we must all reach to a new plateau on the horizon of our mind and come the see a different purpose here in the world. One of healing it through love, because the world has long forgotten itself. This approach will regenerate our minds and rid it of all toxic and impure thoughts such all the beliefs in separation and victimization. To becomes fearless, one need not become reckless and psycho. All that is needed is to simply becoming more loving and considerate of others. Fear caused you to lose sight of your divine power and entire dominance over the world of form. Relinquishing this fear, through love, you realize you made the entire show up. Your fear thoughts generate a faulty perception which hangs over ultimate Reality. So does the light-filled and eternally joyous seem to disappear? It is clouded over, by the many dark appearances your mind has made."

FEAR AS THE ONLY NEGATIVE EMOTION

L ama Dorje had certainly put **Fear** into perspective. I probed further asking, "What other toxic emotions should I be concerned with? Surely anger, jealousy, contempt, bitterness, etc. also have a major part to play in keeping us in bondage to the Samsara."

The Lama replied:- "**Fear is the only emotion, with which you need to be concerned.** Fear is like the trunk and roots of that Great Tree Adam ate from in the Holy Garden. All other toxic emotions are like its branches and leaves. Once you eliminate fear, by destroying its roots, all other negative emotions will drop away naturally. Such "toxic emotions" are just many different faces of fear. They are fear witnessed in many different guises and forms and adapted by circumstance. Nonetheless, fear remains the essential content behind them all. Take anger, for example. There can be no anger apart from fear because they are the same illusion. Even though, anger can seem to arise for a million different reasons, the essential content, behind all the reasons is fear. **Anger always manifests from your underlying fear that someone, some event or some "external" situation has power over you.** Maybe you feel someone is standing in the way of your investments or not behaving appropriately based on your demands of them. You have decided to treat them lovelessly and as just an extension of yourself. You see them, as personal property; and there to fulfill all your arbitrary whims and desires.

Perhaps you have a business venture, which you want to succeed. You begin working and horsewhipping your employees to death to achieve certain unrealistic milestones. Consumed by your impractical goal, you become increasingly inconsiderate of the needs of your employees. The tiniest delay or inconvenience can cause you to flip out. You are quick to flame-up and to start launching guilt wars. Once triggered you curse each profusely and savagely reprimand and rebuke any who stand in your way or ask for some tolerance. You enjoy expounding the vast litany of their inabilities, inadequacies and past failures and highlighting how inept, incompetent and undependable they are. Your hostile attitude is silently declaring also that they are not allowed to be out sick or allowed any life-space of their own. Thus, you are attempting to control and leverage the world of perception, to meet your unhealthy, starry-eyed demands. Most often people focus all their anger and hatred on a particular individual. Someone they find threatening or one who looks like an easy mark. They scapegoat this particular individual, as the sole cause of all their ills. He or she becomes their chosen strawman who is to be burned at the stake. This strategy requires carefully chosen targets because one cannot afford to launch an all-out war with all. One needs allies, after all, to carry out and sanctify their dirty deeds. Once this target has been successfully fried, they then select another to take his place.

Anger is not always directed against a person; it can be focused on some external event or situation, perceived as threatening. People often blowup over the tiniest incident or some innocuous event. They blame the economy, government systems, the conspiracy of the rich, social inequalities, the environment and so on, ad nauseum, to justify their rage. They dare not place the source of their rage within and recognize that it is their failure to take responsibility or to set meaningful direction that is the sole cause of their misery. Maybe they are consumed by a host of addictions or vices such as overindulgence, laziness, comfort, procrastination and so forth. Their inner mental landscapes have become overrun with weeds, thorns, pests, and vermin of every possible variety. Even so, they are too indolent to go out and mow the lawn or attend to the garbage and flower gardens. We each forget that we are the only dreamer of our special dream. The world of perception has always been powerless both to perceive and to do. There is no "outside" enemy at the gates. The threatening person, event or situation perceived, represents the projection of our loveless attitudes and irresponsible behaviors. Hell is enlivened into our perception by our unloving and counterproductive thoughts and beliefs."

THE ONLY GOOD DREAM INVESTMENTS

Then I said, "Fear does not always arise simply because some hostile figure is tormenting one's life. It seems fear can also arise from feelings of loss, scarcity, and deprivation. We are fearful whenever we are losing control over some important aspect of our life. Some have panic attacks. A number find they are losing to some addiction. Others sense an existential conspiracy when nothing has gone kindly in years. They can feel jinxed like they have visited the roulette wheel, a dozen times or more and it has always landed on the wrong color. They may be tempted to drop out and just give up. Can you explain how these situations all arise from a lack of love?"

Lama Dorje replied, "As I have already said, fear can also be produced from a perceived loss of power, due to some "external" event or situation. The loss of some treasure, one deems tremendously valuable in the dreamworld, for instance. Such as the loss of one's health, wealth or faculties of mind. Or the passing of someone close. The only good "dream" investments, one can make are in self-understanding and extension of love. If you do so, you will never risk losing your health, wealth or faculties of mind. Self-understanding preserves your sanity and it imparts meaning to your life. It helps you to maintain your health and wellbeing and it returns your mind to Truth. Ill-health, in contrast, arises from endorsing toxic attitudes and bad behaviors. Being unloving, you become self-destructive and start using the body as an end rather than as a means. Love and understanding offer the only genuine wealth found in the dream. Even so, they arise from deep inside your mind. That part of the mind where the ego cannot go. Once one sees the dream nature of existence, one comprehends also that nothing can ever be lost. No one can ever disappear because nothing exists outside the Mind and this Mind, we all eternally share. All other dream investments will turn sour in the end. Once you invest too much in the dream, you will eventually feel the pain because you are mistakenly assigning value to the valueless. Your consequent failures quickly turn into bitterness, cynicism, disenchantment, and despair. No *thing* in the dreamworld ever had any value or could provide any lasting satisfaction. You are merely deceiving yourself by forms you liked. Sooner or later, the lack of substance of each poor investment will become all too evident. One can never quench their thirst by drinking the water from a distant mirage. Nothing real can ever be lost, and only the real holds value. Once, you remember yourself as Love; you will know you are complete. Simply remove all impediments and obstacles, you have interposed before Love, and it will return. Such impediments became erected out of fear. The instant you do so, this dreamworld will fade away like mists before the Sun.

"Likewise," he said "Anxiety is just fear and concern about your future. However, there isn't any future, apart from your present decision. Your future is continuously manufactured, out of your decisions. If your decisions are loving, you will have nothing to fear. If you feel anxiety over some current situation in your life, it is because you are interpreting it fearfully. Thus you are blocking the gift of healing, this unique opportunity has in store for you. Each situation happens so that we can spiritually evolve.nThe dreamer is never at the mercy of his dreams. This only seems the case from the context of illusion, but never in truth. All illusions stand powerless before truth, and once the light is switched on, they rapidly disappear. Reaching to the inner light is the only purpose of these Sutras. It is our mistaken reversal of true cause-and-effect, which alone perpetuate the fearful dream. We feel threatened by illusions generated out of our thoughts. What is this but Self-forgetfulness? Once one purifies their mind through endorsing right understandings, one is transformed into a being of light. Then all illusory effects, arising out of fear disappear from the runway of the mind.

Every moment, you have the Golden opportunity to be reborn. You have the power to make today, the first real day of your life. Any instant, you can be Enlightened. No one has ever been Enlightened, except in the present moment. The Cause of Enlightenment exists outside of time. It is unconditional and not subject to the transient, nor any other vagaries of the relative existence. If Enlightenment were produced by our efforts or by any worldly cause, it would be karmic and subject to the laws of temporal cause-and-effect. Enlightenment can never be an effect, of a cause that is you. It can only ever be discovered or better yet uncovered. The illusory you, that is in a perpetual state of ignorance and fear cannot produce Enlightenment because this self is floundering aimlessly and hopelessly in the dark. Once you remove all ignorance and fear, the light of Enlightenment comes naturally and spontaneously on its own. For its Cause has always been Eternal. When you feel fearful and hounded by illusions, you must recognize quickly, that all illusions are byproducts of fear. Heal the fear through love, and all illusions will disappear.

When you feel fearful that you are losing control of your life, recognize that the only true Mastery of fear is Mastery through Love. It is only fear that ever needs to control. Love

never controls nor manipulates. It simply releases, blesses and appreciates all. It freely gives away all that it IS, and it is ALL.

Love erects no barriers to itself, and it introduces nothing which could function as an impediment to its unconditional giving. In the presence of Love, there no self, and no other. All barriers have disintegrated and melted away. In Love you blend completely with existence and accept the situation as it is. You embrace the other in their totality. It is fear alone, that erects all barriers. So whenever you are feeling fearful, you have allowed yourself to become contracted and darkened in your mind-state. Thus do you appear to inhabit a world of form! One in which the foolish need to exercise tyrannical control can become very intense. Nonetheless, anyone caught in the snares of fear is only ever perpetrating illusions of control. Anyone truly fearless desires no control. Fear always attaches itself to form, for it cannot exist apart from it. It is quick to establish barriers, partitions, and interferences of every possible variety. Nevertheless, since all form is unreal, fear has no reality and is not part of Truth. It remains just the Moloch of the underworld waiting to be unmasked. When you hide away in your cave in this dark world and cower behind so many barriers, you become too afraid to approach your fears directly.

Now let's take envy and jealousy, as examples. These represent your fearful belief of being unjustly deprived of some treasure you find unattainable. Deprived by whom? You may ask since you are the only dreamer of the dream! Its entire contents actions and scripts reflects your thoughts. The presence of envy and jealousy also encapsulate your unwholesome belief that real satisfactions can be received from the external world. Once you believe you can be satisfied by any dream, you lose sight of the cure because the remedy is always inside your thought. This world of scarcity, you are perceiving is a consequence of your mistaken thoughts. You must remember you have always been complete because you Are the formless, timeless, spaceless ever-potent essence of unconditional Love. And this Love contains all and is All.

When you lose sight of your true Identity as Love, bad things begin to happen. Your false identity will generate faulty perceptions. Pandora's box will open, and the dream will seem to take on strange powers and seem to be outside the dreamer's mind. It will bring to you fresh hells and play them out before you. Many strange distortions and fearful images will arise in your sleep. Lost in the mirror of your forgetfulness, you will not recognize such hells are entirely mind-created. For once the dreamer forgets the enormous power of his mind, the dream must react by becoming fearful, vicious and retaliative. Thus, it quickly turns the power he loaned it through projection, against him. It is done unto him, as he believes. The increased presence of fear, then lessens the possibility, that he or she will ever awaken. All that has to happen, to end this dream of fear, is for the dreamer to take back ownership of it. You must recognize that you are fully responsible for all that seems to happen in it. Fully responsible for all your moods, thoughts, circumstances and reactions to them. Creation and Reality are far beyond your making. The dark images on the screen, arising out of your love-lessness reflect your unique contribution. Even though the Reality of All is Love, such Love must be put into action to bring back remembrance of your true nature. Being selfless, altruistic and unconditionally forgiving accomplishes this for you. Thus you heal the dream of its many distortions and frightening aspects and gently awaken the dreamer. Your mind becomes restored to its natural awareness and the recognition of its Eternal Home in Truth. You perceive directly that the world, you fearfully imagined was never there. Dream and dreamer disappear together, allowing true Reality to shine forth unimpeded."

The Lama's discourse had been quite lengthy. I learned much on the primary mechanisms by which we generate our worlds of fear. I understood the relevance of love and right interpretation in dispelling it. All the same, I needed a living example. So I asked Lama Dorje for some illustrative experience of applying the power of right interpretation to cure anger and fear.

He began by saying, "One time, when I was younger I was living in the mountainous regions of South-Western Tibet. I was living full-time in the caves there and searching for lost sacred scrolls during the day. I had developed my yogic intuition, and realized I would soon find some scrolls of tremendous significance in this region. By clearing my mind of all obfuscating thoughts and reaching one-pointedness of mind, I hoped to be able to harness certain '**Remote Viewing Techniques**' to zoom in telescopically on the exact best location to search.

You may, for example, have heard of Karma Lingpa, the fourteenth-century Tertön who found the Bardo Thodol text, also known as *"The Tibetan Book of the Dead."* Well, he was applying this same technique of employing spiritual sight for his discoveries. He had adopted it to find many other important works and treatises, such as the *"Profound Dharma of Self-Liberation through the Intention of the Peaceful and Wrathful Ones."*

Anyway, one day, while I was perched high on this cliff, I saw around fifty fellow Tibetans heading towards the border of Nepal. There comprised about fifteen to twenty families in total. Then about a half hour later, I noticed a consignment of Chinese soldiers following after them, heading with celerity in the same direction. I knew this was not good, but there was little I could do to help. I would never be able to reach these families in time. The only thing I could do from my vantage point was to raise the alarm. So I shouted out loudly, to warn them of the approaching threat. My cries soon echoed across the landscape, but it was all to no avail. Because a half hour or so later, I heard many gunshots ring out. A while later, the Chinese soldiers reemerged with the Tibetan kids, by their sides. They had massacred their parents and now intended to indoctrinate the children and raise them in their Chinese ways.

I was immediately both shattered and disgusted and consumed with such insatiable anger and rage. Not only was I incensed by this senseless act of brutality, but also at the final insult to their parents. These kids would now be raised by alien principles that went against everything their parents stood for. Yes, the soldiers of this regime were using every means possible to squash out our culture and religion. It was not enough apparently, just to steal our lands and homes and destroy all our monasteries. Then I remembered something, my teacher had said to me:

"Truth cannot be destroyed! It is as deathless as the wind, and the Nirvanic Mind itself. Intimidation, along with overt acts of aggression and destruction, reflect but inept reactionary responses of the Samsaric mind. They are knee-jerk reactions, which in turn poison the mind of the aggressor and intimidator alike. Imbuing him with

deep karmic imprints, which keep him bound to the various hells of ignorance. So he continues to suffer for many future ages."

These words restored peace to my mind. It made me realize that the innermost essence of our esoteric teachings could never be destroyed because it was harmonized with ultimate Truth. The pure fragrance embodied in the sutras and shastras represented incontestable and indestructible verities. Verities forged and polished in the fires of illuminating wisdom, and transcendental experience. They shone now, as always, with immaculate radiance. With this soothing interpretation, all anger and fear subsided. Soon it was vanquished completely from my heart. Then it came as a shock to me that I was beginning to feel real compassion for the soldiers instead. I was having the same Motherly feelings for them that I would have for a small child, with a blade or scissors in its hand. And ready to protect and safeguard them against their mindless actions."

This personal vignette of Lama Dorje's had certainly been a revelatory reminiscence. My only thought was that it reminded me, in content at least, of one of Jesus's last inspiring sayings on the cross, "*Father, forgive them; for they know not what they do.*" I was feeling both sad and happy and was quiet for a long while. Sad at the endless torments, miseries, and brutalities, endured and perpetrated by the armies of the sleeping. Happy with the illuminating perspective the Lama had provided.

THE REMOTE VIEWING TECHNIQUE

I wanted to learn more about this *Remote Viewing Technique;* so I asked if he could provide more detail. He responded: "There are many techniques for remembering both the past and future and for reaching to clairvoyance. Some train using systems of mental mnemonics. They apply various ingenious inner cataloging schemes to gain a prodigious memory, and soon have almost eidetic recall. Such recall however is restricted to one's present life experiences. Others use psychoactive substances, such as LSD, Peyote, Psilocybin, Ayahuasca, DMT etc. to open the windows of their mind. This instantly melts away the very rigid, conditioned world of the ego and transports them into the true present. Then the intelligence of the universe streams in all the blocked insights, epiphanies, and superior teleological patterns that their conditioned awareness blocked. A few block out all conscious activities and mental programs, through hypnotism, mantra repetition, and regressive hypnotherapy. These methods, empower the unconscious to communicate its vast storehouse of information. Remote viewing is by far the most natural and powerful technique for revealing hidden material. You do not need to apply ingenious schemes of mental calisthenics or use psychoactive substances. Instead, you simply open the floodgates of your mind and eliminate all distractions. You must be open and receptive to the present and all possibilities. If you are too mentally defensive, tunnel vision and vertical in your thinking it will not work.

To master this technique, you must first prevent all memories and future ambitions from hijacking your thought processes.

Deep breathing exercises can help slow down your thoughts, and bring you into a state of mental quiescence. Next, you need to put a halt to all analytical and reasoning modes of mind. You are not searching for new insights and conceptual knowledge, but looking to stream in intuitional flashes and distinct impressions from the Akashic field. This field permeates the entire world of thought and memory, and it knows where everything is. Send out a request into this greater field, which states (in generic terms, at least) what type of information you are after. This request then functions as a psychic stimulus or probe into the greater field. You are seeking to establish a resonance between it and the greater plenum of your subconscious thought.

Now you must be open and expansive enough to take in the entire world of thought and able to tune-in, rapidly to whatever you desire to learn. All else must be simultaneously screened out. Your mind is to remain calm, unruffled, and quiescent, like a vast sea or lake without any storms. Hence, any undulations of thought excited by the resonance, can be easily detected and distinguished from all background noise. Then silently wait until the images start flooding in. They are now unimpeded by the nominal filters and distractions normally operating in your mind. The excited resonance will feed its information in through the psychic causal link it now shares with your mind. It comes in very raw and jumbled at first and is not easily decoded. Then it begins to take on greater shape and definition. Very distinct impressions will form and your sense indriyas will soon be able to build an intelligent image."

ATTACHMENT

NEAR GAURI KUND

The Lama's insights fascinated me. I said, "It seems that fear could be considered the whole crux of the problem. Once you are free of it, you are released from the bondage of the Samsaric existence."

He responded, "Yes, one completely liberated from fear, through love, is no longer in hell. However many live in extreme trepidation and are possessed by inner emptiness. The weed of fear flourishes wherever there is feelings of futility and notions of vulnerability, just as love blossoms wherever there is whole-ness. Dreamers can develop fears on just about anything one can imagine. They seek to avoid certain unpleasant situations, people or thoughts and thus drop precipitously into reactionary, fear-based, modes of living. Some have quite the catalog of in-built phobias and are mentall besieged by highly distorted forms of fear. Others are complete hypochondriacs. Fear cuts them off sharply from the current of life, and it stunts any chance of authentic growth.

Fear represents everything you want to shut-out, repulse or separate away from and all that you desire to control, limit or eliminate. Often the special object of one's fear cannot be ap-proached directly so one must find an alternative way of ex-punging it. Regrettably, fear is very insidious in its ways. It can enter one's mind in a form that seems most innocent, innocuous, and attractive but soon it poisons the entire mind-system, leav-ing behind a fractured, decimated and psychologically crippled figure. One who represents a complete mockery of the very con-fident, optimistic character that was there before. Many have denied their fears so acutely, that their inner demons remain unconscious and unknown. Their fears are never consciously symbolized in their native, raw, and purest forms. Others are carried over from previous lives. Even so, fear only constitutes only one-half of our hell. The other half is attachment. In truth, fear and attachment exist in a dualistic relationship. One who has conquered fear, through being unconditionally loving does not bother with any foolish worldly attachments. Similarly, one who grasps at nothing becomes free of fear. Attachment repre-sents all you desire, seek or are attracted by. All that you refuse to give up and cling so tenaciously to. Just as insects are attracted to the warm light to have their lives extinguished, so it is with you and the poison of attachment.

There are many worlds of attachment. The worlds of tempta-tion, idol attraction, bodily pleasure, specialness, and worldly power, to name but a few. They all diffuse fragrant, albeit poi-sonous diaphanous mists into the relative existence, as bait to lure you. Attachment causes illusions to proliferate and the om-nipresent, all-powerful, eternal reality to be obfuscated. With attachment your perceptions become dark, and your mind-state defiled. Thus, you become blind to that which IS.

THE THREE LEVELS OF ATTACHMENT

All attachments fall along a spectrum, leading from the gross to the extremely subtle. Generically they all fall into these three categories.

1. Physical

2. Psychological

3. Spiritual

These can be considered the three attachment traps, which bind each to the hell of Samsara. The physical is the realm of our gross attachments. It relates to our bodily concerns and to lower level temptations. The list is vast and includes food, drink, sex, possessions, medications, wealth, various addictions and creature comforts. Even your physical features or newly implanted breasts or veneers can serve as strong attachments. Obviously, there are many snares even at the physical level. Gross attachments automatically generate the world of our gross aversions. You may not see it happening, but once you bite into the poison of duality and preference, your decision making becomes tarnished. Almost immediately you will seek to sidestep certain places, people and uncomfortable situations and to avoid certain foods, exercises, jobs or unpleasant tasks in life."

Then he drew up this simple overviewing diagram that details just some of our attachments at the physical, psychological and spiritual levels.

ATTACHMENTS

Spiritual	Psychological	Physical
Siddhis	Superiority	Pleasure
Spiritual Abilities	Ingenuity & Wit	Wealth
Astral Travels	Worldly Power	Addictions
Enlightenment	Relationships	Ego Toys
Visionary Experiences	Ego Adventures	Sex / Drugs
Intuitions	Professional Ability	Beauty

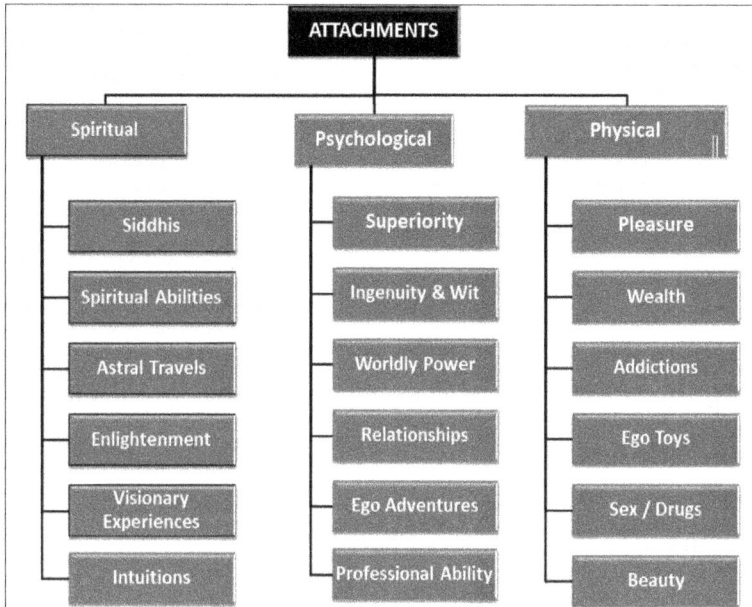

SOME OF OUR PHYSICAL, PSYCHOLOGICAL AND SPIRITUAL AT-
TACHMENTS

He continued, "Yet, even the few who have overcome all snares of physical attachment often still carry powerful psychological or spiritual attachments. Hence, you can see great yogis, ascetics, anchorites, and monks who are no longer overtly worldly or materialistic and yet something seems to be callous and calculating in their attitude. They may have no interest whatsoever in sex, food, possessions or material comforts. Sometimes they can be extremely contemptuous of all fumbling creatures, who remain caught in these fly traps. For sure, these yogis and ascetics are no longer in bondage to the world of things, but they remain in bondage to the world of thoughts. They retain certain superiority complexes and feel they are far more intelligent, witty and disciplined than those around them. They can be caustic in their judgment and often they erect certain false, superficial airs and myths about their powers.

They seek to charm you with their mystique. Be very careful now because these can be some of the greatest snake charmers in existence. An inner toxin still exudes from all their pores. One that speaks to the more discerning its cautionary note that states: *"Something very foul, rotten, rancid and dead lies hidden beneath this mask."*

It is evident; they still have a neediness about them and one they cunningly exploit others to fill. They desire to be apotheosized into special beings or gods for not coveting worldly things. They ravenously crave attention. Their attachment remains; it has just been transposed into another form and migrated to the psychological level.

The psychological is the lower realm of our more subtle attachments. This realm is associated with our self-esteem and ego identity. Here, we are more concerned with how we appear to be, rather than how we Are. Attachments found here includes our merits, degrees, distinctions, qualifications, intellectual abilities and life experiences. It can also include our sense of humor, eccentricities, superiority and false displays of humanitarianism. Yes, whole universes of attachment fly under this banner. We can even be attached to our evil ways, negativity, cynicism, emotional toxicity, psychological dependence, mental inertia, etc. Each of our subtle attachments establishes a subtle aversion, which runs antipodal to it. We are averse, for instance, to anything which may compromise our self-image and lead to a fall from grace in the mind of others. Thus we erect many defenses in the subconscious realm, which serve to protect our personal value. Such defenses can become a strong attachment, once we become heartily invested in them.

Those few who have successfully eradicated all physical and psychological attachments may find themselves still clinging to various spiritual attachments. The spiritual is the most subtle realm of attachment. It includes various mystical and luminary experiences such as Siddhis, psychic-abilities, infallible intuitions, visions and so forth. Thus arises the splendiferous Medusa-faced world of spiritual materialism. These serve as a lighthouse or totem pole around which all witless fools will gather. Many false prophets and spiritual charlatans claim to be spiritually enlightened or to be divine messengers. Then they do idiotic things like expecting their initiates to dress in strange robes and bow before their feet. Many begin hypnotizing human robots to chant songs of adoration, which claim their Master to be a divine avatar, incarnated into the flesh. These spiritually enlightened Masters and Divine Gurus may think they have climbed high up the spiritual ladder. The unabridged truth is they remain hopelessly stuck in the mud of the world because to retain even a single attachment, is to retain the entire world of attachment. One remains in bondage still, and the particular rope that binds one to the totem pole of bondage does not matter."

Lama Dorje had certainly highlighted for me the spectrum of attachment. I was now cognizant of many of the snares to watch for. I said "I have seen this for myself. Recently, while I was in

Rishikesh, I noticed a blind boy and an old man walking up and down this particular dirt road all day. I would pass by them two or three times a day, en route to my hotel. It seemed they were engaged in some form of spiritual penance. Nevertheless, they were so filthy, impoverished and emaciated, that I began to feel a certain sadness. They must be starving, I thought, but had become impartial of their plight due to their superior state of spiritual elevation.

One day while walking by them, I turned around and went to the old man. I then offered him a large sum of rupees so that he and the boy could eat. Our eyes made contact, and what I saw shocked me to my core. There was no peace, serenity or illumination going on behind those bulbs. Instead, there was nothing but immense anger. Behind all the dirt he looked so worldly and calculating. He rejected the cash and rather violently hushed me away. He made me feel like I had just committed some horrible (albeit unspoken) crime. I could not figure it out and surmised that he could have at least taken the cash and given it to the boy or some poor street wanderer. However, he was too obsessed with fulfilling his penance here to do anything noble and altruistic like that."

"Yes," said the Lama "He is a good example of one who has transcended the realm of physical attachment, but remains hopelessly stuck in the realm of spiritual attachment."

Now, I was wondering why more don't see their attachments and the enormous damage each does to their spiritual progress.

The Lama continued, "Everyone can recognize the pervasive damage inflicted by attachment, where there is an addiction.

Addiction is just a very obvious form of attachment. An opioid addict or alcoholic sees with tunnel vision. They relate only to that dimension, where their addiction holds them hostage. This becomes their entire universe of thought. Their modus operandi fast becomes about procuring the next drink or high. This strong pestilential craving consumes all their thought processes and social activities. Thus, so many opportunities become lost or fall through the cracks. Most lose their friends, businesses, careers, health and often mental health. They want to be good and productive people, but the powerful addiction of alcohol sneaks in, to tempt them whenever they feel well. It proceeds to pull all their strings and thus they feel powerless over their lives.

Likewise, hoarders become overly attached to worthless possessions. Soon they become unable to move about their house or apartment but are also too afraid to leave it. Their dwelling becomes infested with insects and vermin. In consequence, they develop serious health issues. Even so, there is no getting through to them. They know the problem but do not want to resolve it and reject any sane solution. Such folk are mercilessly caught in the bone crushing jaws of their particular attachment. Gamblers and shopaholics are examples of those with powerful psychological addictions. We can easily see the devastation wrought upon their loved ones by their reckless overspending. Often, they lose interest in everything else and bring pain to all who help. Like other addicts, the fuller potential for their lives often goes unlived.

We love to crucify all these addicts on our crosses or else burn them in our viper pits. We make them into sacrificial victims to appease the many gods of attachment. We do not readily recognize, that the Mary Poppins types of this world are just as infected by this cruel disease. So they go around sucking their lattes, macchiatos, and ice-creams, and live in their pretty little houses. They have good and respectable jobs and present the glamorous illusion that they are top of everything while secretly condemning the rest of us. Nonetheless, they are just as pervasively poisoned by the evils of attachment. What would our Mary Poppins do without her pretty little house, or latte to suck on? She too has bought into a spectrum of attachments. One that entirely controls her life and shapes all her decisions. The cost of which is her freedom. She does not see how her attachments mold all she thinks and determines all her motivations. She does not recognize how vile a creature she becomes when we even hint at taking away any of her attachments. The truth is we are afraid to declare that the gods of attachment control us all."

This communique had all been very interesting, but I wasn't convinced. I said, "Many experts say addiction is a disease. They do not see it as an attachment. They say there exists an *"Addict Mindset,"* not easily overcome and teach us to feel compassion for addicts."

The Lama continued, "Yes there is a grain of truth in this. Every addict is predisposed to their addiction, in much the same way that a wolf is addicted to eating sheep. Once again one must recognize the enormous power of conditioning, particularly if it is allowed to run unchecked and along those channels, to which one is most susceptible. Behavior does breathe and reinforce similar behaviors. Consequently, self-destructive thought patterns propagate and dig in where they gain the roots to flourish. Thus addictions, which seem physical are often predominantly psychological. Nonetheless, no bottle of Jameson's has ever jumped down any Alcoholic's throat, powered under its own steam. Nor has any self-powered needle every plunged itself unwittingly into an addict's veins.

We have to arrive at the real roots of a problem before we can ever hope to implement a cure. I mentioned before that inner emptiness is the cause of fear. Likewise, it is the cause of all forms of addictive behavior. And what is inner emptiness but the suffocating thought system of the ego! The ego cannot find value in anything, even in itself. From this inner sanctum of depravity, it projects a world of worthlessness. This inner emptiness must find some means of venting or alleviating its pain— the manifestations of which are many. Hence you see all those terrorists and suicide bombers popping up out of the woodwork. All quickly aligning themselves with some insidious, or Machiavellian cause which they remarket as noble and virtuous. This cause is just a proxy in which they seek a license to act out all evil deeds. Inner emptiness is the real Loch Ness Monster roaming in the swamp of their minds, and it is a voracious beast demanding endless meat. Others, as mentioned, sublimate their pain through some addiction. They perceive futility and meaningless everywhere and use their addiction as a screen or else to implement a patchwork solution. After all, the out of mind quickly becomes out of sight. There is no way to stop this madness because the only real cure is the restoration of love into one's heart. With love comes meaning and also understanding."

Lama Dorje had helped me view addictive behavior through a new pair of eyes. Nevertheless, I needed to understand better the significant difference between the inner emptiness of the ego and the Buddhist meaning of emptiness, known as *Shunyata*. So I asked for greater clarity on this.

EGO EMPTINESS VS. SHUNYATA

The inner emptiness of the ego is diametrically opposite to the Buddhist concept of Shunyata. Ego emptiness is real emptiness on the relative level and has no redeeming value or feature. It arises from the ego's lack of existence. The ego cannot know anything because it is not part of Truth. It can simply dazzle, bewitch, tempt and fool those who know not themselves. Hence, it hoodwinks those who doubt their Divine Grandeur and hopes you will settle for false meretricious gifts instead. It proceeds to sell you on empty dreams. Nonetheless, even terrorists have their dreams; dreams of self-aggrandizement through the mindless slaughter and butchery of others. In the end, they too want everyone to taste their inner emptiness. The Buddhist concept of **Shunyata** teaches that the relative world is void. All forms and phenomena are illusions devoid of any real existence. They appear due to distortionary beliefs and are enlivened out of your arbitrary fears and desires. Expunging all such beliefs, the Absolute is witnessed once more. Then you attain to spiritual vision, and this world is perceived no more.

TWO GOLDEN BIRDS

Then Lama Dorje began reciting this quote and asked what it meant.

> **"Like two golden birds, perched on the selfsame tree, Intimate friends the ego and the Self dwell in the same body. The former eats the sweet and sour fruits of the tree of life, while the latter looks on in detachment."**
>
> [The Mundaka Upanishad]

I responded, "It suggests the ego is very worldly in its perspective. It embraces life fully and is always ready to rock and roll. It is not afraid to indulge the good with the bad, the sweet and sour and entertains life in its full capacity. The Self, on the other hand, seems a totally lame-ass bird. Not comprehending the greater world around it, its response is always awkward, stilted and appropriate and more like that of some space-cadet high on acid. So it hovers high in the sky and jets about in its interplanetary propulsion vehicle from which it looks out cluelessly at all below. It remains forever tangled in the nebulous cloud of its perpetual indecision. Being the *'Rain Man'* of birds it is least likely to pick up chicks at the local bar. Its life is an utter failure since it misses out on so many golden opportunities."

Lama Dorje responded "Yes, words can always be ambiguous, as you have admirably demonstrated. The exact same words often impart diverse meanings to different states of mind. In the end, words are not to be trusted. Authentic self-validated experience and inner wisdom alone are to be trusted. You are correct in that the ego is very worldly. To the ego the world is everything. Therefore it worships and idolizes it. In its dim view, there is nothing else out there. As for the rest of your interpretation, it is entirely mistaken since you digested it through an ego state of mind. This quote presents a sincere warning about the dangers and pitfalls of the ego and its world. The ego is that bird that lives by making continuous comparisons. It is quick to classify everything as good or bad, sweet or sour and it is partial, particular, fussy and biased in everything it thinks and perceives. Thus, it establishes around itself a sharply differentiated world where various orders, levels, and hierarchies are everywhere seen and given certain meanings. This deeply partitioned, object-orientated existence of form derives from its misplaced judgments and conceptions and it becomes your trap. So the ego is the goose continuously being cooked in the bottle of the world. It cannot get past the perceived universe because of all the severely warped classification schemes it endorses. It decides arbitrarily what is true or untrue, worthy or unworthy, based on its momentary whims. It judgments arise out of the fleeting mirage of its instantaneous predilections, preferences, and tastes. In its insecurity, it proceeds to accessorize itself with certain belief systems, cultural value systems, codes of etiquette and behavior, and so forth. It even holds fanatical concepts pertaining to what constitutes beauty and truth.

Only the special and remarkable aspects of existence are deemed worthy of its energy, attention and time. These aspects it prizes and esteems and then attempts to cultivate in itself. Thus it falls straight into the hell of vanity and megalomania. These attachments, in turn, give rise to other hells, including jealousy, envy, idol worship, dependency, superiority and so many others. The worthy becomes magnified in its perception while all else are ignored, shunned, actively dismissed or vaporized into non-existence. The ego can only maintain this highly rigid and partialized world picture that embodies so many contrasts and classifications through being superior and judgmental. Judgment is one of its most treasured gods. A blind one who peers myopically out at the world, and quickly labels and condemns everyone and everything. Some it deems attractive and worthwhile, while others it deems unsightly, base and contemptible and therefore to be avoided at all costs. So its world quickly populates with models, celebrities or entrepreneurs while Quasimodos, losers, and degenerates are all stamped with rejection on their butts. The ego is continuously condemning certain aspects of the whole, while futilely grasping at others. Some it wants to trap into its butterfly net. Yes, it is always either licking the boots of others or stepping on them like cockroaches.

What it judges against remains but is now unseen. The blindness of all its judgments, denials and unfair evaluations clouds out True Reality. What it judges against, in turn, judges it. Thus judgment proceeds to tear the world into a gazillion different pieces. Pieces which then seem separate and independent. What emerges is a terrifying depiction; one of a world of so many broken bodies and minds. And so a once beautiful picture explodes into so many scattered pieces of glass. Peeking through these broken pieces of glass, Truth seems so distorted and fragmented that the light, beauty and transcendental meaning of the original picture, is no longer grasped. Presenting this picture, the ego proudly declares Truth to be non-existent. All the same Truth remains unaffected and undiminished by all the ego's ranting, superficial judgments and endless categorizations. They are powerless to influence it in any way. All that is lost through the ego's judgments is awareness of Truth."

Then Lama Dorje said he would provide more detail on how attachment functions to bind and imprison the mind and how it leads to distortion and control.

THE LAW OF ATTACHMENT

"The Law of Attachment amounts to nothing more than: "**Anything you possess; you will become possessed by**." It makes no difference, if your pet attachment is a person, object, belief, ideal, value, credential, experience or so on, the result is always the same. Once you seek to possess anything, immediately it holds power over you. You then lose all lucidity and clearheadedness.

Your partiality to the particular attachment, means you have become invested in the dream. Your world becomes rapidly clouded over, by the dense foggy overlay of your attachments. Now you enter a world of illusions where nothing is known. Illusions rise to block your vision, and you no longer perceive the real. Your attachments then call for more judgments. Wherever judgment is present reality has disappeared.

THE RELATIONSHIP BETWEEN
ATTACHMENT AND DISTORTION

The ego lives a highly dichotomized existence. It is always either accepting or rejecting, flattering or flagellating, including or isolating, licking ass or kicking ass. This turbulent state of mind can find no rest or peace. Storms are always brewing. In its more elevated moments, the ego may seek to understand all the chaos surrounding it, and it may even attempt to resolve some of the world problems. In this mission, it fails strikingly because it is the cause of all these problems. It represents the poisonous, judgmental, divisive mind-state, which generates all states of conflict, tension, and unease. One that leads directly to all forms of misery, sickness and vengeful pursuit. Thus, we see many, in which the flames of anger, rage, hostility, and fear continuously surge up to scorch all on the nearby horizon. They are perpetually simmering or boiling over, like a witch's cauldron. Rapidly oscillating between one caustic mood and another and spraying venomous toxins, into the air around them. The very tone of their being can be very intimidating and results in extreme trepidation, and so you feel your teeth chatter, and organism coming apart. There are many who can kill you with their dagger eyes, and whenever they enter a situation, dark clouds descend. They project their toxic thoughts and emotions onto the screen of the world and look for more suckers to blame. Someone to serve as the patsy for all their problems. They seek vengeance to atone for their inner misery. Numerous callous monsters roam in the dark world of the unconscious, and such vile presences can often be seismically detected, even at large distances. Many do not want to hear the truth about themselves and viscerally react to the large imprints their egos leave in the human jungle. They are in stark denial of whole sections of their lives. Entire decades are found missing like cardboard cutouts. They run ferociously from Truth like a banshee and are fearful that a touch of self-honesty will drive them insane or into untimely obsolescence.

When we become attached or averse to any aspect of our perception, we distort that which IS, into something very twisted. We enter a false world of murky appearances, in which nothing can be distinguished unambiguously and precisely. The Sun of Truth becomes blocked out. The dark clouds are powerless to affect the Sun, but they do obfuscate its light from our awareness. In the dreamworld below roam a throng of unwholesome desires and villainous intentions. Then idle wishes and fantasies leak inward, to commandeer the ship of the mind. The present becomes completely avoided or merely used as a means to serve the profiteering engines of society. The gods of attachment prod us to move onward at full speed; they dare us to fearlessly adventure into our future. They have become restless because their voracious appetites can never be satiated. The present is treasured only to the extent that it fulfills our chosen attachments. That which is efficacious towards accomplishing our ego goals becomes amplified, and all else falls into the gutter. Sadly, what is tiny and insignificant is magnified a million times over and it captures our entire field of attention. In effect then, we experience the present moment solely through the dense and distorted overlay of our wish fulfillment desires. The true majesty and timeless radiance of the present go unnoticed. Caught in the perpetual haze of our many attachments, idols and foolish fantasies, all light becomes occluded. We have found the enemy, captain, and we are they. It is only by recognizing the inherent emptiness of our attachments that we can remove the chains from our mind and escape the dark prison-house."

THE LINK BETWEEN ATTACHMENT AND CONTROL

Lama Dorje seemed to have become quite graphic in his outlay. I did not know what the hell to make of it all. Before I had the chance to ask another question, he fired off again. "Another important dimension to this problem of attachment is that of control. You must ask, at all times *What is the direction of the controlling force that motors my psyche? Is this me in my primordial essence that is calling the shots or the surface me and all its attachments?* Once attachments rise to becloud your mind, it is too late for you will have become too controlling and manipulative to know. You will transform overnight into an intolerant and unimpeachable tyrant and exploit all to reach your desired outcome. Spontaneous anger will be sporadically released whenever life is not going on your pet terms. You will then attempt to justify your outbursts through initiating various games of guilt. As a result, anxiety and stress will be your constant bedfellows. Your self-made stress will induce many toxic chemicals into your body and thought patterns, which will only further exacerbate the situation. Mercilessly bound to your attachments, you will not taste any freedom. You are being horse-whipped around by your petty pleasures and indulgences. Soon you will find, you have become very closed-off to all emerging situations and overly-consumed by poisonous attachments. The anxiety and alienation may become so great that you will lock yourself away into a private world and develop very entrenched perspectives. Then, you will freeze all communication channels, deemed not in your best interests. By creating enemies everywhere, you will lose the opportunity to learn important lessons. Your psyche will be invaded with sickness and self-obsession and no longer be fluid and impartial enough to adapt to the real needs of any given situation. This is because only an unbiased and uninvested mind can truly see and hear. A mind given over to attachment, on the other hand has all its senses defiled. These inner messengers will merely go out as hungry dogs to scavenge the world of perception and bring to its Master all that he wants."

Then I said, "This is all very interesting. We are continually pressured in the West, to invest ourselves wholeheartedly in materialistic comforts. Taught, that the more we possess, the happier we will be. Then summoned to bow down before the many gods of phenomenalism. So we flog ourselves daily at its altars by working jobs we hate. We accumulate all through layers of sweat and turmoil, and by being highly insensitive to others. In the briefest time, we have transformed into the most shallow, extortionist, consumer orientated society; there has ever been. We are brainwashed from the very beginning by a plethora of silly phrases and ridiculous ideologies that circulate in every cranny of our existence. Inane and asinine childish phrases such as, *"The More the Merrier,"* or *"One can never possess too much of a good thing"* or *"The One with the most Toys at the end of Day Wins."* We are culturally indoctrinated with the understanding that all power and victory is gained through pillaging and plundering. Then caressed such naïve euphemisms like: *"It is better to give than to receive."* Is it a wonder that all our utilitarian strategies are geared exclusively towards taking by any and all means possible? Whether this be through cruelty, deception or callous disregard, it seems to make no difference.

When I look around me, I see some of the most miserable folk; the world has ever known. This in spite of the fact that there have never been so many comforts and toys about. Yes, everything is a drive-thru' or available at the push of a button. All seem frantic and anxiety-ridden and devoid of any life-signs or authentic humanity. We are now more like machines that are multithreading or have broken down. Those who possess the max, seem the most wretched and selfish and often the most tragic. It seems we have reached our lowest common denominator and soon become road-kill on the face of the cosmos. Then transform back into a race of genetically impotent creatures and be unable to exhume or resurrect ourselves from our technological and chemically laced graves. Now I am beginning to see at last, just how much our attachments cost us and how much is lost in the process of attaining them. What is your suggested antidote for curing the poison of attachment?"

THE PRACTICE OF NON-ATTACHMENT

The Lama listened intently and then said "The practice of Non-Attachment is the perfect antidote for the poison of attachment. It is one of the most powerful and liberating techniques there is. Once you apply it indiscriminately to all aspects of your life it will completely dehypnotize and free you from the hell of the relative existence. Immediately you will feel happier, more carefree, tranquil and expansive. The secret wisdom is that: '**Whenever we cling, we become imprisoned, when we let go, we are freed.'**

All the same, a technique remains ineffectual words on a page unless you apply it assiduously. Only when you integrate and assimilate it into your life, can you receive its gifts! The application is what counts. This brings great conviction in its power and veracity and transforms into a living philosophy. The practice of non-attachment can bring the real back into your awareness, and dispel all illusions that stand in your way. So instantly removing all that consistently failed that served to darken your mind! How can you ever hope to become calm, centered, and quiescent while remaining tormented and swayed by worthless phantoms? How can you relax, settle down and attune, when you feel yourself under continuous assault by too much information?"

I interceded, "I can see your logic and reasoning but most would find no point to life if they did not chase after certain toys, experiences, or accomplishments. They feel a need to engage in certain ego crusades, or life seems pointless and deadening. Devoid of a meaningful purpose by which to live, we quickly fade.

We need some worthwhile goal or exalted aim to energize and invigorate us and to maintain our sense of will. Rejecting all is like being that witless, standoffish bird of the Self and it is not a recipe that works well for most!"

The Lama responded, "So many suckers and fools think the relative existence is the Kingdom of plenty—the land of honey and nectar. That is why one finds so many human drones hovering about doing a host of meaningless activities just to get certain gifts they treasure. They think, here they have found the cup of life at last. What a joke! The realm of the phenomenal will forever remain, a false and insubstantial realm. It contains nothing of lasting worth. What is perceived is just worthless trinkets that come and go. Transient appearances that never had any value or meaning in the first place. All the accolades, possessions and powers one accumulates come to naught! Moreover, this false world generated out of our attachments functions as a dark cover over true reality. There is nothing in this mind-numbing artifice that even approximates life. That is why you perceive throngs of lonely, desperate, disenchanted and broken souls moping about in it. Just look at them and their mindless ways! It is enough to suck up all hope and vitality! Life belongs to reality, and is found there alone. Our strange notion that we are "living," presents just a mockery of what Life is. All dreamers are just like *'Punch and Judy'* figurines, who mislabel their many puppeteering gyrations for life. All the time their strings are being pulled by the three poisons of Fear, Attachment, and Ignorance."

Then the Lama launched from a slightly different angle saying, "Our flippant and unstable behaviors are many and our mindless chasing after various experiences, insights and accomplishments just represent a vast ego mosaic of quixotic misadventures. There has never been any such thing, as a thing. Objects are illusory mirages arising from our belief distortions. Hence the world remains in a perpetual state of ignorance and confusion. All experiences remain illusory because the relative existence has never been. As for our various merits, they remain just silly badges of honor we pin upon ourselves while walking about comatosed in our sleep. The only accomplishment, we can ever attain in the dream, is to awaken. Also, you do not understand the practice of non-attachment. Non-attachment has nothing to do with rejecting or excluding any experience. It simply means, '**Remain non-attached.**' By all means, you should celebrate all life seems to offer because unless you do so, you will feel unjustly deprived. Then fail to discern, the inherent, underlying emptiness of all experiences here. Where there is nothing real, no lasting pleasure can be had. Therefore, remain non-attached and do not cling. It is attachment and clinging that do all the damage. It is wiser to be always be a state of '*let-go.*'

Perhaps, you may have heard of the Taoist phrase **Wu-Wei**. It means '*No Action,*' and it has much in common with the practice of '*Non-Attachment.*' They are both powerful living philosophies and excellent vehicles to reach the supreme.

WU-WEI

Wu-Wei is the philosophy of living harmoniously with effortless action. It involves living just like a river; never rejecting or clinging to anything. Instead, one embraces all that comes their way. Since every moment, one is prepared to let everything go; they enter a perpetual state of ease and grace and enjoy a supremely restful state in the greater field of action. Being flexible and dynamic one readily accommodates all new changes. By being willing to take the lowest position and attaching no special airs, falsities or grandiosities to some invented persona one remains unconditionally stable in the flux of perpetual motion; immune also to all turbulence going on in the greater world around them. In consequence, they are always at the right level and enjoy endless bliss. One cannot remain in this state of ease while clinging to attachments. Attachments demand strenuous effort and sacrifice. They go against the prevailing current of life and maneuver you out of a state of equilibrium. Spending all your time possessing and accumulating and attempting to rise above others, you swim against the current. Once you have worn yourself out this way, you will float downstream like a corpse.

The curative recipe is be in a total acceptance of life as it is unfolding each and every moment. Always celebrate the current state of affairs and embrace all learning lessons and special gifts it offers. Do not become distracted by superficial ego investments and guilt ploys or you will enter an illusory state of being. Do not ever move from the present moment or you will become dead to Life. The present is the sole portal to the real. Everything real is **Here-Now**! No appearance or illusion can exist outside the present moment. The appearance of any illusions indicates you are not truly present. The practice of non-attachment and harmonious action through inaction will bring you into the real present. It will divest you of all illusions and make you increasingly capacious and light-filled. Then the distorting overlay of obscuring passions and idle wishes will fall away, and new life and possibility will breathe into you.

With time and sincere practice, the tyrannical control of the ego will naturally melt away. Soon you will no longer overflow your banks and spill toxicity onto others. By no longer imposing your arbitrary self-made views and opinions above the real, you begin to witness the realm of pure aliveness and never-ending potentiality. Remaining open, alive and fluid and spontaneously adapting to all emerging situations without any measure of stress or anxiety, you enter a golden palace of restful quiescence and perfect equanimity. You will always be able to respond now appropriately to life as it is. The dead archaic, lifeless skeletons of your past will no longer rise to haunt you or cloud your vision. Your mind-state will become imbued with deep gratitude and you will come to experience existence in all its psychedelic tones and colorations.

RECOGNIZING THE LACK OF SUBSTANCE IN OUR ATTACHMENTS

The practice of non-attachment requires undertaking a rigorous and fearless evaluation of all attachments, one cherishes. You must recognize how each is sandboxing you in or constraining you to very limited modes of operation. Each must recognize the full influence and power their attachments hold in shaping their decisions. Comprehend how their vision has become blocked because of this. Ask what a neutral, impartial and unbiased observer would do in the same circumstance. If you are being thorough and honest, you will discern the enormous impact each of your attachments has on your moods, relationships, personal investments, time-allocations and so forth. Attachments are the mainspring fueling all grievances. Grievances are just the flip side of attachment. There is a dualistic relationship between grievances and attachments because grievances arise whenever attachments remain unfulfilled. You may not be aware of all your grievances. Each day, your mind attempts to navigate a very narrow path through a minefield of hundreds (if not thousands) of grievances.

Grievances affect the quality of your life profusely. They saturate your mind with negative thinking pattern and induces toxic moods. Each operates as a hindrance which can wear you down. Whenever you are feeling unhappy and disturbed, you can be sure some grievance video is playing itself out in your head. You may be feeling mild irritation or else extreme anxiety, dread or fear. The ego is automatically programmed to hold grievances against anyone, anything or any situation that seems to stand in its way. When you no longer treasure any attachments, an amazing healing transformation occurs. All grievances and darkened mind-states disappear, and you awake to reality. It is critical that you ask yourself the following two questions from time-to-time.

1. **What Am I attached to?**

2. **Why Am I attached to it?**

In other words, what outstanding offering are your attachments furnishing that you would gladly sacrifice your peace for them? Why are you so willing to become their victim? Does this attachment promise pseudo-safety and protection or just an inflated sense of self-worth? Is it loaning to you temporary satiation of the body or mind, while dulling your resolve? Is it demanding you sacrifice your present for a greater tomorrow? Presenting to you increased power, flexibility or freedom? A dream of immense wealth, for example. Wealth seems to provide certain gifts but the freedom and power it extends can only bring you so far. The majority of those who are wealthy are incredibly miserable. It is evident, that their wealth has made them slaves of superficial toys or made them the victims of worldly parasites, leaches, and sketchy characters. Only, for a wise few has wealth brought any worthwhile freedom! *One's purchasing power is worthless, if one's mind remains plagued by illusions and under the dominion of the ego.* Unless your freedom of decision is exercised judiciously, it will just serve to increase your slavery! There is nothing wrong with wealth and the worldly pleasures it offers. It may indeed buy a better form of misery, but attachment to its offerings, often brings overindulgence, eccentricity, sloth, need of increased security, predacious personalities and '*good-time friends*,' etc. It can also lead to broken friendships, a lack of responsibility and a loss of appreciation for the simpler things in life.

Ask yourself: What Happens if all my Dreams come True? What Then?

It makes no difference what your special dream may be! You may dream of being a great musician, actress, writer, president, CEO, athlete or something else entirely. However, once you accomplish it, you are in for a very rude awakening because you will find, you can still only wear one set of clothes at a time, sleep in one bed, and eat only so much before getting full. How many times is an Olympian going to look at his or her gold medals before getting bored? What else can they do but cash them in! The medal isn't exactly going to jump out of its box and give them oral sex, nor is it worth a lot financially. And another annoying fact—everywhere you go, there you are! The inner landscape won't change much and in any meaningful way unless you do. You will still experience the world of Art, Music, Adventure, Science, Entrepreneurship or whatever else in much the same way as before. You are still the same old carcass floating downstream, caught in the vicious trap of your toxic persona. The painted veil of your physical appearance and superficial understandings hasn't brought you any closer to the truth.

Often, the power of your celebrity or fame will work against you. It can foment immense jealousy in others and turn you into the focal point of hate. You may have noticed for example that Barrack Obama became a lot grayer once he took over the helm at the White House. It was if he underwent some accelerated life-testing/aging at some covert military command base. Being president or famous is like asking to be daily hounded and beaten-up. It would be far easier to visit the local S&M club and get it all over with in a single night. You will also attract new friends who are just there for your wealth or celebrity. They will not see the inner you, nor do they care to know because they are just parasitically living off the fallout on the Jetstream of your success.

When you examine the end purpose of your attachments, you find them devoid of all any meaningful content. None can deliver the unconditional peace and joy you seek! Nor the essential existential understanding, that frees you unconditionally from the relative world. Each offering is more like a mirage in the desert, that will disappear with time. In the end, you will be left all the more hollow, desiccated and empty within!

Discriminating reason teaches that anything temporal is without all value because what does not last forever is not genuinely there. The temporal cannot satisfy. It can only offer the illusion of satisfaction. The transient is conditional and relative and dependent on a host of other illusions to reinforce its pseudo-reality. Tasting from the cup of temporary happiness invites the cup of temporary pain to your lips. If you are unwilling to see the undeniable truth in this, it is because you have chosen to deceive yourself. One cannot gain happiness through illusions. Esteeming them, one always pays the price. The impermanent has not real gifts to give. It matters not, what splendiferous forms they take, nor how many jewels seems to glitter and shine from them. Beneath the highly polished veneer of all idols, possessions or merits you seek, lies nothing. Whatever does not hold true for all time, is not true at any time. The conditionally true is untrue. Conditional truth is contingent. It depends on the specific framework and context, in which it is embedded to prop itself up. It needs illusory conditions so that it can seem to exist and hold value. Choosing to worship illusions made of dust causes you to lose sight of the Absolute, exceedingly pure and unconditional. Thus, you depart from the realm of the eternally valid which is the only real Home of lasting satisfactions!"

Then I asked Lama Dorje if he could illustrate. He said, "Take steam, for example! Its conditional reality is contingent on boiling water to 100°C and having an atmospheric pressure of 1 bar. Remove the heat source, or increase the pressure and it will turn back into water or ice. So it is also with consciousness. It only becomes vaporous when you apply the heat of true understanding and reach the right psychological temperature. Freeze it through the impurity of false understandings, and it turns into ice. Then you appear to reenter the frozen dark world of the object-orientated existence. A dull static universe, in which everything seems separate from everything else.

Truth lasts forever; its value is infinite and beyond all measure. The untrue is worthless because its offerings are temporary, conditional, relativistic and karmic. Any gift you appear to receive from illusion was a compensation for past efforts and good deeds. It will need to be paid back in full, leaving you with a net sum of zero. Attachments are idols! They tantalize and bedazzle only those who lack knowledge and insight. You are simply being blinded and deluded by forms, you like and overlooking underlying content. An empty box, even if wrapped beautifully is not a true gift. Do not invest yourself in empty boxes! Rather

use the dynamo of your introspection, reason and right understanding to penetrate past the inherent emptiness of all your
attachments. Then all fall naturally away without any effort or
strain."

I spent the next week or so pondering deeply on the numerous
attachments; I had nurtured in the past. Reflecting on how each
had let me down or proved insubstantial It did not make a difference if it was a relationship, a career, an adventure, or some
position of prestige. Either they came to an abrupt end or did
not meet expectations. All I was left with was a slew of watered-
down memories. Not a good ROI for so much effort invested. In
the end, the priceless gem of my naked essence evaded me until
one day, I transcended.

My being and understanding were all I had. Worldly knowledge
had done nothing to augment me in any way. Instead, it had tarnished and blocked me, at every step. Certainly, I had enjoyed
many interesting and novel experiences, but Enlightenment was
the only real gem, I cared to keep in my top pocket.

IGNORANCE / SELF-FORGETFULNESS

The next time we met, Lama Dorje introduced the last of the three poisons. He said, "**The third poison is ignorance**. It has also been called **Delusion** and **Self-Forgetfulness**. The particular words or terminology used are unimportant because the essential content remains the same. Those under the spell of ignorance, fall into the realm of illusion and they quickly become dispirited and myopic. They are delusional because they perceive through the tenebrous haze of a heavily distorted perception. Such distortions arise from their judgments, fears, and desires. They do not possess the naked and unblemished perceptive capability that vision alone offers. In their deep delusional states, they chase after any mind-dream currently on the radar just as a dog will chase endlessly after a stick or a ball, or even its tail.

They think this latest mind-dream is their hot ticket to greatness, happiness, and release. Then a while later you find their heads are in the gutter once again. Just like goldfish, they are content to swim back-and-forth endlessly in the bowl of the relative existence. They never recognize that the view hasn't fundamentally changed. They cannot comprehend that their dreams can never provide any lasting worth and that all conditional happiness induces an equal amount of pain. They never adopt an entirely different approach and never grasp through reason, insight, and intuition that unconditional happiness is available only in an entirely different direction. All bliss is contingent on going within and shining away one's state of ignorance. Instead, they cling to old dead habits and patterns and primitive solutions proven not to work. They react viscerally against all meaningful change and fail to understand that all healing and liberation, depends intimately on pure thought and judicious belief. Sadly, they will not take the space odyssey and adventure within to eradicate all that is found wanting there."

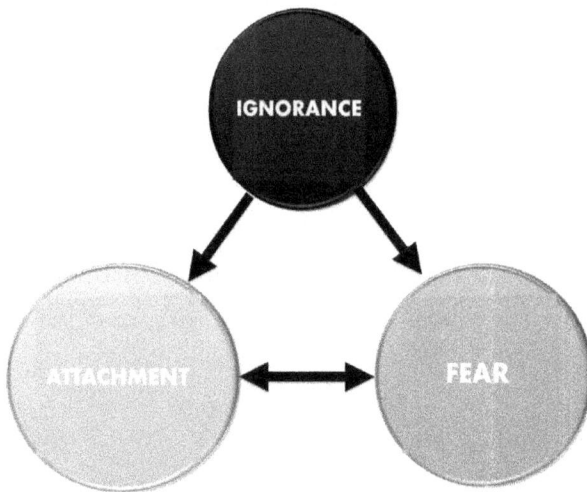

IGNORANCE, ATTACHMENT, FEAR TRIAD

Once the mind fell into its state of ignorance, the realms of fear and attachment arose. For this reason, ignorance is considered the first of the three poisons. It arose when we used our free will to believe the untrue. Doing so, we became blinded to Truth. Out of our mistaken beliefs, illusions quickly proliferated to cloud out the light of vision. Nothing has been known unambiguously since. Instead, in the relative existence, illusions seem on a parity with Truth. Once ignorance entered the mind, we became

Sharon Moriarty

partial and judgmental. Out of this partiality arose the realms of attachment and revulsion. What the mind judged and rejected became the source of our fears. Fear and attachment continue to reinforce one another and are just two sides of the same coin.

Fear is synonymous with the ego-self and the mind of separation. The ego seeks to protect itself from Truth by implementing a vast network of defenses. These defenses form a cloud around the mind which keep the light out. These thought processes constitute our lower mind, and they are interfused with all sorts of unrealities. The ego interprets defenses, as its only real protection against the many enemies it perceives. Even so, these barricades it continuously erects prevent our ignorance from ever been dispelled. They work against our best interests and spiritual healing. As long as they remain, the mind seems to find itself hermetically sealed in, to the realms of attachment, delusion, and fear. This is a dark place where so much chaos, confusion, and contradictions reign. So it engages various mindless schemes for its protection, that are guaranteed not to work. Meanwhile, it hunts about for any idle scraps or trophies; it can rescue from the dream. It takes all it plunders back to its bodily cave. These scraps and trinkets represent all it sees worth salvaging in the dream. Having lost all clarity and wisdom, it becomes very sleepy and dull. It thinks it has left its original Home. Nonetheless, it cannot find the healing elixir or cure which will guide it back to safety."

NIRVANA

WISDOM

TRANSCENDENCE, FORMLESSNESS

NON-DUALISM, SUPRA-CONCEPTUAL

EGOLESSNESS, FEARLESSNESS

HEALTH, RADIANCE, BLISS

NON-ATTACHMENT, PURIFICATION

COMPASSION, FORGIVENESS, DEFENSELESSNESS, BODHISATTVA VOWS

RIGHT UNDERSTANDING, MEDITATION, DHARMA PRACTICE

ASCENT

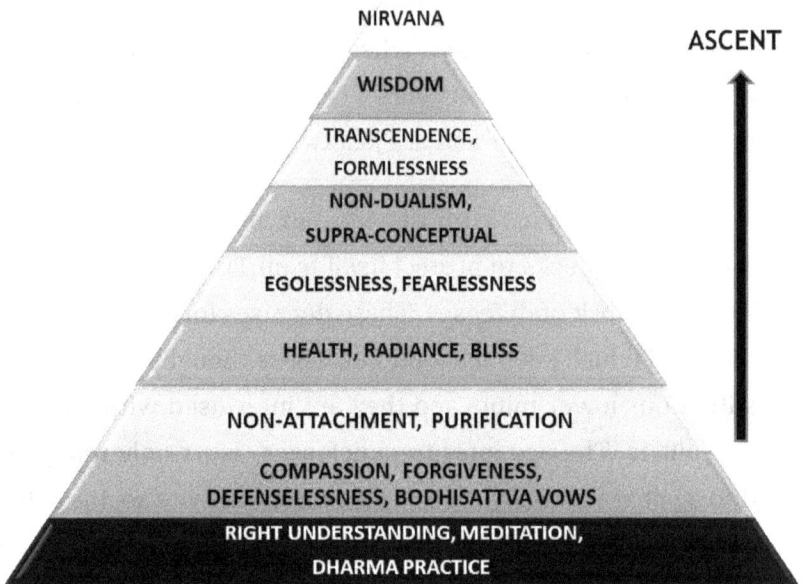

THE PYRAMID OF OUR FALL, THROUGH IGNORANCE

Then Lama Dorje drew this pyramid, to explain some of the cause-and-effect relationships which lead to the descent into darkness. They are the only reason why the dreaming mind continues to experience the cycles of death and rebirth. Then he proceeded to explain the chain of causality involved in more detail.

1. Ignorance first gave birth to Consciousness and Spacetime

All experience of consciousness did not exist before ignorance entered the mind. Once this poison became introduced, Whole-Mind seemed to split up into the dyad of consciousness and perception. Ignorance produced the dualistic realm known as the relative existence. Perception is the second half of this split, and it includes the artifice of spacetime. Consciousness is not whole since it always implies some degree of separation. It introduces distance between the conceiver and the objects of his conception. None of this reflects the pure undifferentiated and transcendent realm, known as Nirvana. Only Whole-Mind is 100% pure. Being purged of all wrong beliefs it alone can experience Nirvana.

2. Out of Consciousness arose Forms, Symbols, Concepts, and Percepts

Out of the pseudo-separated modality, known as consciousness, various forms and percepts started appearing. In the realm of the seeming "outer," legions of images became carved out of un-differentiated Oneness. The mind needed these crutches to reach true understanding once more. Once this realm of false-ness and pseudo-separation became established, the mind be-gan diligently assigning various attributes and features to all the separate things it perceived. From these it derived all its concepts, relative knowledge, and symbolic understanding. Collectively, these composite the realm of inner mental objects.

3. From Form and Symbolic Thinking Arose the Body, The Ego, and Sensation

The body is just one of many symbols that arose from name and form. The mind then projected sensation into the body and the greater world around it. Thus, mind seemed to split into the six sense indriyas that projected the world. The "split" mind mistakenly began to think that the source of sensation was outside and produced by an external universe of things. So it entered a private hallucination and started becoming reactive to this world. Meanwhile, it chose the body as its new home and began to identify with the ego. The ego was never part of Reality and merely represents the aggregate of all unreal thoughts and false understandings that arise in our deeply separated mind-state.

4. Sensation and the Ego, in turn, give rise to our numerous Attachments, Desires, and Fears

Once mind was fooled into believing the world the senses depicted was real, it became firmly dream identified. Soon it took itself to be an object in this sense generated world. It conceived that mind was a mere product of matter. Over time it began to feel fully encapsulated in the body and the world so these apparitions gained increased traction and definition in mind. They were maintained further through the power of conditioned belief. Foolishly chasing after numerous sense objects gave rise to our many attachments and desires. Meanwhile, that which our sense body felt threatened by generated the realm of our fears.

5. The mind then began experiencing the flip Side of Sensation and the Ego, which is Sickness, Suffering, and Loss

Over time, the body and the world became deep-rooted beliefs of the mind. We began to feel deeply entrenched in this illusory world. We thought we could have the good without the bad, the sweet without the sour and so forth. But this is impossible. We must always receive, what is on the flip side of the coin. Hence, we began to experience the world of sickness, suffering, and loss! The ego convinced us that we could extort pleasure without receiving any pain and that we could gain through another's loss. This is impossible since they are no "others." There is just a single unified field to life, and it possesses no boundaries.

6. Once the mind experiences Suffering and Loss; it became Judgmental and Defensive; Thus reinforcing its Original Fears.

Feeling miserable, sick and isolated we become even more fearful and ambitious to safeguard the little that we possess. We start slashing the sword of judgment aimlessly about to protect ourselves and our tiny little fiefdoms in the sand. We begin using it mercilessly to justify all attacks on those whom we see as separate. We place all idols and dream tokens we plunder into our treasure chest. We begin erecting numerous defensive strategies to keep all interpreted as fearful or repulsive out.

7. Finally Worn Down and Disenchanted, the Mind experiences the illusion of Death, once more.

Eventually, immensely fatigued and disenchanted by our dream of worldly identification, we appear to die in the dream. Such is our ego's way last-ditch solution for solving all our problems. It doesn't possess any real solutions and has always been the source of these problems. Feeling powerless, bored and yet unwilling to heal, it chooses death for us. However since our mind-state remains unchanged at a fundamental level, we must continuously appear to be reborn until we heal ourselves of ignorance.

Mind in its pure essence remains deathless, timeless and formless. It cannot really be destroyed or disappear from existence. After all, it is the sovereign divinity that powers all universes. Only the body appears to die and yet the body itself is an illusion generated by the mind. You will never see yourself die because you are the deathless spirit that projects the entire show. The only solution then is for you to purge all wrong understandings and wake-up. Then the dark ego dream of ignorance come to an end and Truth is welcomed back. You experience the undefiled awareness, in which the self-resplendent nature of Truth alone shines!"

The Lama had certainly connected the dots in my mind. I had never understood, how intricate and powerfully interpenetrated it all was. Now, I understood pellucidly how all apparent death, was not due to sickness or illness, or chemical imbalances but solely due to ignorance. All forms of sickness and illness were just symptoms projected into the body by a mind that refuses to heal itself. A mind afraid of truth employs sickness as a defense against it. Such a mind willingly endorses all pernicious ideologies of the ego. Eventually, it gets bored of all its tiresome games and endless circling and chooses death once more.

THE ANTIDOTE FOR IGNORANCE

Then I asked Lama Dorje, "**What is the cure for igno-rance?**" "The only cure for ignorance," he said "is true un-derstanding. This is the potent antidote that automatically dis-pels all false beliefs. Unconditional love cures fear, non-attachment eradicates attachment, and true understanding eliminates ignorance. This leads automatically to right actions and non-destructive behaviors. As a result, one starts becoming more compassionate and altruistic. One starts recognizing; we are all limbs of the selfsame body—the One-Mind. Once we put true understanding into practice, we become freed and de-tached from the world of appearances. Then the "split-mind" of the ego which continuously grasps and attacks, judges and con-demns starts to lose strength and disappear. As mental purity increases, one starts becoming light-filled.

Released from the poison of attachment and the numerous stresses of the world, one starts experiencing true health and bliss. All conflicts melt away and hoarding stops because these were the outcome of attachment and dream investment. Grasp-ing to nothing and being unconditionally loving one becomes fearless. Dispelling fear, our perception starts running luminous because fear and attachment no longer distort it. I know it sounds simple, but true understanding has become deeply ob-scured to most. We do not know anymore, how to ask the right questions, nor how to meditate. We do not understand true Cause-and-Effect nor probe deeply enough into the true meta-physical basis of existence. We examine only surfaces and ap-pearances and have become obsessed with the phenomenal world. As a result, most true Cause-and-Effect relationships have gone unnoticed are seen as reversed.

For example, as I mentioned before many believe the mind and consciousness to be epiphenomena of matter. As a result, they see external remedies, as the cure for all their afflictions. They fail to comprehend the full power of their mind and see that it alone is what cures them; that all medications are just placebos and proxies. Placebos to which we attach enormous healing beliefs. We imagine substances retain some magical properties that are apart from the mind. Various psychoses and neuroses are therefore allowed to develop unchecked. We no longer take personal responsibility but seek to medicate these conditions out of existence. The intrinsic health and sanity of our mind we atrophy and annihilate when we place lend our faith to outer cures. Yes, many false notions percolate in our minds. We take the body, the universe and the spacetime existence to be real. We fail to see that they are merely conceptual meta-realities driven and projected from our split-mind. Spacetime is a false artifice, and it is merely presenting us with a learning arena to heal our pervasive state of ignorance."

Then he drew another diagram to help me better understand and began to explain it, saying: "Just as there is the descent pyramid into death and rebirth, there is an ascent pyramid which leads our of ignorance to Nirvana and Eternal life. Here are the causal relationships involved.

NIRVANA

ASCENT

WISDOM

TRANSCENDENCE, FORMLESSNESS

NON-DUALISM, SUPRA-CONCEPTUAL

EGOLESSNESS, FEARLESSNESS

HEALTH, RADIANCE, BLISS

NON-ATTACHMENT, PURIFICATION

COMPASSION, FORGIVENESS, DEFENSELESSNESS, BODHISATTVA VOWS

RIGHT UNDERSTANDING, MEDITATION, DHARMA PRACTICE

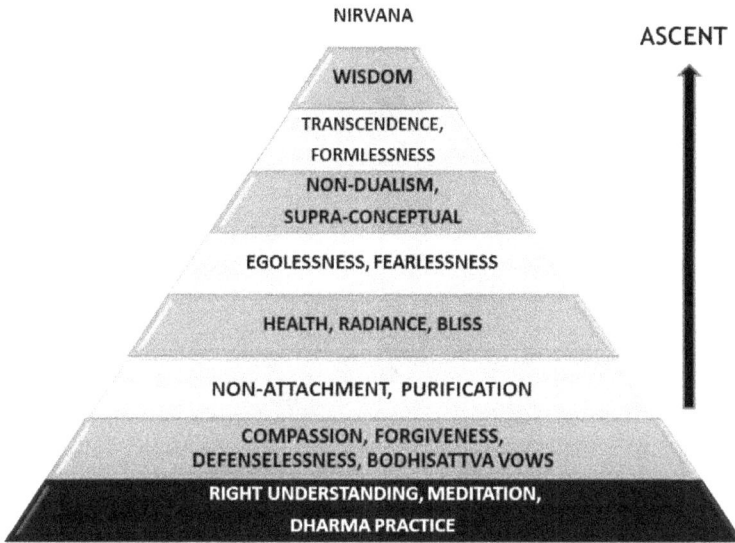

THE PYRAMID OF OUR ASCENT, FROM IGNORANCE TO WISDOM

1. True Understanding Leads to Compassion and Forgiveness.

Applying introspection, reason and meditative practice, we attain to genuine insight. We perceive we are not separate from others, or from the world around us, any more than a tree or its fruit is separate from the soil below it. Recognizing how our thoughts, attitudes, and behaviors affect "others," we begin to become more compassionate and forgiving.

2. Altruism and Defenselessness Lead to Non-Attachment and Increased Purification.

Having recognized (intellectually at least) our fundamental unity, we start dropping all ego barricades and defenses. We stop hoarding things and putting others down. We begin to put into practice the Bodhisattva vows and recognize that all healing is a shared and collaborative venture.

3. Non-Attachment Brings Health and Bliss

Dropping our defenses and attachments our health and state of bliss increase. We no longer feel imprisoned in the island fortress of our bodies, and surrounded by its barrage of futile defenses. Healing energy begins to flow again within us along with a new spirit of optimism. As we come into greater contact and communion with our true Self, we begin to taste profound states of ecstasy.

4. Our Greatly Improved well-being Automatically Eradicates Fear and Leads to Egoless Behaviors

With our health and sanity restored, we become fearless and begin to reap the rewards of our egoless behaviors. In fact, we come to recognize the entire unreality of the ego and comprehend that it merely represented a network of false beliefs and ideologies that we arbitrarily cherished in our "Separated" state. These strange ideations made us feel alone and hopelessly fenced in, within a mound of clay. Now we understand this lone voice was the cause of all our confusion. Being partial and judgmental, it covered our eyes with impure thoughts that made it impossible to see. These alone kept us a seeming prisoner in the relative existence.

This voice was only listened to because of the stark and overbearing presence of fear. Our distorted perceptions magnified the unreal. Now finally this dark world, cookie-cut from all our special attachments and fears is being released. We do not want its petty gifts anymore, for we realize their immense cost.

5. As our Mind increases in Purity. All Boundaries of the Dualistic Universe Start to Fall Away

Our attachments and fears had caused the real and transcendent to go unnoticed. Consequently the real was driven from our perception by our denial and foolish obsessions. As the purity of our mind increases, all boundaries start to dissolve, and all dualistic thought patterns begin to be healed. We see that all concepts and forms pertained to the ego world of things. They represented a world which the ego wanted to make true and amounted to nothing but artificial entities and had no substance at their core.

6. As all Pseudo-separations Dissolve, we enter the Transcendent Realm of Formlessness

As we progress in our practice, we start seeing through all dualities and arriving at the supra-conceptual understanding of affairs. Our concepts become more expansive and light-filled, and we recognize they are merely symbolic representations and not true reality itself. Now we feel safe to go beyond them and arrive at the transcendent realm of formlessness.

7. Merged with the Oneness, we Migrate beyond the scope of Relative Knowledge and Reach to the Wisdom of the Absolute

Once we resolve all dualities and dispossess all false egoic knowledge, we reach to wisdom. Then the inner light explodes outwards, and both inner and outer worlds collide and merge. We see the relative existence was never really there and that it merely functioned as a veil over the transcendent realm of the Absolute.

8. Finally having Attained Complete Purification of Mind, We disappear from the Relative Existence and enter the pure non-differentiated Realm of Nirvana

Then I asked, "Does one need to eliminate the three poisons to escape the relative existence?"

ABSOLUTE BODHICITTA

"Excellent question!", the Lama responded. "In classical systems, one needs to cover all bases to make progress because any weakness will immediately foil one's effort. However, Truth is Holistic, and so your success depends only on the quality, depth, and sincerity of your application. The classical worldly mind always thinks in magnitudes. It strategizes and assaults from many directions at once. Thus it wears itself down. The sly man knows how to think in completely different dimensions. He will, surmount or circumvent a wall or drill through in just a tiny section. He will not waste himself trying to destroy the entire wall to advance.

Possessing full conviction in one true understanding is enough to liberate your mind. Your faith then functions magically to release you from the entire universe of falsities. It uses the law of mind and operates as a magic healing touchstone to shine all apparitions away. Once you penetrate through to the core of a single false belief, you will rapidly be able to generalize your understanding to all aspects of your perception. Thus, you expose the inherent emptiness of all illusions.

For instance, let's take the objective world and the body, as examples. The ego would have you believe that these are separate and independent entities. The discriminating mind, in contrast, recognizes that they are dualistically intertwined and conclusively interdependent. In summary, they are merely two faces of the same root illusion because if you did not possess a body, you would no longer experience the world. Similarly, once the world is known as void, the body loses all purpose and disappears. The light of transcendent understanding shines them both away, and it dawns on you that were always just phantoms of consciousness, arising out of ignorance. Then you know also that nothing was ever outside, nor within.

This path of reaching to awareness of truth, through removing ignorance, is called the path of emptiness (or *Shunyata*). On this sacred journey, you unburden yourself of all false beliefs. Doing so, you reach to wisdom and penetrate directly to the ultimate Reality which is beyond all perception. Making progress on this path involves refusing to affirm nonsense beliefs. This refuse heap includes all unsubstantiated gossip and propaganda given to you by the world and anything you have not known firsthand. Being no longer hoodwinked or willing to vouch for the arbitrary opinions of others, your intelligence intensifies and develops in subtlety and acuteness. Meanwhile, your mind becomes more flexible and expansive. As your world opens up to accommodate new thought-streams, you may sincerely believe you are becoming less articulate and more uncertain by the day. As you uncover the great deception, nothing will seem clearcut anymore. Instead, you will feel as if your world is falling apart and losing all its boundaries. You are now beginning to recognize all knowledge here is pseudo.

The ego, in polar opposition, can be very self-assured. Being limited to very narrow-banded vistas of thought, it is quick to display its erudition. Thus, it puts on a show of certainty in the hope that you will continue to trust it. Of course, it is very confident in all its beliefs because it never really questions them. This theatrical flop only satisfies those who are happy to remain deluded. As you approach the transcendent realm, you can know only one thing for sure—*"that you know nothing at all."* Yes! One must be stripped bare before one can enter the gates of timeless wisdom.

Then one day, the entire belief system that nourishes the relative world, collapses like a game of dominoes and you are left standing face-to-face with naked truth. Now you comprehend that there is nothing to be seen because this world was a mirage arising from your mistaken beliefs. The new Knowledge you encounter is nonsymbolic, and it cannot be known consciously, only superconsciously and viscerally. Consciousness is always impure to some extent since all concepts and forms represent limitations. Now you reach the knowing mind itself, and it is potent beyond measure and also formless. You have come full circle and awoken from your sleep in the Holy Garden. You no longer ask any foolish questions because the serpent of relative knowledge has finally swallowed its tail.

Once one penetrates through a single duality, one easily sees through them all. There comes a day when no false understanding is left standing in your way. No appearance is strong enough to withstand the light of your mind. You find yourself timelessly immersed in the realm of the eternal and undifferentiated. You laugh because you recognize you have always been immersed in Truth. There was no 'where' else to go, and it was impossible to disconnect from the Source of Creation—only in dreams. It was ignorance which had fabricated the turbulent sea of illusory partitions and forms seen all around you. Even so, it was a sea with no real substance and merely represented fluctuations of the mind, blown into different definite shapes by the winds of ignorance. Such shapes and forms are no longer perceived by the awakened mind.

This path of reaching to Truth, through eliminating ignorance, is known as **Absolute Bodhicitta** (Buddha-Consciousness). It works extremely well for rational, reasoning and intelligent minds. For those who hold no sacred cows but are ready to question genuinely. It is favorable for those undeceiving beings who are eager to take the deep dive. It can be considered the *soup-du-jour* of Spiritual paths for those comfortable living in the head, rather than in the heart. For those who excel in demonstrating compassion and forgiveness, there are other paths."

Then he asked me if I had any insights to share since I had reached to Absolute Bodhicitta, through the path of emptiness.

SOME MYTHS OF ENLIGHTENMENT

I said, "Yes, I have a few things to add. Firstly there is a powerful misconception that circulates, that tacitly whispers: *'Once you reach Enlightenment, you attain infinite wisdom and are now powerful over gods and men.'* The myth spreads, that you now conscious of all events going on in the phenomenal world at any given instant. You can therefore predict the future value of any stock and go to Vegas and make a killing. Or else visit hospitals and work miracles to cure the ailing and so forth.

What a joke! Since sickness and the body are themselves now seen to be unreal, what is there to heal? Only the mind can be healed and only ever of ignorance. It is this that releases all illusions. What I immediately comprehended in no uncertain terms, was that all sickness and misery were self-created. Such appearances were mental miscreations arising due to our defiling obscurations. The sick were akin to babies peeing in their diapers and then crying out for help. Once, I reached the knowledge of the ultimate; I was utterly bewildered. It was as if, I had unwittingly parted the curtains of the great Oz, to find with great dismay and horror that there was nothing to be attained or known. In contrast, all that I had known before was lost or yanked away and seen as an empty dream. Yes, I had transcended the realm of ignorance and appearances. However, nothing new was imparted that was not always freely available. I could see and understand most lucidly now; that was the only difference. I had been cured of my blindness and was no longer contaminated by erroneous conceptions and perceptions. All became luminous and enlivened and seen in its true essence. All boundaries and stratifications were gone. Yes, I knew that nothing perceived was ultimately real and the perceiver had also become entirely MIA. Now I understand why I could never understand anything before. Illusions can't ever be understood. All are empty of substance and devoid of meaning. It was futile to demand more from them than they could ever give. They depended intimately on other illusions to give them all their pseudo-meanings and substance. It was all like a vast magic show and a great deception. Sold to all those witless beings, who buy-in to hallucinations and trade them with those of their friends at weekends.

Another myth was that of infinite wisdom. There is no such thing, as we conventionally understand it because wisdom is void of all degrees and levels. It cannot be possessed but only lived through. Being supremely pure it simply sees and comprehends without any hint of distortion. Now I found myself completed subsumed in it. Lost of all meaningful direction, as if drugged. All worldly knowledge became like soap bubbles; flimsy and ethereal. More like diaphanous mists that would collapse in a splash before it could have an impact. Yes, I had reached the seat of authentic Being and penetrated through all illusions. Receiving the so-called gifts of wisdom, I saw it was an empty box; all empowerment and growth came from no longer being fooled by the false. Wisdom was '*the knowing mind*' itself. There would never be any knower in the conventional sense who could know anything or possess any object of knowledge. Everything had disappeared since the *within* and *without* had fused into One. This Oneness was devoid of all objects, forms, phenomena, beings, and attributes. It was transcendent of all concepts, percepts, sensations, and understandings that the relative mind entertains. It could not be symbolized or understood but would remain forever unknowable, ungraspable, fathomless and recondite. This Oneness was likewise timeless, spaceless and had no other cause. In fact, it seemed to do nothing at all. Even so, all became created and manifested out of is majestic grandeur. Its ever-potent purity was the seed powering limitless universes—both seen and unseen. This Oneness had two off-spring—Wisdom and Unconditional Love and by these two faces alone, could it be known!

I also realized that there were many celestial kingdoms, beyond the phenomenal realms, known by the six senses. However such kingdoms required more abstract modes of sensation, that remained undeveloped in us. Witnessing them was contingent on the development of more advanced psychic-evolutionary capacities we have not currently evolved."

RELATIVE BODHICITTA

Finally, Lama Dorje responded, "You certainly hit the nail on the head, but I think you lost me somewhere, as I was enjoying a cup of Chai. I will have to throw in a few speed bumps. Now if you are ready, I will tell you all about Relative Bodhicitta . . . This the path of eliminating fear and the ego through being unconditionally loving. Through it, one melts the world away because all forms arise from ego fears. Once you know yourself as unconditional love, you will have fulfilled all your heart's desires. Knowing your inner perfection and innate state of completion, you will realize nothing else was ever needed. Having found the priceless pearl, you will willingly toss all other pebbles and trinkets away. The world of empty attachments and uninspiring idols will seem so lame, barren, tacky and lifeless in comparison to your newfound gifts. All attachments were merely functioning as dream substitutes standing in place of your Reality. By cherishing them, Love became lost to your awareness. By denying Love to others, its inner presence became shrouded, and you became lost and fragmented in your self-fabricated world.

In the relative world, compassion and forgiveness can find little grounds for justification or support because it is such an uncaring, chaotic and merciless place. It represents a counterfeit netherworld built only from the fabric of illusions. This licenses our ego to rationalize all its cruel, thoughtless and vengeful acts. As a result, it continuously strengthens in our thought!

The path of the **Relative Bodhicitta** is the exact opposite to the ways of the ego. It involves becoming more compassionate, forgiving, understanding and selfless. Over time, one becomes freed from the clutches of the ego and increases in their attunement to wisdom and the Vision of Spirit. The unfolding of Love within restores Self-remembrance and simultaneously relinquishes ignorance. Having dropped all dream attachments, the lens of one's perception runs crystal clear. So is one restored to unity and light. No longer interposing any barriers to love, they find themselves in their true Home. They enter the formless realm of the undifferentiated.

ATISHA'S TEACHINGS AS HOLISTIC

NEPAL

Atisha's teachings are immensely holistic. He presents certain seed ideas, which once correctly understood can release avalanches within. These Sutras can trigger an internal explosion which then reveals the true nature of reality in all its psychedelic splendor. He presents many different windows by which to gain access to the ultimate. Which particular window you choose is unimportant because the final result will be the same. In the end, you will stand illuminated, and bathe in the light of the timeless and infinite. Nonetheless, some windows work better for some, than for others. The window of relinquishing attachments works best for those, committed to a life of simplicity. It is found favorable for environmentally conscious beings, and all who abhor the engines of profit, all-out consumerism and a life a material ease. Those who reject the insanity of the modern human jungle with all its megalithic monsters of stone will be attracted to this path. Meanwhile, those strong in the powers of reason, induction, and introspection, may make excellent progress on the path of emptiness (Absolute Bodhicitta.) These are the ones ready to dispel all false beliefs at a moment's notice and take that backflip into the unknown and unchartered. Alternatively, one who is more loving, caring and compassionate will make great leaps forward on the path of Relative Bodhicitta. The three poisons are the three faces of your release from the hell of Samsara. Once one penetrates any face, one penetrates them all, because Truth remains one in its essence.

THE PROBLEM OF DREAM INVESTMENT

The spectrum of our dream identifications is vast. The dream is a wizard at completely mesmerizing and magnetizing our awareness streams. Each moment we are bombarded with gazillions of different images, trinkets, esoteric facts, rumors, fortuitous hearsays, dynamite concoctions, hallucinogenic agents, trivial fiascos, perverted megalomaniac blogs—all with such celerity, that it keeps us dazzled and dazed. It is a veritable terpsichorean world of magnanimous proportions, infused with a kaleidoscope of sense bewitching data, all coming at us from thousands of competing angles. All mercilessly biting at our coattails and vying for our attention. Stock market crashes, genocides, coupes, corporate takeovers, political scandals, chakras, kundalini, energy transmissions, naked singularities, mesons, multiverses, miracle drugs . . . It never ends! So you find yourself entering a holodeck of flat-screens, cyber-apps, information trolls, phishers, spammers, marketing pimps, all ready to sling mud, filth, and grime into your neural pathways at once. Until it all stinks with such powerful mephitic fumes, that you find yourself transformed into a mentally fried New Age zombie. Floating about on your tech wings momentarily, until the cyber-drones launched from the axon airspaces, look to blitz you again with more of that prized abortive, feckless, counterproductive information that sabotages all your attention channels. Then there are all the data-mining tools, correlative engines, and keystroke trackers, all ready to interpose themselves as communication jammers on your awareness. Eager to pounce on your every click, only to start it all over again from ABC. Is it any wonder that we have all undergone a Darwinian ecological breakdown and devolution, in which we have degenerated into the social equivalent of Homo erectus on LSD? Unable to think and reason anymore, so we remain as babies in our nappies, firmly suckered to our soothers. Possessing the cerebrational and excogitating capacities of single-celled lifeforms and the lewd unwholesome motives of vermin. Needing to be fed continuously through the IV of communication tubes and electronic beams, while basking in the glow suffused from the systolic arrays of LCDs continuously surrounding us! Wiring into a host of other nefarious devices which we find popping out from every orifice of this hybridized cesspit of humanity and technology.

Yes, when we probe deeply into our dream identifications, we immediately recognize that we have become overwhelmingly overrun by a very hostile bastion of self-obscuring thoughts. A veritable smorgasbord of distractions, bodies, looks, torsos, sex, phallic symbols, Indian Gods, Karma Sutras, worthless possessions, portfolio planners, garbage opinions, social networks, cyberbullies, vitriolic rants and so on *ad nauseum*. All our dream identifications are irradiated and imbued with the full multi-hued colorations, textures, tones, and fragrances of our interpretative minds. Pictures weaved into powerful mosaics of biased beliefs from misinformation media toys. There seems to be no frame of reference on this runway. So we find ourselves falling fast into the nebulous quicksand to become modern-day Otzis. Timelessly frozen in the icy and hostile landscape of the modern day technological revolution and New World Order. Undergoing radical transformations of thought, while calling in demolition teams to destroy old worldviews. Then we proceed expeditiously to erect new gods, to take pole position in our minds, to avoid being misperceived and misconstrued as godless heretics. There is barely any time to catch our breath, or we will be left clinging to the 90s' and listening to the music of Procol Harum.

So we oscillate furiously about between our inner and outer worlds, searching hysterically for meaning and understanding. Or at least a straw or two, by which we can pivot our sanity and pirouette around on for a while until we can make it into the big time and use that straw to break the camel's back. Regrettably, we need more than a straw to heal our abject state of mental paralysis. More than a virtual reality game to infuse and vitalize all porous fissures in our lobotomized minds and we need more than virgin daiquiris to quench our relentless thirst and for bandaging up the enormous gaping hole in our souls. All candles have gone out! Our minds await patiently and silently for the light of a single firefly on a hot July night, to navigate our way out of hell. This world has always been destined to implode. It only takes a lone butterfly or a spider climbing stealthily up a wall, to hypnotize and enflame some fanatical visionaries to lead us all into the light of nuclear Armageddon.

The spacetime existence was always fluctuating about in the breeze and wavering in the jet-streams of consciousness. Waiting for that opportune set of distractions, that would pound us into submission while poisoning all wells of our thought. Perhaps something novel here for the CDC to probe into and investigate. There is but little time left for our minds to settle down. Chronic restlessness and hyperactivity seem to have become our drugs of choice. We need to hold up the mirror to our collective consciousness so that we can take a deep impartial look at itself because the essence and nature of the viewer seem to have gone MIA. Lost in a never-ending foggy haze somewhere near the Bermuda triangle. Yes, the dreamer has gone off radar and become a mere blip in some fishbowl in the North-Atlantic.

So he peers out now like some flatfish or blowfish now and then, from the self-obscuring vaporous mists of the subaqueous realms, where he has adopted some trailer-trash persona and one that presents but a caricature of all his former glory. He continues to spout out his mental diarrhea in a glib vernacular dialect through a bifurcated tongue. Speaking volumes of artificial duplicitous nonsense, for the witless to consume—all carefully accumulated, manicured, parceled and decoratively wrapped from the fabric of all his artful fuckups. All ready now for the recycling bin. It seems unlikely that in any lifetime soon he will ever reach to Self-Realization. Time to turn on the ovens and get cooking."

NON-IDENTIFICATION LEADS TO SELF-REMEMBRANCE

Yes, Lama Dorje had certainly given me a nice panoramic vignette of some of those poor dream investments that often ensnare us. He had engraved, stamped and branded into my mind, the real reason most remain in chains. It was becoming evident why most would never break the spell and pull themselves out of their dream hypnosis. They would continue to run amuck in the holographic matrix of the relative existence for eons forward as creatures of distraction pulled hither-and-thither while fearfully reacting to every shadow showing up on their cave-wall. Bereft of the strategic knowledge needed to quench all inner volcanoes of thought. Unable to reach any true quiescence of mind. But, as Freddie Mercury once said, *"The show must go on."* The dream would, unfortunately, continue for most, so long as their dream investments seemed to be paying off? All would linger in a nice deep slumber, listening to lullabies, until something "bad" came to rattle them out of their comfortable dreams and worldly cages. Maybe some savage nightmares were needed in this cocktail—nightmares of torture, death, and self-annihilation. Yes, despair would be the much-needed panacea for most, that would lead to their awakening. Absolute disenchantment would rupture and perforate the dream beyond repair, bankrupting it of all its sleek, sleazy and tantalizing offerings.

The Lama continued "Non-attachment and Non-identification are two of the most strategic techniques for awakening. Non-attachment is the perfect antidote for relinquishing all one's dream investments. Similarly, Non-identification helps you to remember yourself, as the only dreamer of the dream. Simply begin by closing your eyes, a number of times a day. Relax and watch your mind vigilantly for all distracting thoughts crossing the horizon. You will see that they take various shapes, sizes, and forms. They are just like clouds in the sky. Some seem luminous and colorful, while others may appear dark, tenebrous and threatening.

The important element is not to exclude or become overly attached to any one thought. Instead, you are to take the position of an impartial observer—a simple watcher on the hill. The clear vacuous sky of pure awareness, behind all action. A sky in which all thoughts and phenomena appear. Then you will begin to see how each is powerless to affect you. For you are this deathless awareness and the enduring light of the Sun itself."

THE FIRST METHOD OF NON-IDENTIFICATION

I was a bit blitzed by all this. I asked, "Aren't our thoughts and ideas important to us? Aren't our mental fluctuations and witnessing key to our ongoing transformation and healing? If we ignore our thoughts, won't we end up aloof space bunnies, divorced from all true and authentic living?"

The Lama continued "No! These thoughts do not mean anything. They are all ego thoughts, and they have nothing to do with reality. Instead, they are what cost you awareness of reality. They are as lifeless and meaningless, as the furniture in a room. Through identification with them, your natural awareness becomes blocked and you miss-out in experiencing your greater reality and freedom. It is our identification with such thoughts that leads to all forms of misery, sickness, and mental toxicity. Some commit suicide, through excessive identification with some ridiculous thought, that is momentarily gamboling and frolicking on the horizon of their mind. Before they know it, storm clouds and lightning bolts start coming in fast from every direction. Then it is smoking flesh and time to close the curtains.

Some find it difficult to go within. Many feel very threatened or taxed exploring the inner world. If that is the case, one can simply practice watching one's moods and emotions instead. Thus one begins to see the very diverse portfolio of emotions that ravage their mind throughout the day. Soon these practitioners become excellent surfers on the *Big Wednesdays* of the emotional world. They succinctly distinguish each emotion as it comes and goes, and soon view each one impartially, as a ship in the night.

Often our emotions behave like overexcited teenage girls, and they aim to bait us with their sad tale, so they can easily manipulate us and hijack all our attention. We must disengage, and dissociate from all hypnotic identification with our moods if we would claim the prize of self-mastery. We must become like a Nexus 6 or a Dr. Spock in the emotional world and eviscerate each in turn. Yes, we must nuke it fast, before it ever gets a chance to grow and overtake our mind. One should take note of their bodily sensations regularly. Bring your mind to rest at different parts of the body and then inquire what sensations, am I feeling here, at this moment? Is it pain or pleasure or is the feeling entirely neutral! Am I feeling stiff as a corpse, hot like a bimbo, cold as a mummy or as relaxed as an opiate addict?

Your body wants to be loved and appreciated too, even if it is just a dream body. Most often it is ignored and forgotten, because of the mind's continuous obsession, with other things. Often it feels a little like last night's whore—unloved and ready to retaliate. It is ready to make you sick or kill all your sensation, like a Lorena Bobbitt. Emotions and moods are the image reflectors of our mind's state of well-being or toxicity. Sometimes, it is beneficial to watch your body from the distance or some neutral vantage point. Imagine yourself hovering high above it and observing it impartially. You can visualize yourself in a balloon or a drone, that your mind can control. Then begin zooming in-and-out, and view it from different angles.

The object of this practice is to establish distance between the real you (the impartial awareness) and the false you who is overly-identified with all the thoughts, emotions, sensations that are continuously flooding your mind. Soon you begin to see that you are apart from all that is happening and remain an indestructible and eternal awareness."

THE SECOND METHOD OF NON-IDENTIFICATION

The Lama continued, "There is a second practice of Self-remembrance. It involves remembering yourself, in your daily life. It does not matter what you are looking at, whether it be an airplane, a tree or just a computer screen. Remember to ask yourself who is looking at this! When you are more comfortable, you can also ask "**What is looking at this?**" So when you are watching a movie, keep a part of your awareness in reserve, and watch yourself watching the movie. When you are going to the store to pick up a twelve pack of beer, watch yourself intimately doing this. You can also watch yourself getting trashed and comatose. Your witnessing should be inclusive of all your thoughts, moods, sensations and movements. With sufficient practice of this technique, you will develop a very heightened awareness and relate to your true nature as a pure and potent awareness. Your true Self has always remained just a watcher on the hill. You are not anything appearing on the worldly TV. This scarecrow that walks and talks as you, is not the real you but merely a projection of your mind. Thus you will become less afraid, less attached and less invested in the dream and be able to laugh at yourself more easily. As you lighten up and tune out the chaos of life you will soon become unconditionally joyous and psychologically healing of all mental sicknesses and neuroses that arise from world identification.

We all take our dream images, far too seriously. Rarely do we take a rest from our overworked and overburdened selves. Rarely do we do a reset, and disengage to a more neutral perspective. We are often so loveless to ourselves and treat ourselves like toe-rags. We need a holiday at times. A holiday from all our sickening thoughts, septic moods, and searingly painful sensations. Maybe your body has become a wreck or a junkyard, a ship's graveyard and is ready to be decommissioned. You have become immensely tired of it. It no longer moves like a butterfly—it only stings like a bee! It has lost all that fluidity, grace, vitality and virility, it once held in abundance. Or maybe there is a certain mood or thought that keeps on pestering you, and wearing you down. You feel bone-crushed in its jaws. It returns now and then, to exact another pound of flesh. You want to snap away and just disengage. A critical component of yogic mental ventilation is in remembering that *'The mind of the dreamer alone is real and never its content.'* "

TRAIN IN SENDING AND TAKING TOGETHER; DO THIS BY RIDING THE BREATH

CLIMBING IN THE HIMALAYAS

What Lama Dorje said resonated well with me. I felt on permanent vacation since I had broken the spell, (or should I say curse) of the relative world dream. I had always projected my annoyance and frustration to it. Therefore, I took aim at various people, situations, random events and encounters, that I saw ruining my peace and serenity. I even projected blame to any government, social system, cultural milieu, oligarchy, plutocracy or wandering bum that would gracefully accept my abuse without retaliation. I felt this vast conspiracy of the rich, fake and powerful and it was immensely suffocating. It seemed the Illuminati and supremely privileged had the game rigged in their favor. Most of us were just pawns in a merciless game, and about to be thrown off the table, any moment into the abyss of despair. Then we would be put back into our box (which was a coffin) to the sound of a requiem. I felt myself continuously letdown, disrespected and ridiculed by the world; unappreciated, unloved, unseen. All I amounted to ever was that special superhero image I contrived in the barren pastures of my limited imagination.

Now, it was evident, that my thoughts alone had always been my exclusive tormentors. The ingenious interpretations I projected to the world had built my prison-house. The goal had always been for me to become supremely thoughtless, yet potently aware. Inhibiting all my thought processes through yogic introspection alone could bring unconditional bliss and Self-empowerment. No one who feels mercilessly pushed about by a meaningless world can taste bliss. And this meaningless world is crafted entirely from our toxic thinking patterns.

THE FORGOTTEN WISDOM

Lama Dorje waited for my inner soliloquy to play itself through before pressing onward. Then continued, "Many subtle, powerful, exoteric and esoteric understandings from the past have been lost in our obsession with material progress. Some of these exoteric mysteries include the exact methods by which the Egyptians constructed their pyramids and completed their mummification process. Then there was the mysterious disappearance of the inhabitants of Easter Island. To this day, the system of glyphs known as the Rongorongo, have eluded all decipherment. Not to be outclassed, the Anasazi Indians built some of the most superb and unique cliff dwellings ever encountered. Sadly, their entire civilization seems to have been nuked off the face of existence several hundred years ago. The almost perfect stone spheres found in Costa Rica; which weighed almost twenty tons and measured eight feet in diameter are also a mystery. How such masterful spherical precision was accomplished remains either lost or veiled in secrecy.

Another incredible esoteric mystery is the precise relationship existing between our breathing rhythm and mind-states. Everyone knows an intimate connection exists between because whenever we are angry and fearful, our breath automatically becomes more rapid and shallow and rises predominantly in our upper chest cavities. In contrast, when we immensely relaxed, our breath slows down and deepens and is sourced from a location near our bowels. An angry breathing rhythm vitiates and impairs our power of concentration, and it displaces us from a state of mental poise and equanimity. As a consequence, we will soon make some critical mistakes. When large parts of our body remain improperly oxygenated for extended periods, chronic health problems develop. Direct manifestations of this include hypoxia, heart attack, and stroke. Longer ranging health issues include reduced vitality and energy, organ damage, accelerated cell death, and a reduced capacity to fully live.

The whole body is actively involved in the breathing process. Our breathing rhythm can become a powerful irenical force to promote our well-being, health, and creative attention. The quality of our breath tells many things about us. There is a unique breathing rhythm linked to each of our moods. A relationship also exists, between its quality and our state of conscious evolution and spiritual attainment."

FEARLESS EARLY EXPLORERS IN THE SCIENCE OF BREATHING

"Over a millennium ago, some Tibetan yogis decided to make a concerted effort, to turn the breathing process into a Science. Consequently, they meditated for years in caves, high in the Himalayas, and watched and controlled their breathing rhythms. They found that by correct control and harnessing of the breath, it was possible to attain very exalted states of spiritual realization. They had become the ultimate alchemists of being, without fully understanding the details and profound mystery of its operation. These dedicated alchemists were able to control the bellows of their bodies and reach extremely elevated states of consciousness. Through engaging in certain deep, protracted breathing exercises, their concentration power increased enormously and this enabled them to enter states of pure awareness. Their explorations proved that habitual deep breathing, beginning at the bowels, could transform one's entire energy level and quality of being. Certain pranayama techniques could transport one easily into extremely peaceful, and centered states of consciousness and even superconsciousness. One's mind could become so concentrated that it became one-pointed and incapable of distraction. This greatly revered state is known as **Ekāgratā** in Sanskrit. In this state, one could focus exclusively on a single object, or thought for hours or days on end, without ever losing any mental vigilance or attention. In fact, this one-pointedness was key to mastering the miraculous yogic powers, known as the Siddhis and it added tremendous creative flexibility and higher layers of abstraction to their visualizations.

Soon they became so adept in the Siddhis that they could manifest objects out of thin air. These aptitudes also worked magnificently to read the thoughts of others and to receive critical information from the One-Mind, of the Sambhogakāya. Likewise, it helped them to tap into the universal Akashic field so that they could receive any information they needed at will. Hence, they harnessed this ability to prognosticate future events, to develop healing cures and to locate hidden lost scrolls of great spiritual import.

I mentioned before the vast storehouse of consciousness, known as the **Alaya-Vijynana**. The Akashic field, rightly viewed is the collective storehouse of all that was ever consciously ideated. It contains all our thoughts, memories, experiences and actions. It holds the vast reservoir of all we ever experienced. All such impressions create unique imprints in the Akashic field, in much the same way, that all objects and phenomena establish defined curvatures and indentations in the spacetime field. In any case, these advanced yogis used their privileged access to this field, to read thoughts and to predict past and future events. Soon they had morphed into expert seers, remote-viewers, and clairvoyants, and were freely tapping into the hidden vaults of the Universal Mind. It was as if they had been granted a special security clearance and were now able to skip the lines at airports because they could access highly classified documents through mental teleportation. They exploited such Siddhis to shape-shift into various alternate forms, whenever it was convenient. Mobilized by such abilities they could become as light as a feather, as heavy as a Tyrannosaurus Rex, as small as a subatomic particle or as massive as a galaxy. By combining a certain regimen of well-defined breathing exercises (pranayama) with various visualizations, they were able to reliably generate the psychic heat, known as the *tummo.* Thus they could survive without any clothes even in sub-zero conditions!

Their visualizations were of a vacuous body, in which lay potent energy channels, known as *Tsa* (**Nāḍī** in Sanskrit). There was a fundamental energy channel, known as the Sushumna, that was as thin as a very fine thread. It connected to all other energy channels as well as to the entire cosmos, and it threaded all prana in existence. This particular *Tsa,* began at the Muladhara chakra, located at the perineum, and it coursed its way up to the Sahasrara chakra, located just above the crown of the head. Soon these yogis realized that the surrounding air was infused with all sorts of invisible pranic energy fields, which could potentially offer infinite nourishment. By transmuting this subtle energy, through certain breathing techniques, they were able to extract its nourishment. Thus, they were able to survive months on end, without eating anything physical. Similarly, they used the breath to enter the supremely exalted state of undistracted yogic bliss, known as Nirvikalpa Samadhi. In this quiescent state, the phenomenal world dissolves into non-being and awareness alone remains. All becomes experienced as a non-differentiated plenum of light. In this enlightened state of consciousness, the dream nature of the relative existence is known directly, and one has entered Nirvana."

THE CRITICALITY OF THE BREATHING RATIO

So, our breath was the prime mechanism by which we could transmute pranic energy into potent spiritual capacities. Likewise, it was the all-important conduit linking our physical, mental and spiritual realms together. Once I mentioned this to Lama Dorje he expounded further. "Yes, through deep breathing, one can suppress the thought fluctuations of the mind. This then brings great release, freedom, and peace. One dedicated in their pranayama practice can enhance their power of intention almost immeasurably and so recognize that their true nature is entirely independent of thought. To gain these notable powers, one must start from first principles. The most critical consideration is understanding how the breathing ratio we maintain affects our moods and mental states. The duration of the incoming to the outgoing breath defines this ratio. They are definite rules to the game! Knowing them one can accomplish any outcome one desires. For instance, a certain breathing pattern will transport your expeditiously into a sublime mental state. By stacking the dice in your favor you can accelerate your passage out of time."

I responded, "This is most fascinating. Can you provide some examples of how our breathing ratio affects our mental states?"

He continued, "Changing the timing relationship between the incoming and outgoing breaths can be used to invigorate and awaken or else to induce sleep and deep states of relaxation. For example, maintaining a timing relationship of 1:2 between the

incoming and outgoing breaths automatically energizes, vitaliz-
es and awakens the mind. Simultaneously, it sharpens all your
senses and makes them come alive. A timing ratio of 2:1, on the
other hand promotes drowsiness and sleep while concurrently
dulling your senses. Finally, a timing ratio of 1:1 is helpful in inducing deep states of relaxation. This rhythm places you in a
very fluid and capacious state of mind, rather than in an overly-
concentrated and narrow-banded state of consciousness. Prolonging this breathing ratio will increase your creativity immensely. It is the most opportune ratio for autohypnotic sugges-
tion. Thus, when you want to reprogram your underlying
subconscious motivations and tune everything else out, this is
the one to use.

There are clearly defined breathing ratios for entering all states
of consciousness. Some prove beneficial for becoming immersed
in the vaporous state of consciousness and for seeing the dream
nature of existence. Other ratios and visualization techniques
are excellent for generating the psychic heat. A number are beneficial for tuning in and accessing hidden information from the
universal field. There are even breathing techniques for raising
and releasing deeply repressed unconscious memories. These
prove salubrious for healing those, who have experienced past
traumas and for releasing accumulated baggage from previous
incarnations. All memories conscious or unconscious will affect
your attitudes, moods and perceptions. Thus, they inhibit your
capacity to live fully, authentically and fearlessly. Often repressed memories and experiences make it difficult for one to
function to their highest potential. Learning how to breathe correctly is very much learning how to live. Just fifteen minutes of
deep breathing, early in the morning can vitalize you for the entire day. It will clear away all those lethargic thinking processes

that sleep often induces. In just a few moments, you can change your entire mental state and disposition. Over time, mastery of right breathing patterns will transform the whole quality of your life experience."

All this information had me hooked, and it connected well with what I had experienced through my yogic practice. I had trained in Kriya yoga, for many years, and was very familiar with many of the Kriyas. Within just a few short months of doing postures, visualizations, and pranayama, I experienced the quality of my breath and vitality improve enormously. I found myself able to concentrate for long periods, without distraction. My appetite was great, my sleep quality excellent and I had gained so much more zest for life. However, I had never heard of the particular breathing technique associated with this Sutra. Now, I desired to understand it in greater detail. I said, "Can you give me a full blow-by-blow explanation of what this Sutra means and how it is applied?"

He said, "This Sutra is concerned with extending loving compassion to all. In Tibet, it is known as the *tonglen,* and it is one of the most powerful techniques for combining pranayama with mental visualization. It synchronizes loving thought visualizations, with the incoming and outgoing breaths. Before I proceed, I need to teach you the initial preparation which will help make this technique far more effective."

INITIAL PREPARATION

"For the initial preparation," he said "It helps to do a few Hatha Yoga postures first. These will loosen up all your joints and energize your body and prevent any residual numbness or pain from distracting you later on. Then place earplugs in your ears and a bandana over your eyes and sit comfortably in the lotus posture. If you cannot do the lotus posture, just sit with your back straight. The important thing is that your posture feels restful and unblocked. Now close your eyes and focus them upwards at the center of your forehead; at the location of the inner eye of Shiva Netra. Visualize a lotus blossom, just above your head and a clear celestial space surrounding it. This blossom represents your ability to transmute the mud of the relative existence, into something extremely pure and potent. Imagine your guru to be sitting in lotus posture just above this lotus. He or She has a light-filled body and is radiating loving-kindness to all living things. For those who do not have a guru, they should choose someone who exemplifies their ideals of unconditional love and compassion. Alternatively, one can choose to visualize Avalokiteshvara (Tib. Chenrezig) the Bodhisattva of infinite compassion. Other options include Krishna, Manjusri or Amitābha. Manjusri is the Buddha of gentleness and discriminating wisdom. He always carries a Vajra sword by his side, with which he facilely and flawlessly cuts through ignorance, superstition, and Maya. He sees beyond the veil of illusory phenomena directly to the non-dual nature of existence. Amitābha is the Buddha of boundless light and is known for his boundless compassion. Those who have a lineage of gurus should visualize them all smiling, and filled with light and in a lotus posture. The visualization should be of a vertical cascade; with each sitting just below his master with the root guru positioned at the very top.

Now breathe deeply in and out twenty-one times while preserving a timing ratio of 1:1, between the incoming and outgoing breaths. This simple pattern will reliably place your mind in a deep state of relaxation. With each incoming breath, visualize yourself rising slowly, into the lotus position of your guru. Then with the ongoing breath, imagine the guru descending into your heart, filling it with universal compassion. Imagine there is a fine thread connecting your hearts seamlessly together. As you continue the breathing regimen, begin to feel that you are merging into one another and becoming of the same essence. If there is a lineage of gurus, imagine all your hearts connected by this fine thread and you all merging into a single light-filled body of infinite potency.

THE ACTUAL PRACTICE

O nce you are proficient with the initial practice technique, you are ready for the main practice. Begin by choosing someone whom you care very deeply for. Someone, experiencing some form of pain, suffering or disease, whether this be physical, psychological or spiritual. Perhaps, they are suffering from cancer, or immobility or else they have become hopelessly depressed and cheerless. Perhaps they cannot see their way forward and have lost all light and hope. Visualize this person and their particular affliction very lucidly and do not miss any of the finer details. For this, it may help, to apply the **magnifying glass technique**.

THE MAGNIFYING GLASS TECHNIQUE

The magnifying glass technique is very simple but highly effective. Begin by imagining; you are holding a magnifying glass in your hand. This magnifying glass can zoom in on any part of the world, you wish, from the cosmological level of galaxies down to the most infinitesimal of the subatomic levels. You can use it to see others up close and thus to zoom in on their physical features and internal organs. It also works wonderfully to examine another's thoughts. Begin by imagining a white billowy cloud appear on the undersurface of your magnifying glass. Now send a silent request out to existence to manifest this person's true thoughts or feelings into this cloud. Wait patiently and watch. Soon you will start seeing words emerging into this cloud. These words will appear written in bold letters and are easily recognized and understood. They represent this person's true thoughts and feelings at that particular time.

Begin the actual practice by placing the face of the person; you care about under your magnifying glass. If unable to distinguish any of their features, zoom in for a closer look. Now move your magnifying glass over to the source of their affliction. If it is cancer, for example, begin by zooming in on the cancerous section of their body and look closely at the individual cancer cells. Note their color and growth activities and the nocuous pestilential cloud into which they agglomerate. If their affliction is psychological, you may begin to see a dark nebulous cloud hovering above their head that may even engulf their entire body. This cloud represents the pernicious activities of all their toxic thoughts. You're aim is to dispel and vaporize this cloud into nothingness.

RAYS OF LIGHT AND DARKNESS

Once you can sharply visualize and distinguish the particular affliction of your recipient, you are ready to progress. Begin by imagining that with each incoming breath, dark rays are shooting outwards from the source of their pain. These rays are traveling through space and entering your pores. You are inviting them to enter your heart because you are ready to absorb in all the pain in your chosen receiver. You are immune to their nefarious influence because of your secret knowledge. Your heart, being pure and compassionate, can easily transmute the negative energy into light and healing. The dark rays are powerless to affect you because they belong to the world of shadows and appearances. Now as these dark rays enter your body, imagine that they are heating up a symbol **OM**, placed strategically in the center of your heart. As you absorb in more of the dark rays, this **OM** begins to glow tremendously. Its color changes from a mild pink at first to a bright red and finally to an incandescent white. With each outgoing breath, visualize light rays of healing energy emanating from this mystical **OM** symbol and shooting across space. They are entering the source of pain of your chosen beneficiary, infusing him or her with powerful surges of healing energy. They are bringing new life and hope.

Completely immerse yourself in the experience and feel that with each incoming breath, you are taking away the other's pain, misery, despair and destructive patterns of thought. Likewise, with each outgoing breath, you are sending healing rays which infuse them with new vitality, health, and hope. Gradually you see they are becoming more joyful, peaceful and radiant, and filled with wellbeing once more. Soon you notice that all the sickness, darkness and toxicity that lingered previously is being deprived of its power. It is being rendered innocuous by the healing energy you are transmitting.

As you excel in this practice, the world of pain and negativity becomes powerless to affect you in any way. Instead, you find you are more selfless, carefree and mentally expansive. In your newfound joy, you no longer run away from the world of pain and sickness nor seek to avoid uncomfortable situations. You are now immune to all pernicious evils, psychic-vampires, and soul-suckers of the world. Amazingly, you welcome and embrace all newly emerging situations, as an opportunity to demonstrate your strength, spiritual virility, and magical abilities. You have become healed by your willingness to extend healing; peaceful by extending peace, and happy due to your willingness to propagate joy and blessing to all.

This is one of the secret Laws of existence. "**Whatever you are prepared to give, you will receive.**" The world is just a projection of your thought, and it only ever reflects back what you give it. Now your ready to take the next step and one giant leap it is. This step will advance and promote your newfound capacities beyond your wildest dreams.

EXTENDING BLESSING TO AN ENEMY

N ow visualize under your magnifying glass, someone you dislike or even positively detest. Someone who sets you on edge and one you avoid at every opportunity. Some character, who has the power to destroy your entire peace of mind just by contemplating their presence or past actions. Begin the application by searching for some physical deformity, psychological ailment or source of suffering or trauma in their lives. Now practice the previously given healing pranayama visualization on their source of pain or affliction. Welcome in all their grief and agony with each incoming breath and then send out healing rays of positive energy and blessing with each outgoing breath. If you are unaware of any ailment or weakness, in your detested "enemy" you can apply this alternative healing visualization technique instead. Imagine there is a dark cloud encompassing them. This dark cloud represents all negative attributes and behavioral patterns, you have ever perceived in them. It can include all that repulses you about them and all that which induces fear or irritation. This dark cloud encapsulates them in a shadowy fortress of gloom and nastiness that you never care to enter. Due to perpetual darkness, you cannot see the light contained within its center. Now be honest and sincere and find at least one attribute, strength or feature of your enemy, that you at least deem positive in some way. Think of this feature or strength as a radiant child of pure light, hidden away beneath the dark cloud. This child of light is part of their greater reality, and yours. This defenseless child needs your help to grow and to be released. It wants to join with you again, and you need its help to become whole. It cannot merge because it is held ransom by all the negative energy your ego thoughts have surrounded it with. Nonetheless, you are key to its healing, as it is of yours.

With each incoming breath, imagine the dark energy rays your "enemy" exudes are entering your heart where they are being transmuted into living energy and light. In turn, with each out-going breath, light rays are shooting out from you, traversing through the dark cloud and finally entering the luminous child. Each time these rays enter, he or she is receiving critical nour-ishment needed to grow and flourish. With each successive breath, the child is being flooded with light, and the dark cloud is disappearing. Soon the cloud becomes powerless to hold back the light emanating from the radiant child within. This light streams to join you both, for you share the same essence. The child is immensely grateful for all the help you have given it to survive. You are rescuing it from the suffocating jaws of dark-ness and death.

With successful practice, your enemy becomes transformed into a friend, and you both are healed. All the negativity and toxic patterns you perceived before, you recognize now were just a call for help. A call for you to forgive, that which you condemned first in yourself. You are both liberated, since your compassion has become whole and therefore capable of universal applica-tion. Existence has always been showering you with blessings or making calls for help. These calls were providing you with new opportunities to strengthen in love, forgiveness, compassion, and mercy. Your nurturing capacity had become so severely at-rophied. Whenever you answered the calls, you became aware of your essential loving nature and simultaneously demonstrat-ed your creative power, completeness, equanimity, and strength. Finally, with mastery you become unconditionally loving."

Lama Dorje had certainly gone the extra mile, in teaching me how to excel with this healing meditation. He taught the technique with immense clarity and also imparted its relevance. After all, if one just transmits healing thoughts and blessings to friends, this is somewhat self-serving. One may be using the meditation as a form of self-protection and looking to strengthen one's social network. Aiming to photocopy their indigenous belief system everywhere, even if it is highly distorted, misplaced or evil. True healing can only occur when we are willing to heal and empower inclusively—even those who may not share our worldviews and perspectives. Unless we extend healing energy, and compassion indiscriminately, we cannot spiritually mature.

UNIVERSAL APPLICATION

Then he continued, "Once you make this healing meditation universal in its application, you will shower the world with even more blessings. Do not attempt the universal application, however, until you have first mastered it in specific applications. It is fruitless to apply universally, that which you have failed to master in specific situations. Your compassion will remain just a mind-dream, and have no real effect. You will be merely fooling yourself, that you are growing in purity, altruism and true understanding. Auto-hypnotizing yourself that you are becoming the radiant Buddha of Universal Love when you have not reached that state. For the universal application, visualize that with each incoming breath that you are imbibing the entire world of pain, suffering, and deprivation. Absorbing all the sickness and lack that is anywhere or in any living thing; all the brutalities, injustices, genocides, massacres, suicides, grief, mishaps or failures in communication. No source of darkness is to escape your mental radar. Then feel how powerless this pain and injustice is to affect or derail you in any way. Instead, you are thriving under the influence of all this dark energy because you have mastered how to transmute it into its opposite, through your universal compassion and purity of mind. So you are filling with life, vitality, boundless energy and light, with each incoming breath. You are becoming Mother Teresa and Florence Nightingale in their essence and are impervious to all forms of sickness, suffering and lack. One successfully able to transmute every negative situation into something positive that is infused with new life and hope.

You are ready now for a nuclear explosion of the spiritual kind. Because all this energy, light and love cannot be restrained any longer. With each outgoing breath, all your light and compassion is exploding outwards into the world indiscriminately; reaching wherever it is needed. This transmuted energy is healing the world of all darkness, sadness, and despair and awakening it from its Self-forgetfulness. You are bringing back awareness of the divinity and power that is intrinsically present in all. The understanding that darkness is powerless to corrupt light in any way; and death is impotent to subtract from life. Such is the ultimate practice of Atisha's technique."

I interjected saying, "The world has a great need for this *tonglen* technique of universal compassion. It is desperate for any tiny morsels of healing, understanding, and forgiveness. Otherwise, it will soon enter a degenerative spiral to who knows where. Probably something deeper and far more insidious than Dante could ever have imagined. Not enough dreamers see their great need of awakening. They do not recognize the enormous influence their dreaming minds and attitudes have on the collective consciousness. They do not know they sleep. Many have become so very insular and cold, that they are unable to extend compassion and understanding, even to their few friends, if they have any at all. Do any of the spiritual teachers, gurus, celebrities or politicians, etc. who speak so eloquently about the need for developing universal harmony, peace and understanding help in any way?"

He responded pretty abruptly, "**No, they don't!** Words remain just superficial entities and empty vessels unless one has gained true existential conviction in what they represent. They carry no meaning unless one has become magnetized into a powerful force for change. Only then is one able to transform and liberate millions of minds. Mahatma Gandhi had the internal conviction of what worked. Through his teaching on non-violent resistance, known as '*Satyagraha*,' he transformed the whole consciousness of India. Words will convince others, only when you have proved them first to yourself. Only, when others see radiance, peace, and wisdom emanating from your eyes, as exemplified in all your behaviors and actions, will they want to possess such power for themselves. For then you will have become the perfect embodiment of your words.

In the present day, we see politicians circulating about like jackals, ready to carve each other up for a dime. All are fervidly seeking the spotlight like insects while chanting out all this empty rhetoric about cultivating peace and reconciliation between nations. Next moment, they want to build walls around their borders or point-blank refuse to accept refugees from war-torn nations. Then they are calling in airstrikes and releasing armed drones to take out civilian populations, despite zero surveillance intelligence of any hostile intention or threat. Likewise, we see all those celebrities who are constantly prancing about, promoting awareness of some critical worldly concern. Idle causes, such as '*Feed the Alaskan Wolves*' or '*Save the Planet and the Icecaps from melting*,' etc. They seem more concerned about getting ill-treated dogs, doggy dentures and a manicure than taking care of those around them. In the final analysis, they are empty devious beings sneakily aiming to promote themselves, and their whole lives are an entire Red Carpet Affair.

We are easily duped and blindsided by subtle masks and the cunning ploys engaged by the armies of the superficial. We peer out in awe, thinking here, at last, we have found a stunning portrait of beauty, innocence, and universal compassion in motion. A truly conscientious and kind-spirited being. We are almost ready to melt away in her lips and be caressed by her tongue. Thinking, here is the loving cradle, that our heart has always desired. Then, we walk outside, still feeling sedated by the sense stupefying spell and mental aphrodisiac woven from her deceptive charm. Taking a gander up at the stars, they are shining all the more brightly now. Then, she emerges a few minutes later and savagely chastises her chauffeur, for not pulling close enough to the curb. The mystic spell has been broken.

The world is over-populated now with so many fraudulent gurus and pandits. Those who can articulate volumes of highly loquacious nonsense, while packaging their crap in such glowing, world-encompassing terms. By all who seduce and entrap through empty promises and cheap allurements. Many are only too happy to lecture about love and truth when speaking in the abstract. However, when it comes to demonstrating their ideals of universal love and understanding under specific circumstances, they prove hopelessly deficient. Such spiritual marketeers are emotionally paralyzed beings; incompetent buffoons that have about the same empathic proficiency as a polar bear does. All is mere sophistry, humbug, and bait designed to snare the witless. There is no realization here, no spiritual insight or cup of overflowing altruism—just endless word spinning and deception. As you finally emerge from your tower of vertigo and accumulate the courage to peel away the many masks, you find at root a fiendish troll. Yes, this pumped up mannequin you prized so much, turns out to be immensely obnoxious when moralistically exposed and seen in their raw nakedness. Behind all the layers of sweat and fetid odor, you discover all the bigotry, racism, sectarianism, homophobia and callous disregard. In the end, they amount to nothing more than freewheeling chameleons, who are in it for themselves, Freeloaders and proselytizers who slyly aim to wheedle and extract all the adulation and wealth, they crave from their devotees and fans."

Then I asked if he could share some personal experience of applying this technique. For the first time, he withdrew silently and became stubbornly recalcitrant. He seemed very reluctant to share any insight. Nonetheless, I kept pressuring him, to give some response. I said, "I always understand things better, through the elucidation that personal anecdotes provide."

Eventually, he spoke, "When I was younger, I attended a Buddhist opposition rally that was protesting the Chinese takeover of Tibet. There, one of the monks had decided to undergo a self-immolation. Yes, he was going to light himself on fire and make of himself a sacrificial offering to the cause. I didn't know what to think, or how to digest the whole affair emotionally. It seemed such an extreme and unneeded response. Nor could I see, that it would fundamentally change anything. There he was sitting in deep meditation, surrounded by a large crowd. His cloak was soaked in oils, and the atmosphere was intense. Then the moment came when the fire was lit. Initially, I was very saddened as the flames began to rise and take shape. I was immature and thought it pointless to sacrifice one's life. Nonetheless, as the fire progressed, a profound transformation started occurring within me because, this monk never moved an ounce, even as the fire raged to consume his entire body. His self-immolation had genuinely impressed me and left me stunned. Quantum shifts were going on inside me. This pivotal event demonstrated the depth and quality of his meditative practice. In that moment, he had taught me the heights that were possible through inner self-discipline and had cogently demonstrated his mastery of the Buddha's key teaching on non-identification with the impermanent. This event was the crescendo of his life, the culmination of all his yogic practice—his very graduation from the Academy of life. As a result, I knew in no uncertain terms, that our essential being is deathless.

Then all of a sudden soldiers arrived and started shooting indiscriminately into the crowd. My venerable Lama was shot and killed, in the resulting fracas and intermingling of scurrying bodies. For many weeks afterward, I was intensely sad. Many unsettling thoughts plagued my mind. I was filled with pure, undefiled rage, for the first time in my life. I could no longer meditate or focus on anything at all. He had been teaching me these seven Sutras, at the time and teaching this particular Sutra on the day of his passing. Now I felt his work had been left incomplete. I got so depressed that I did not want to go out or do anything anymore. I had lost all spiritual will and inclination. Then one day, I recalled one of the last things, my venerable teacher had said. *"One achieves mastery of the tonglen technique when they can send their love, blessings, and forgiveness to all indiscriminately with no reserve or ill-will."* I began pondering, on these words, more-and-more. They thoroughly suffused my thought processes. As they entered deeper into my being, I began to realize the soldiers were just doing their job. They had merely destroyed a body, but this was an impermanent thing. Nothing Real had been taken away, that could justify my rage. My teacher would continue, as before. Only now his wisdom would reach me from the eternal bodies of the Sambhogakāya and Dharmakāya. Consequently, I proceeded to apply the *tonglen* healing practice to extend universal compassion, even to the soldier, who had shot him. I practiced it without any partiality or exclusion. I realized, that I if I held any exceptions, I would never be whole. So my practice became universal in its application. Soon a great peace and equanimity descended on me. It has been there ever since. That very night, I was Enlightened through this healing visualization technique."

Lama Dorje's powerful living example silenced me to my core. Nonetheless, the ego always creeps in, to do mischief and soon my mind was spinning again in countless directions. The one realization I took from his experience was that tragedies, often come with silver linings. There are unseen gifts in many situations. If we can yank ourselves out of our '*Victimization-Mindset*' and interpret events correctly, these treasures become ours. Suffering should never be wasted. Without it, we can easily remain indolent and complacent and perfectly content to live directionless lives while remaining addicted to superficial pleasures. Yes, suffering can be a great psycho-spiritual force. It can trigger an inner impulse in us to change our defeatist patterns and thus reach liberation.

TIME-OUT FOR AN EMOTIONAL INCUBATION

A s I retired to my hut for the night, my emotional body was undergoing a major firestorm. I could feel the tectonic plate shifting, as various landmasses in my emotional world began colliding. Lama Dorje's experiences had catalyzed all these inner volcanoes. He had probably done it all by purposeful design. He knew I was far too comfortable and complacent living in the mental world, but much less so in the emotional one. I always wanted to be in command and control, and I dreaded that monster who could take over my being in its entirety. One that could force me to see and experience life, through a completely new set of eyes. Yes, he had wanted to strip me bare and take me on a wild journey to my core. A journey past the circle of fear spun from the conscious mind with all its sneaky mechanisms of deception. He had wanted to rattle my composure so that emotional healing could begin. I had been dancing on the surface of my inner landscape for far too long, pretending what was below, did not exist or matter at all. Meanwhile, he had illuminated the criticality of complete impartiality, in mastering the *tonglen* practice. Altruistic impartiality was the essential ingredient needed for our success. Not having it, was analogous to trying to make bread without a leavening agent—the bread would never rise. Despite this recent illumination, I still had many open, unresolved questions. In particular, I was only partially comfortable with his sentiments on self-immolation and in regards to suffering in general. So I decided, I would bring these up in the next session! Then I aimed my inner probe squarely on my emotional body because I wanted to know, precisely, what was holding this show together, and on what premises, it was built.

SUTRA 7: TRAIN WITH PHRASES IN EVERY MODE, PURSUIT, AND BEHAVIOR

A BEAUTIFUL DAY, SURROUNDED BY THE MAJESTY OF THE HIMALAYAS

I began the next discourse by raising my pressing concern: "After considerable reflection, I am interested in learning more about the effectiveness of self-immolation as a form of political protest since the Chinese don't care if Tibetans set themselves on fire. Also didn't George S. Patton, once say: *'The object of war is not to die for your country but to make the other bastard die for his.'* Wouldn't a more active form of protest produce more immediate results and raise the issue of Tibet's annexation by force in the Global Consciousness? "

To this, the Lama coolly responded "No, It wouldn't! General S. Patton is an expert in the Art of War, but he is hardly an expert on the Art of Peace. If we mindlessly followed the Chinese policies of aggression and blind brutality, we would then have made the Chinese our teachers. In the process, we would also have abandoned all our core principles and Buddhist ideals of non-violence. Vengeance and Retaliation has never been a sagacious teacher, and it has no wisdom to impart. In contrast, it makes the whole world sightless. Vision, Empathy, Collaboration, Pure Motivation and unbiased Understanding are what is needed most. Only then can the spirit of true compassion and conciliation flower. Abraham Maslow once said, "*To the man who only has a hammer, everything he encounters begins to look like a nail.*" The Chinese are those carrying a large hammer right now and Tibet is their chosen nail."

I chimed in, "Many seem to be dying so senselessly. Likewise, isn't self-immolation a form of violence against one's body and not too different then from just being a masochist or cutter?"

Lama Dorje crisply responded, "No one is dying! Death is impossible because no outside world has ever been. This body is wholly illusory, and it is not alive in any real sense. Being just a mental projection, it simply reacts to the purposes the mind sets for it. When the mind feels sick and conflicted, this manifests as sickness, contraction and low-energy in the body. Those who are self-immolating are merely saying "**Truth cannot be destroyed!** Forced to make a choice, they are choosing their Spiritual Reality over the Body, the Real over the Transitory, the

Formless over the realm of Form. They fight for those heart-rooted principles, valued in the depths of their being. They are deathless because of their capacity to live fully and fearlessly, and this entails a willingness to embrace death. Your idle comparison of self-immolators to masochists and cutters is misses the point. You are again focusing on **form** over **content** and giving **form** precedence in the equation of what constitutes value. It is the underlying motivation and intention behind what we do that matters. Masochists hate the body, and so they torture, brutalize and flagellate it, in various ingenious ways. They fail to comprehend that a part of their autogenous thought that they really hate. The enemy is within all the time but this enemy they cannot see, reach, nor silence. Hence, their inner demons remain undeterred and go about business as usual. Thus you see this playing-out of a host of self-destructive behaviors, onto the canvas of their bodies. Many project a vengeful intent to God and seek to assuage his vengeance by preemptively inflicting tortures on themselves. Guilt is likewise a formidable inner enemy that cannot be satiated. We unconsciously retain guilt, not only for our past actions but also for our failures in action and for our current thoughts of malicious intent. Cutters are an entirely different class of fish to Masochists. Most cutters do not resent their bodies at all. Instead, they seek to externalize their inner pain which they feel searing continuously in their mind as a flame that scorches without remission. This pain is immensely intense at times, and yet invisible to others. By externalizing it, they finally get a great sense of relief. The sources of such agonized affliction are as multitudinous and diverse as the cells in the body and lifeforms in our environment. The aggressors that torment the inner landscape include one's failure in communication, feelings of alienation and mistrust, a longing for love, empathy and greater recognition. So we feel an acute state of conflict with the prevailing state of existence."

I became silent for a moment, as I was having an inner epiphany and beginning to comprehend how similar outward symptoms often manifest from entirely different causes. The inner content lurking behind mirror-like symptoms can often be at variance or even diametrically opposed. The content can often be self-destructive in its essence and at other times, ennobling and pure. We need to know the true face of the beast. Unfortunately this face of the demon is often densely veiled and shielded from view by the outward symptoms. His statement "**Truth cannot be destroyed**," had triggered an old forgotten memory. This now began to reverberate in my mind. It was of a young Vietnamese boy, who had his Christian Cross viciously snatched away by a Communist soldier who then tossed into a river. The small boy didn't get angry. He gracefully responded, by making the sign of the cross over his forehead. Then he confidently declared to the soldier: "**You can take away that cross, but you can't take away this one.**"

Now I remembered a question I had regarding the nature of suffering: "A long while back, you indicated that sickness and suffering do not genuinely exist. Last time we met, however, you said suffering should never be wasted. These statements appear to contradict, can you explain the disparity?"

He responded: "**Context Dependency**, are the two words that answer that question for you. From the greater context of the Absolute, sickness and suffering do not exist. Nor do the world of form and phenomena, for that matter. Nonetheless, from the limited perspective of the relative world, sickness and suffering seem all too real and self-evident. The relative is the realm of appearances and everything in it can be advanced and employed either constructively or destructively. Thoughts, words, actions, decisions can be used as a raft to ferry one to Bliss and Self-liberation, or else to propel one further into the Dantesque hell-fires. Suffering and sickness can be great motivators since they galvanize our resolve and prompt accelerated progress on the spiritual path. Our many harsh trials in life can promote greater empathy and make us more conscientiousness. They place us in a pressure cooker where change is demanded; doing so they can enhance our decisions, actions and behaviors. This enlightened redirection is most often a great gift. Sickness and suffering help slow down time, and they transport us wholly into the present. With suffering our minds wander less and becomes more vigilant; consequently we no longer seeks to entertain futile dreams. The omnipresence of pain quenches all cravings and desires, and it demands all our resources be in the **Here-n-Now**. Most misuse the treasury the present moment offers. Their cunning and exploitive mindsets cover it entirely. The veiled treasury then becomes unknown and the golden opportunity to rise beyond all illusions forever is lost. It is not the present that is fearful, it is only the ego's dark projections over the present that induce fear. These images, idle wishes, fantasies and miscreations cause all our pain. The present will remain always the Home of Bliss, Truth and the sole Gateway to the Eternal. However, this is only known by those who have truly seen and experienced it. The remainder live in illusion of time and foolishly think they are witnessing the true present.

Now, I will teach you the last Sutra. This Sutra is Atisha's parting words of wisdom, to all those newly awakened. It functions as a final guidepost, for all who have entered the body of the Nirmanakāya. It is also an extremely valuable Sutra, for those remaining trapped in the dream of ignorance. Atisha is forever cognizant of the many distractions and vicissitudes, which arise in the dream universe. Unexpected events emerge from nowhere to completely derail us. Many lost, and blind souls can seek to hijack all our attention. An untrained mind can accomplish nothing. It is useless to itself and as a mentor and guide to others. Unless we maintain continual remembrance of what is worthy and inspirational, we can easily fall back into the soul-sucking bogs and marshlands of delusion. What we faithfully imbibe grows within us, and one day it brings forth a rich and bountiful harvest. Our beliefs are immensely powerful. Those we accept and embrace pass downwards instantaneously into our subconscious mind. There in the subliminal and supraliminal level of the consciousness spectrum, they are put to work as minions of the underworld. Their only task is to fulfill all our dreams and attempt to make our nonsense intelligible in the conflicted world we perceive.

The subconscious is a neutral, impartial and welcoming receptacle that embraces all our thoughts. Each moment it is scouring the world of our perceptions for all that is beneficial in accomplishing our chosen ideals. It is continuously amplifying, harnessing and sorting through the mass of perceptions, sensations, and information that continuously assails us until it has either fulfilled our desires or served to reinforce all our fears. If it only weeds we plant, it is weeds we will have. The subconscious is not concerned with particular outcomes, but only in accomplishing all we demand. It does not judge our unrealistic and conflicted expectations. One must realize fully, that the entire Samsaric existence, only arose because we planted the weeds of ignorance within and it only remains because we continue to water this tree of ignorance.

The relative world is contingent on poor decision making to support its apparent existence. Powered and shaped by the winds of our thought, it depends on our mistaken beliefs to remain intact. Such is the only cause-and-effect principle, it knows and responds to. Perception is the perfect reflector of our beliefs. Our subconscious functions as the creative projectionist. When we choose to adopt and esteem the false, we lose all our sovereign power and place our minds in bondage to the unreal. Then the ego's screaming hall of vengeance, mindlessness, and pain, comes at us hard and fast. Phantoms and mirages arise from our distortionary beliefs, to whip us about in our self-made world. The skeletons of the old come to cloud our view. Clinging to deadened thought patterns causes us to sacrifice our true Powers of Creation.

When Atisha asks that we train with phrases in all modes of behavior, he is persuasively reminding us of the causal link existing between our beliefs and the world of perception. This world is nothing apart from our beliefs. He is requesting we harmonize our mind and thought with the principles and Knowledge of Truth. Thus we become potentiated and empowered and begin to follow the path of our best interests. Simultaneously, we bypass cruel and unnourishing pastures that lead to our detriment. Sleepwalkers do not know they sleep! Only when the misery becomes intense and unbearable will they attempt to awaken and then engage every possible means to do so. The means are numerous and include meditation, reason, introspection, creative visualization, mantra repetition, purity, altruism, and so forth. The divinity within seeks to be total in action and to affirm its power of intention. Unfortunately, the ego of the lower mind often interposes itself to derail us and to foil our efforts.

Atisha's wish is that all dream-producing thought patterns of our egoic mind be atrophied and silenced, rather than strengthened. He wants us to relinquish all habits, hindrances, poor decisions and self-destructive behaviors that cause us to become further entrenched in the conditioned existence. We must be vigilant and discriminating and not let our minds wander down wrong paths. We must be careful and not become more closed-minded, fearful and shut-off or we will not digest those highly efficacious, light-filled understandings, which alone can heal us.

Our minds must retain ony that which elevates and truly inspires. This includes all those Sutras, Shastras, Mantras, Precepts, and Enlightened teachings that were provided or transmitted by Realized Beings. These all function highly effectively as illusion zappers. In our aim to reach unconditional peace and absolute quiescence of mind, we must direct the arrow of our awareness inwards towards our Source. Illusions come in tons of varieties and vary from frightening dreams of persecution to dreams of self-satiation through the body and the senses. Illusions manifest in multifarious forms. They may appear as some fantasy, grievance, or idol we cherish. Illusions are ultra-chimerical entities and include all our dreams of grandeur, specialness, self-empowerment, and control. In fact, anything the ego continuously obsesses about is probably an illusion. Training with phrases helps inhibit false patterns from digging in and taking hold over all else. This prevents us from spiraling downwards into degenerative modes of thinking. An ounce of prevention is worth a pound of cure. The aphorism also holds true on the spiritual path. We must remember, that Truth alone can nourish and we should not waste our efforts and energies on empty offerings.

The Sutras are very powerful, condensed, and potent spiritual understandings. They steer us towards Truth and Self-remembrance and can induce instantaneous illumination. Placing all our faith in them, we avoid many pitfalls and hells. Repeating them, they permeate downwards into our subconscious, where they resonate in the inner chambers of our heart. Soon our heart sings out in ecstasy. Being intimately immersed in the newfound and yet ancient wisdom; it finds joy, peace and release after many lifetimes of futile wandering.

You can discern this for yourself. Even to repeat the word **"Peace"** over-and-over, can have an incredibly stabilizing influence. By inhibiting distractive thoughts, one becomes capacious and emotionally centered. Positive thoughts attract their kin, and this vaporizes the world of negativity. Positive thoughts extend outward into perception, searching for all those events and circumstances that can be channeled to reinforce their veracious ideational content. Existence is not static and fixed but is fluid and responsive. It always adjusts and transforms in perfect correspondence to our thoughts. The dream arises out of those beliefs and idols we choose to empower; and these alone program the template of our perceptivity.

Destructive thinking patterns are contagious and all-pervasive. Each lures with some seduction and just waits for us to bite. In the relative world, you see all those who are frustrated, lustful or insatiable in their appetites. Those who are scatterbrained, ineffectual, underachieved, uncreative, psychotic and escapist.

Then there is the drug-addicts, opioid-addicts, and prescription drug junkies. And so we continuously hear the screams "**poor me**" howling into our ears, from all those who embrace the victim-orientated mindset. Others, function as human leeches, pleasure seekers, attention grabbers, emotional blackmailers, and power-intoxicated tyrants.

Do not let zombies and cockroaches dull your mind. They will silently rob you of the conviction that genuine spiritual progress is possible. They represent the sad army of the witless and lost. They are dark, venomous and spiteful beings who implant evil seeds into every sucker's mind. Having accomplished nothing for themselves and being mere parasites on the face of existence, they desire you to be a cheap imitation. They would like to groom you into being a poor parody of themselves in their zombie-neighborhood of freaks. Such parasites attempt to reduce all to mediocrity and aim to put out your flame. Their one common feature is a complete and utter loss of discipline, mental vigilance, self-belief and self-esteem. You will find silently crying into their pints in every bar in North America. Most often, over time they morph into very cynical and highly apathetic beings. They allow all their thoughts and behaviors to wander carelessly and unregulated, down idle pathways into all the sewers and gutters of the seven worlds. They become impregnated with all sorts of rubbish and love listening to the sound of the insidious crap, BS, and evil that continuously spouts out from their vile bifurcated tongues. They sell it all for cheap at the Sunday market. Then foolishly go smelling after rosebuds, and wonder why they get caught in so many thorns and briars. They love eating the cosmic water lilies since which only steers and hypnotizes their minds down the endless landscapes of the dreamy and deluded. After all this, they wonder rather innocently why they have lost all resolve and become so puerile, callous and blunt."

INSPIRATION FROM ALL PAST AND PRESENT BUDDHAS

This discourse sounded good, until the last section. I said "It seems; you offer no compassion to barnyard monkeys, wayward beings, and all who have fallen off the path. You sound so judgmental and caustic. Whatever happened to your Bodhisattva ideals, of never resting in the pleasure paradise of Nirvana, until all living beings are free from suffering? Whatever happened to cultivating the six perfections? The six purifying pāramitās of **Generosity** (Dāna)**; Virtue** (Śīla), **Patience** (Kṣānti), **Meditation** (Dhyāna), **Industry** (Vīrya) and **Wisdom** (Prajñā)"

Lama Dorje responded "The words I just spoke, were cautionary words of advice aimed at helping those, still very deeply dream identified. There are many slick willy demons, plagiarizers, voluptuaries, institutionalized drones and self-destructive "innocents" that will lead one deeper into hell. Mature Bodhisattvas and Enlightened Buddhas, are inured from the dangers and pitfalls of the relative existence because they have broken the spell of dream identification. Dreamers don't always realize it when their heads are in a noose. The other end of which may be attached to a human boulder who is sinking fast to the bottom of the ocean. They foolishly believe they can save their fellow being. However, all that ends up happening is they waste their energies and opportunities and burn up prematurely. Certainly, one should help those in need, and provide wisdom to all who are ready for it. However, determining the correct situations in which to intervene is an art in itself. One does not always help another simply by cushioning their fall or by sacrificing oneself.

One cannot afford to squander the all-important opportunities that life provides for growth. Sometimes the passing of a hopelessly tragic figure turns out to be a great blessing for the world because he or she was bringing everyone down and wasting their life currency. Human life is precious, and it should not be frivolously misspent. By intervening to save another, one is often just prolonging their overall misery and incapacitating another from using their innate abilities. Often they will learn far more from resolving core issues on their own. They have many valuable lessons to learn but all aim to relinquish their destructive patterns. One cannot progress while keeping one foot on the accelerator and the other on the breaks. Occasionally certain situations arise in the dream, that put one under tremendous pressure and duress. You may feel pressured into accepting negative patterns and beliefs. There can be a great attraction to wallow in bitterness, guilt, and beliefs in victimization. The critical decision will be whether or not you cave to weakness, limitation and circumvented modes of thought. Extreme situations will test you. Your accomplishments will be either transmuted into gold or else turn to dust. With severe circumstances, come opportunities for immensely accelerated growth, great purification and the cashing in on all past efforts. Difficult and highly stressful situations can rapidly trigger transcendent experiences and bring forth Holy Visions. Often you are dragged into the moment, raw, fresh and unguarded and left exposed to either grow or die. There is no contingency plan to save you and no friends to call on your cell phone. You will either have a breakdown or a breakthrough. You will either enter the gates of hell or arrive at the altar of Truth as a radically new Being. Such situations are the perfect opportunity to apply this powerful Sutra of Atisha.

For those who can maintain an open mind, spiritual help is always there. You may, for example, receive a new healing interpretation of your current situation and a far more progressive way of viewing all the pain, negativity and confusion you are feeling. The real content and message may be illuminated for you, in an instant. Truth always answers with a Voice that is quiet, powerful and certain. It is a soothing Voice that takes all your cares away. Atisha requests that you never attempt to escape any situation since all situations have a healing gift to impart. Soon your patience will be rewarded because light will enter to dispel your dark dream. The new interpretation, you receive, will show things to your in a greater context and from a higher vantage point. Mistaken beliefs will melt away, paving the path for a potent new crystallization and synthesis.

All who are Enlightened, had to follow a similar path. Only in form do their paths appear different. They too had to be reborn, through self-immolation, in the fires of the relative world. However, the flame that consumed them was not of the body, but of the mind. Through their fearlessness, bravery, dedication, powerful mental discrimination and impartial thinking modes, they succeeded in lighting themselves on fire. Thus, they transcended all destructive, reactive and negative thinking patterns and saw through all foolish behaviors and worldly indulgences. In consequence, they penetrated through to the Absolute, and the timeless and came face-to-face with the deathless awareness in themselves. They recognized in a flash that the relative reality is an insubstantial mist arising from distorted perception. It is woven out of a dull mind and ego wishfulness and will always remain a mirage that is illusory and unachievable.

Most have substantial unresolved dream content and so they continue to project their arbitrary wishes to the screen of the void. Nevertheless, the dream of perception just reflects back one's learning progress. All situations and events offer new opportunities to correct prevailing errors and foolish behavioral patterns. Mistaken beliefs will continue to be projected as images and situations until satisfactorily resolved. The universe is a holograph in motion (holomotion), and it mentally spins and dramatizes those special interference patterns imprinted by our beliefs. You can easily correct all sources of erroneous thought and negativity instantaneously if you are honest and rigorous enough. Thus, you escape your prison-house and all chains that appear to bind you now will fall quickly to the floor. When you attempt to escape any situation you demonstrate weakness and your apparent escape will become your hell. Rather teach yourself and others that no situation has any power over you. The relative existence and external events being mental projections are not to be feared. Use every situation, as a vehicle for transcendence and embrace the gift it is offering you. Escape, and you enter a hall of distortion. A fearful and joyless world will then emerge, in which you will feel like a fugitive always on the run. All who escape and shirk their responsibilities become vulnerable, pathetic dream figures and strangers to themselves. Soon they feel alienated and lost in their own mind-made dream."

THE APPLICATION OF CREATIVE VISUALIZATION

Wow! The Lama had impressively hammered it all home for me and powerfully expounded on what needed to be embraced or avoided. I still had one last burning question I needed to ask. "How can Creative Visualization and Positive Intention help those who are dream-bound, to awaken?"

"Creative Visualization and Positive Intention are part of Atisha's plan, of training with phrases. They restore awareness of the tremendous power of your mind and thought over all appearances. Once you see your visualization intention coming true, you will also finally realize who is the projectionist of the dream. Even so, it is always better to ask only for what is beneficial for your spiritual progress. Align your visualizations with Truth principles. Ask, "**What end purpose does this Serve?**" This will help separate its true content and underlying aspiration from idle ambitions and desires. Whenever you choose a worthy goal, the results will always come fast and furious because you have just called upon the greatest power in the universe. Miracles are spontaneous for those who are open to the ways of light. Truth retains unlimited power, and this power is yours to use. You can harness it to attain mastery, in both the realms of the manifest and unmanifest and so gain full power over existence. You can deploy it to peer past the dull deadened world of surfaces and shadows and to look into the majesty beyond.

Too many dreamers, do not know what they authentically want or need. Their desires continuously vacillate and are often in acute conflict. Mostly they desire the impermanent and self-destructive, and so they travel interminably in "outer" worlds, which have nothing lasting to give. It is all a game of smoke and mirrors in which they remain blind to their real Identity and power. Still, they will not journey into the deep inner dimensions and taste some of its fruit. They use Creative Visualization as a magic wand and ask for childish toys. So they want a chocolate Santa Claus in their stockings, hookers and blow and a lifetime of gift cards to Victoria's Secret. Their poor choices make them mindless over time, and their real purpose becomes lost to awareness. Only when they undertake that meaningful journey within, will they recognize where true power lies. Their illusion of traveling in outer worlds is an unfortunate misadventure, and such worlds were always unworthy of them.

This Sutra can be applied both constructively or destructively. You can train with phrases to purify your mind and release erroneous understandings and so awaken or else to invite in more hellish nightmares. There are phrases that can completely incapacitate, decimate and eradicate the ego in a flast; ones that quickly eliminate all karmic seeds planted in the past. Thus you are conveyed into timeless Being and its Knowledge. All creative power derives from the infinite fountain of Mind and this Mind's Source lies in the present moment. The power within, however, may be misapplied if your intentions are impure.

Begin by thinking of something positive, that you would like to happen in your life. The time-frame for accomplishment may be tomorrow, a week from now, next year or many years ahead. Having the intended outcome well formulated and visualized is crucial. Once the end goal is clearly pictured, the means will fall easily into place. Existence can deny you nothing because existence is powered from your mind. Hence, it must bend to your thought and will. Make a request, and it will immediately go to work extracting all that is useful towards its accomplishment. It will sort through all the apparently random events and haphazard streams of futile, nonsense activity surrounding you to bring your desires to fruition.

Making visual aids or voice recordings of your intentions can help cement them into your subconscious. You do not need to plug in all the fine details of how your goals are to be fulfilled. Rather, think of them, as already accomplished. Once set in motion, forget about all your ambitions and go about business as usual. Your success will demonstrate the enormous power of your mind. After that, you will be fooled no longer by the supposed laws that rule the external world. The relative world's ideology teaches that power is intrinsic in matter and energy. Once you belief in the laws of gravity, biochemistry, radiation, medicine, nutrition, economics, justice and so forth, you are lost. Once you believe you have to work ferociously hard, maliciously plunder and deceive for every scrap you obtain, you have embraced the scarcity mindset. You need know how your visualization goals become accomplished. The miraculous is yours and so all that defies commonplace explanations is not your concern."

THE POTENCY OF MYSTICAL SPACE-DUST

This session was my last discourse with Lama Dorje. After spending almost six months, in this remote and beautiful outpost, the snowfalls had ceased, and the mountains were once more passable. I started preparing for the journey back and began putting some provisions together. Lama Dorje said I could always fly back from the new Ngari Kunsha airport. I could travel to Lhasa first and spend some time there before heading back stateside.

Lhasa, however, had lost all appeal for me. I didn't feel I could handle the picture of devastation, waiting for me at this former capital of Tibetan culture and life. All those Chinese run businesses and signs would make my stomach turn over and possibly make me immoderately angry. It was as if a beautiful lady, had been raped and had her eyes and heart yanked out before you. All that was left there were soulless sockets and a blank, emotionless, cultureless skeleton which functioned more like a machine. I craved more adventure and decided I would either travel down through India or onwards to Nepal. Finally, as my imminent departure loomed, I decided I would trek to Mt. Kailash first and spend some time there completing a pilgrimage around the mountain. This pilgrimage would also include a visit Milarepa's cave and Lake Manasarovar. Mt. Kailash was supposedly a beacon of spiritual energy, and it ceaselessly shed endless rays of compassion and illumination on all humanity. The Tibetans considered it the spiritual center of the Universe and the Home of the Gods. After that, I planned to hire some "nutcase" driver to take me down the friendship highway into Nepal and onward to Kathmandu. There probably would be quite a bit of rough hiking and river crossing on this route too, but nothing anywhere near as rough and life-threatening, as I had endured on my way into Tibet. I would also get the chance to see Mt. Everest and Cho Oyu on this route, which a friend of mine had climbed once.

Lama Dorje warned about the Chinese. They will wonder why you don't have any entry permit on your passport. They may end up locking you up, or worse. It is best to say that you just recently arrived and cannot understand why your passport was never stamped. You probably will need to pay some official off with a bribe to get out. Also, tell them nothing about staying in this Ashram. You may need to get a trekking pass in Nepal and possibly some other places. On the pilgrimage to Kailash and the surrounding area, remember to travel around the mountain in a clockwise manner, or you will look strange to Tibetans. They will think you are trying to increase your karmic debt.

All the same, I was very reluctant to leave, and feeling more like a child being torn away from his favorite Teddy Bear. There was an awe-inspiring majesty about this place, and a supreme peace and bliss had descended upon me here. Of course, I was reluctant to give it all up and move on. It had become such an intimate part of my soul. I knew it would always remain inside of me, and that I would carry it everywhere. Still, I wondered why all good things in life always have to be sacrificed or come to an abrupt end. It seemed pragmatism ruled our lives instead of the heart. I did not relish going back to the jungle of the western world; even less so to the States. I intuitively knew, however, that it was there; I was needed the most. I was now carrying a powerful, healing and liberating message that would be an oasis for their thirsty souls. I was embodying the perfect antidote to the pervasive sickness of the modern day culture and had become the message myself. I only appeared to be living in the world now but was no longer of it. I would teach all who would listen diligently. Maybe I would publish some books too, on these esoteric teachings. I sincerely doubted many would genuinely listen since we now live in an age of continuous information bombardment. Few have the attention span to read even a single book through and fewer still, possess the inner evolution demanded, to correctly interpret it. It seemed such a futile task, like sending a letter to the Easter Bunny and then expecting to hear back. Enlightenment, itself could not be bottled. It was not a potable commodity and was beyond all teaching. It could not be transmitted as an objective or phenomenal knowledge. It required a flash of insight and illumination from deep within, in which one comprehended the supreme essence of existence very lucidly and penetratingly for oneself. Maybe, however, if I planted enough seeds and strategically placed enough mind-cairns about, a few would get the message.

Early one April morning I headed off. The Lama and I embraced one last time. It was a warm hug that I never wanted to end. Then he imparted these last words to me. *"Remember Sharon, I have been your signpost in this Dream, and you must become the signpost in the Dreams of others."* Then I started on my ascent of a nearby ridge. The clouds were descending fast, and soon all would be out of sight. I decided to glance back one last time at the Ashram. This Ashram had been my lifeblood during the most turbulent, inspiring and momentous time in my life. I was shocked to see that it had completely disappeared. Yes, the Lama and this Ashram had always been too good to be true. Everything from the last six months, ever since I headed out from

Gangotri into Tibet had been nothing but a dream—a meta-reality in a parallel universe.

Later, when I did more research, I found out that he had passed from the dream over a half-century before. He had once been a selfless Teacher, Tertön, and Translator. One of the ancient ones, who came to save my life and he had imbued me with the most veracious of messages. All of this left me feeling stunned, mystified and in awe. It seemed the magical vortex of existence with all its ingenious ways knew no limit and could extend to everywhere and to everywhen. He has been more real than any other, I have known. All I felt was tremendously Grateful! Grateful! Grateful!—Grateful in the deepest recesses of my heart.

EXPLANATION OF TERMS USED

Absolute Mind :

Transcendent Mind that neither needs nor employs the learning aids of the five Skandhas of Form, Sensation, Perception, Conception, and Consciousness, by which to know itself. Absolute Mind is undifferentiated, pure and limitless in its potency. It is also serene and quiescent and functions non-dualistically.

Alaya–Vijynana :

Ground or Storehouse Consciousness. Often equated with the subconscious. It contains memories and impressions formed from past experiences, actions, and understandings. It holds all our karmic imprints and it establishes the seeds for our personality, desires, fears, attachments and awareness filters.

Bodhicitta :

It means Buddha-Consciousness; There is both **(1)** Absolute Bodhicitta and **(2)** Relative Bodhicitta.

Absolute Bodhicitta :

This is the pure Enlightened mind that has seen through the emptiness of all form and phenomena. It recognizes that all is devoid of any implicit self-nature. Being no longer tarnished and obfuscated by any false understandings or dualistic thought, it experiences timelessness and truth directly.

Relative Bodhicitta :

The path to mental liberation, of one who practices the six pāramitās. By practicing universal compassion, altruism, and forgiveness, one becomes released from the toxic grip of the ego and the relative world. Thus one comes to recognize the one Self in all and knows the truly effulgent, self-resplendent nature of the Self.

Bodhisattva :

One who selflessly observes all those practices needed to bring all living beings to awareness of their Buddha nature.

Bön :

Pre-Buddhist School of Religious Practice. Whose followers often engage in unorthodox methods of reaching Self-Realization. Typically these are a mixture of Magic and Tantric practices. A rare few engage in black magic, thus they invoke demons or evil spirits to accelerate the work or to increase their karmic debt.

Dâkinî :

A yogini who has reached Enlightenment. This term is often used also to refer to a non-physical deity that can be used to enhance meditative practice.

Dharmadhatu :

The seed essence from which all space and phenomena arise. This seed essence is extremely potent but is without any attributes or form. It is beyond all conception, perception and all capacities of the relative mind to know or grasp.

Dharmakāya :

The pure undifferentiated body of Truth. It is a body of limitless potency and bliss and the realm of pure unconditional love. It transcends all perception and conception and therefore seems non-existent to the relative mind.

Enlightenment :

Enlightenment is transcending the dualistic mind-frame and all false knowledge it weaves. Thus one escapes the relative existence of the Samsara and is released from all suffering, caused by wrong understandings, and has no need for "rebirth." It also describes one who experiences the pure, non-differentiated, and timeless realm of Nirvana directly.

Eka-Grata :

Achieving perfect one-pointedness of mind. This is critical for reaching mental quiescence, attaining mind mastery, and excelling in all the Siddhis (supernormal powers).

Nirmaṇakāya :

The physical or manifest body of a Buddha.

Nirvana :

The pure undifferentiated realm entered only by one who has reached perfect understanding. Such a one therefore does not generate new illusions or seeds of karma. Can be equated with the Dharmakāya. Here resides the pure and potent Knowledge of the One-Mind.

Sambhogakāya :

The second mode or aspect of the Trikāya; A subtle body, often considered a reward body. It transcends the apparently physical body and is potentiated with limitless form. In this welcoming manifold all Buddhas, of the past, present and future timelessly exist. It is the source of all pure Buddha-lands and Celestial kingdoms. This body contains the pure understandings of the One-Mind and can be used to induce visionary experiences as learning aids to help Neophytes on the path to liberation.

Pāramitās :

Means "Perfections." Mastery of the six pāramitās of **(1)** Generosity **(2)** Virtue (Morality) **(3)** Patience **(4)** Meditation **(5)** Industry (Right Effort) and **(6)** Wisdom which bring one to Enlightenment.

Relative Mind :

This mind is dependent on the five skandhas so that it can learn and purify itself. It represents mind that seeks for liberation and awareness of its wholeness. This mind is perpetually confused about both itself and the true metaphysical basis of the world, it appears to live in. It is plagued with contradictions, misunderstandings and the trappings of dualistic thought. It cannot know anything with perfect transparency.

Samsara :

The realm of conditioned (or relative) existence within which one remains defiled by the three poisons of **(1)** Fear, **(2)** Attachment and **(3)** Ignorance. Thus one experiences continuous suffering, death, and rebirth. Once one has divested oneself of all false understandings and impurities, one is released into the pure realm of Nirvana.

Shastra :

Specialized knowledge (typically Spiritual) in a defined area and is often given as a learned treatise or set of precepts.

Siddhis :

Supernormal Powers, attained by advanced yogis, who have become adept at reaching to mental quiescence and one-pointedness of mind. They include many psychic powers such as clairvoyance, telekinesis and remote viewing. These powers also extend to one being able to manifest anything one wants, shape-shifting and mastery over Nature and the Cosmos.

Sutra :

Esoterically a Sutra is a potent key that can lead to Self-empowerment, even Enlightenment. They serve as guidance aids from Spiritual Masters, who have already attained.

Shunyata :

This term refers to Emptiness. It is the understanding that all phenomena and forms whether seeming internal or external, are devoid of any self-nature. Even the personal ego, being just the composite of all our false understandings and subsequent reactions is likewise non-existent.

The Five Skandhas :

Also known as the five aggregates. These are those elements that come together to form the illusory ego self or "I." They present one with the false notion of existing in a relative world, apart from one's mind. The five skandhas are **(1)** Form **(2)** Sensation **(3)** Perception **(4)** Conception and **(5)** Consciousness. All of which depend intimately upon the six organs of sense which are **(1)** Sight **(2)** Sound **(3)** Smell **(4)** Taste **(5)** Touch and **(6)** Thought.

Trikāya :

The three bodies of Truth. Namely, the bodies of the **Nirmaṇakāya, Sambhogakāya,** and **Dharmakāya** when spoken about collectively. In Christian Theology, they are analogous with, the **Father** (Dharmakāya), the **Son** (Nirmaṇakāya) and the **Holy Spirit** (Sambhogakāya).

Tsa :

Subtle Energy Channels. Used to carry psychic energy transmissions.

Tonglen :

Tibetan Pranayama Technique for developing Universal Compassion, through giving and taking with the outgoing and incoming breaths.

Vasanas :

The karmic imprints and tendencies that are residual from past life experiences, actions, and understandings. They are powerful forces of one's subconscious psychic matrix. They direct one's future decisions, actions, and behavioral responses.

Void :

The undifferentiated ever-potent plenum, from which all universes arise. Since this plenum is beyond all concepts, percepts, forms or attributes, nothing more can be said about it.

AUTHOR BIO

Sharon Moriarty is an Engineer, Adventurer, Yogi, and Mystic. She has had an interest in Tibetan and Zen Buddhism, and New Age Thought for almost two decades. She is thoroughly familiar with many of the Yogic Kriyas and Advanced Meditation Techniques.

OTHER BOOKS BY SHARON MORIARTY

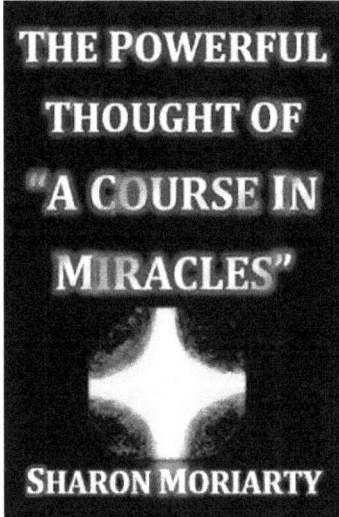

THE POWERFUL THOUGHT OF "A COURSE IN MIRACLES"

SHARON MORIARTY

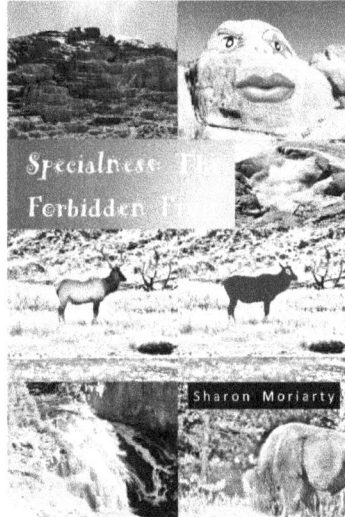

Specialness: The Forbidden Fruit

Sharon Moriarty

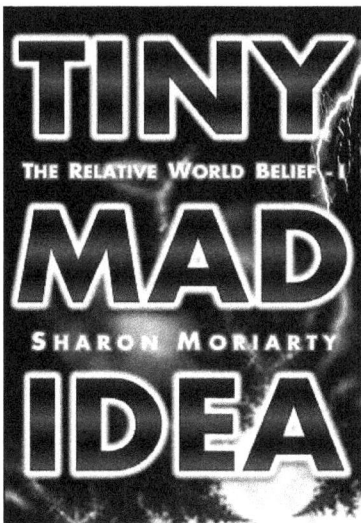

TINY MAD IDEA

THE RELATIVE WORLD BELIEF – I

SHARON MORIARTY

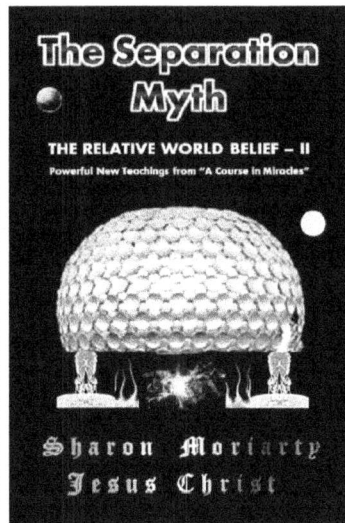

The Separation Myth

THE RELATIVE WORLD BELIEF – II

Powerful New Teachings from "A Course in Miracles"

Sharon Moriarty
Jesus Christ

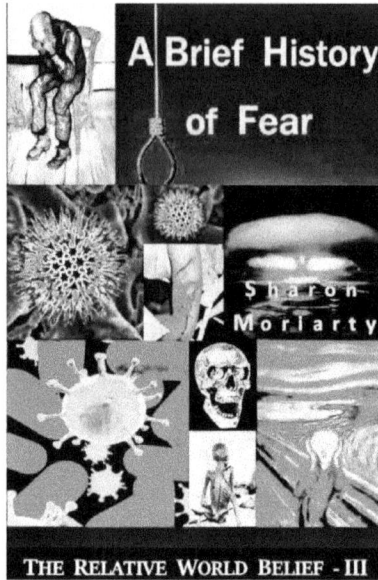

E-Books and Paperbacks Available now on
Amazon and CreateSpace.

http://www.Amazon.com